D1426041

THE COMPLETE GUIDE TO
CLIMBING AND
MOUNTAINEERING

THE COMPLETE GUIDE TO
CLIMBING AND
MOUNTAINEERING

PETE HILL MIC, FRGS

David and Charles

To my parents, for putting up with my wanderings for so many years.

Learning
Resource Centre
Stockton
Riverside College

796.522

A DAVID & CHARLES BOOK
© F&W Media International LTD 2008, 2011

David & Charles is an imprint of F&W Media International, LTD
Brunel House, Forde Close, Newton Abbot, TQ12 4PU, UK

F&W Media International, LTD is a subsidiary of F+W Media, Inc., 4700 East Galbraith Road
Cincinnati OH45236, USA

First published in the UK & US in 2008
This paperback edition published in the UK in 2011

Text copyright © Pete Hill, 2008
Images copyright © Pete Hill, 2008, with the exception of p. 130t © Derek Boggan; pp. 11b, 214, 216, 217, 219, 222–3, 225, 226b © Di Gilbert; p. 85 © Rebecca Hill; pp. 176br, 191 © Samantha Hill; pp. 10tr, 11t, 178L, 180, 185 © Scott Muir Collection; pp. 206, 208tr & br, 211b © Jonathan Preston

Pete Hill has asserted his moral right to be identified as the author of this work in accordance with the Copyright, Designs and Patents Act, 1988.

All rights reserved. No part of this publication may be reproduced, stored in a retrieval system, or transmitted, in any form or by any means, electronic, mechanical, by photocopying, recording or otherwise, without the prior permission in writing from the publisher.

A catalogue record for this book is available from the British Library.

ISBN-13: 978-0-7153-2842-2 (hardback)
ISBN-10: 0-7153-2842-5

ISBN-13: 978-0-7153-2844-6 (paperback)
ISBN-10: 0-7153-2844-1

Printed in China by RR Donnelley
for F&W Media International, LTD
Brunel House, Forde Close, Newton Abbot, TQ12 4PU, UK

10 9 8 7 6 5 4 3 2 1

Commissioning Editor: Neil Baber
Editorial Manager: Emily Pitcher
Art Editor: Martin Smith
Designer: Jodie Lystor
Project Editor: Margaret Body
Proofreader: Michael Coveney
Indexer: Lisa Footitt
Production Controller: Kelly Smith

F+W Media publishes high quality books on a wide range of subjects
For more great book ideas visit: www.rubooks.co.uk

CONTENTS

PREFACE

The idea of presenting a book to the reader as being 'complete' is, of course, problematic. As soon as you commit a skill or technique to the page, it has changed, moved on or been radically overhauled and updated. To be 'complete' about topics such as snow structure analysis or expedition tentage is also impossible, as they are vast subjects themselves, each requiring a number of tomes to cover them properly.

However, this book is 'complete' in that it covers the whole range of disciplines that can be grouped together under the banner of 'climbing and mountaineering', from bouldering through to expedition climbing. Each section outlines what is involved, and a number of relevant skills are introduced that will allow the reader to make their own decision about whether to pursue that particular aspect of the sport, or to move on to other areas.

One of the great pleasures of climbing and mountaineering is that anyone taking part is rarely limited by any official bureaucracy, rules or regulations, perhaps with the exception of expeditions to the greater ranges. This leaves us to do our own thing, climb when and where we like, do whichever route we choose, travel to wherever takes our fancy and mix with like-minded people. It is this flexibility that is such a great attraction for many people, and friendships born from chance meetings at remote venues often endure for many years.

We do, though, all have a responsibility to be technically prepared, so that we may look after both ourselves and any climbing companion that we choose to share our particular route or adventure with. This will only be possible after a lot of practice and experience, as to be able to swiftly set up a suitable emergency hauling system when our companion is hanging over the edge of a cliff above a massive drop will only be possible after rehearsal in a controlled environment.

The technical skills demonstrated in this book aim to cover the range of common, and not so common, emergency procedures that you may come across. The included day-to-day skills are myriad, all of which should go towards making your time in the hills and mountains a lot safer and more enjoyable. There will be, of course, a great deal of variation possible within each skill scenario, and it is up to you to decide which technique works for you in any given situation. A number of the diagrams have unashamedly been cloned, reworked and included from my previous publications for David & Charles, as I felt that their clarity could not be surpassed and they demonstrate the technique admirably, so apologies if you recognize one or two here and there.

At the end of the day, we choose to climb because we enjoy it and, as long as we give relevant thought to the impact of what we are doing and strive to lessen our overall effect on the environment, then no one else should have a problem with what we get up to.

I hope that you find the contents of this book useful, perhaps even inspiring you to go out and visit areas or try skills that may have eluded you in the past. Whatever you get up to, be safe and it would be great to see you out on the hill one day.

Pete Hill

ACKNOWLEDGMENTS

The number of people that are involved, directly or indirectly, unwittingly or otherwise, in a book such as this is huge. A general vote of thanks must go to anyone who has been caught on film and ended up on these pages, as without them our sport would not exist. Specific thanks should go to the people who have let me peer over their shoulder with a camera lens whilst they have been indulging in their pastime of climbing in either summer or winter. In no particular order, Samantha Hill, Rebecca Hill, Michael Bachner, Niki Treitl, Colby and Jen Frontiero, Tony and Jen Yao, Will Kelsall, Greg Chandler, Lucy Atkinson, Kate Wilson, Geoff Hibbert, Yuki, Tony Ball, Giles Stone, Chris Pretty, Sean Cattanach and Ian Broadley, all of whom put up with the probing lens, thus my heartfelt thanks to them all. If you have had my lens pointed at you but your name is not here, my gratitude is extended to you as well.

I am also very grateful to a number of people, in particular Jonathan Preston, Di Gilbert and Scott Muir, for allowing me to use some of their photographs (see page 4).

Jonathan Preston, MIC, BMG, and fellow *Monty Python* devotee, also kindly agreed to proofread the more technical sections and check that I was staying on the rails as far as skills are concerned, and for his input I am grateful.

Arranging a book such as this needs a lot of equipment, so I am very grateful for the support of a number of companies.

Frank Bennett at Lyon Equipment (www.lyon.co.uk) put up with me bothering him a lot – thanks Frank. Beal (www.bealplanet. com), Petzl and Petzl Charlet (www.petzl.com), DMM (www. dmmclimbing.com), La Sportiva (www.lasportiva.com) and Berghaus (www.berghaus.com) all contributed equipment used in shots and related trips, and I'm very grateful to them. Petzl also let me recreate some of their technical diagrams, which has been a great help. Information from Beal has also been used in a couple of technical sections; thanks to them for letting me do so. Blyth Wright at the Scottish Avalanche Information Service (www. sais.gov.uk) kindly let me reproduce sections of the avalanche hazard scale. I am also grateful to Alan Halewood and the staff at the Ice Factor (www.icefactor.co.uk) for my time there taking photographs.

Finally, and as always, the long-suffering Paula Griffin spent many an hour reading through my initial scratchings, rounding them up into something resembling a readable pile of text. She also accompanied me on trips abroad and took part in many photo sessions, from ice-covered landscapes to parched earth, without complaint. For that, and for still being the perfect climbing partner, I am eternally grateful.

INTRODUCTION: ROCKS, ICE AND MOUNTAINS

The mountains and crags that cover the globe present us with an unending series of locations and opportunities to take part in our chosen sport. From inner city quarried rock walls suitable for bouldering, to the highest ice-covered walls of the greater ranges, there is plenty to go round, with an infinite amount more to spare.

These places where we like to play are made from a host of rock types, igneous, sedimentary and metamorphic, some of which we love to climb on and some that we would travel miles to avoid. Snow and ice can vary greatly too, and even in the same location they can change from day to day, if not from hour to hour. Being able to adapt to these changes, alter our plans or extend our expectations as appropriate, is fundamental to having a safe and successful time on crags and mountains across the world.

Bouldering can become competitive but is always a social occasion

Placing gear on the lead on atmospheric sea cliffs

BOULDERING

Bouldering is a huge sport, both for the participant and, more recently, for the spectator as well. From isolated mountain boulders where solitude is guaranteed, through to popular areas and competitions, bouldering is seen by many to be the ultimate statement of stamina, skill and achievement. The minimalist approach is one of the great attractions, as little gear is needed to start, simply a pair of rock boots and some chalk being sufficient.

TRADITIONAL CLIMBING

The leading of a route, either single- or multi-pitch, where running belays and anchors have to be placed by hand as you go, is many people's idea of climbing. The freedom to climb almost anywhere and at any height, armed with a formidable array of protection equipment, is the staple of many people's climbing careers. Many enjoy the technical process of selecting and placing runners, and working out the best way up the route ahead. Having a companion along is also part and parcel of the sport, and gives you someone to share the experience with, good or bad, enjoyable or simply terrifying!

The huge stalactite of Trela, 6c+

Snow-covered cliffs give excellent sport for gully and mixed climbing

SPORT CLIMBING

Rock climbing without placing protection, as it is already drilled and bolted into the rock, is many climbers' choice of recreation. This allows you to climb a lot lighter, unhindered by the large rack of gear that goes along with climbing traditional routes, and so push your grade more and make moves that may otherwise be impossible to attempt. A climber on a sport route is at the mercy of the person who originally bolted it, as the drilled placements will dictate where the protection can be placed. For that reason it may not be to everyone's taste, but most find that clipping bolts in the sun on otherwise protectionless rock is one of the great climbing experiences.

VIA FERRATA

With its origins in troop movements during World War I, this method of transporting people across steep and rocky terrain has evolved to become a very popular pastime the world over. Climbing up ladders, traversing bridges and sliding along zip lines are just a part of what goes to make Via Ferrata circuits so enjoyable to many.

WINTER CLIMBING

Once the snow covers the mountains and crags, so many opportunities arise for climbing and mountaineering that there will be something for everyone to enjoy. It may be just a walk in the snow up a favourite peak, a simple climb up a snowed-up gully, or an attempt on a new route right at the top of its grade. Whatever you enjoy doing, most will agree that winter presents the ultimate set of opportunities and demands the highest degree of skills in a variety of disciplines. Navigation, competence with axe and crampons and the ability to negotiate snow slopes are just the start.

Via Ferrata routes offer a host of interesting sections

The author on an ice route in Norway

Dry tooling routes cover some audacious ground

ICE CLIMBING

Climbing on pure water ice is an acquired taste, but once it is acquired aficionados will travel far and wide in search of the ultimate stretch of frozen water. This could be found in a remote mountain setting many hours walk from a base, or may even be in a roadside setting, literally allowing you to belay from the towbar of your vehicle!

MIXED CLIMBING AND DRY TOOLING

These athletic disciplines cover the ground omitted by many rock and winter climbers, and are for many the peak of physical and technical perfection. Mixed climbing, with its use of both rock and ice, explores some spectacular scenery across the world and gives rise to some of the hardest routes ever climbed. Dry tooling routes will often end up making their way across seemingly blank cave roofs, using the smallest of cracks and edges for tool placement and requiring the highest level of skill, judgment and fitness.

ALPINE CLIMBING

The Alpine regions of the world give access to stunning scenery, often without too much hardship involved in getting there. Although many routes of great difficulty, requiring a number of days to complete, do exist, there are also many that are accessible to those who wish to challenge themselves at a lower technical and physical level. In many areas the infrastructure is in place to allow swift access to mountain regions, with cable cars and chairlifts often taking away the initial hard work of gaining the snowline.

Alpine mountaineering gives access to spectacular scenery

Big wall climbing

BIG WALLS

Multi-day routes on very long rock or ice climbs make up the big wall genre, although a number of classic big walls have now been climbed in a day by very fast parties, and some even soloed. Mental preparation is very important, as spending days and nights on a route, living on a small portable ledge with your world in two dimensions instead of the normal three, demands not only technical skills but also the ability to deal with sleeping, cooking and other related daily necessities in a very exposed situation.

EXPEDITIONS

Spending a long time away from home, being out of contact with the goings-on of normal daily life and sharing your time with a small group of others is only part of expeditioning. Trips away demand a huge amount of time organizing, with the logistics of transporting people and equipment to a remote country and then dealing with local issues such as permits and transportation having to be completed before any climbing or mountaineering even starts. Dedication is important to succeed in an expedition scenario, but the benefits to those who persevere are huge and often life-changing.

Many people's idea of the ultimate mountain, the summit of Mount Everest

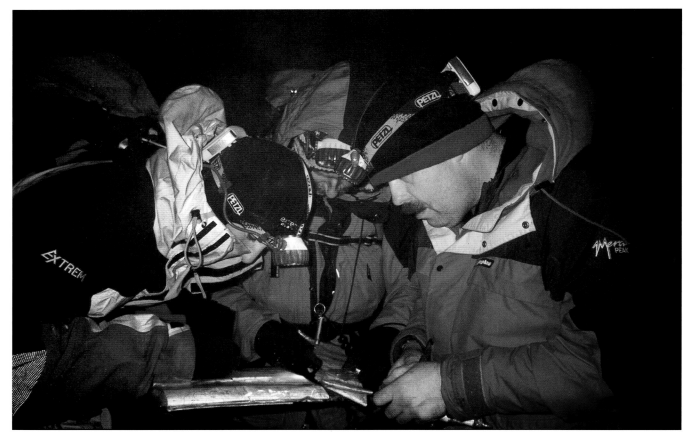

Night navigation in poor visibility

1: BASIC SKILLS

NAVIGATION

The ability to navigate effectively over a variety of terrain in poor visibility is fundamental to a safe time in the hills and mountains. However great a climber someone may be, if they are setting out for remote terrain and are unable to navigate effectively then they are putting themselves, and their companions, in danger.

It is one of the most important disciplines to practise, and this should be built up in stages until you are confident in your own ability to navigate accurately in poor visibility over all types of ground.

EQUIPMENT

MAP

The basic piece of kit, maps come in a variety of sizes and scales, with the commonest being 1:25,000 and 1:50,000. The former works well when very small features need to be identified and navigated to with great precision. The latter is fine for a wider scale of navigation, still performed very accurately, but perhaps where small individual features

such as streams have been covered by snow, contour interpretation becomes important, and there is often less clutter on a 1:50,000 map, making it easier to decipher.

MAP CASE

If your map is not laminated, it is worth doing it yourself with transparent book cover film, obtainable from stationers. This will make it last many times longer than a standard paper map. If you are travelling and don't have time to laminate, the use of

a map case will keep its contents in good order. Buy one that has a rubbery feel to it. These are more expensive but will last a lot longer than cheaper models, which quickly tend to crack and disintegrate.

COMPASS

There are many styles of compass available, and selection is normally down to personal choice. Minimum requirements are: a large, clear base; a housing that is easy to turn when wearing gloves; highly visible markings and a scale or millimetre graduations along the side.

Attach it to yourself with a long loop of string, either around your neck or fixed to the map pocket zip on your jacket.

COUNTER

When pacing, explained below, you need to keep an accurate count of the distance you have walked. To accomplish this, you can buy a small device that is attached to your compass, which can be clicked up from 1 to 9. Alternatively, attach ten pull-toggles, the grippers used to hold cord tight on your jacket, to the compass lanyard. These can be slid down each time a number needs to be ticked off.

STOPWATCH

For timing, covered below, you need to have an idea of the time that you start and then stop a navigational leg. A normal analogue timepiece would do, but it can be difficult remembering when you started. A stopwatch, either as found on a digital watch or one bought for the purpose, would be better. Small digital timers, designed for kitchen use, are lightweight and do the job admirably.

PEN

A thin-tipped permanent marker pen, such as used on overhead projectors, is excellent for writing not just on laminated maps, but any other shiny surface. This allows you to work out timings and other information that is a bit tricky to do in your head, as well as noting other bits of information, such as bearings, that may be needed later.

GPS

These devices are excellent aids to location and for finding your way around the mountains. Extra features such as a 'breadcrumb trail' are useful for backtracking through crevassed terrain, for example, at the end of the day.

A concern with GPS units is that, as they are electronic and require batteries for operation, things can go wrong and they can break. Thus, most would agree that having a good grounding in basic skills of map and compass work is still essential, with the GPS unit being used as a back-up, either for moving rapidly to a place of refuge or for checking your location, transferring the information to a map and using that to continue your journey.

ALTIMETER

Similar in use to the GPS, an altimeter can help you to work out your location but should not be used in isolation for positioning. The exception to this would be when following a long snow ridge at altitude, for example, where no navigational features exist and you are simply ascending or descending.

Altimeters are notoriously fickle when it comes to changes in the weather. Generally very accurate when correctly calibrated, they need to be reset at known altitudes during the trip, as often as every couple of hours in certain conditions, as changes in barometric pressure will cause the altitude reading to become inaccurate.

Altimeters that use satellite tracking to obtain altitude readings are not susceptible to small barometric shifts, but they only work accurately if you have a good view of the sky, and thus satellites, all around.

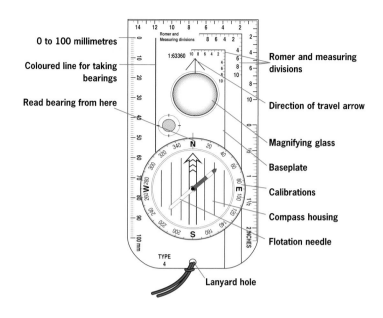

0 to 100 millimetres

Coloured line for taking bearings

Read bearing from here

Romer and measuring divisions

Direction of travel arrow

Magnifying glass

Baseplate

Calibrations

Compass housing

Flotation needle

Lanyard hole

A good compass for mountaineering use

READING THE MAP

This is such an important skill that it cannot be overemphasized how essential practice in varying conditions will be to become competent at navigating. In a controlled situation, try using the map alone in poor visibility to see how well you can interpret the information that is given.

SETTING THE MAP

This means orientating the map so that it fits in with the features on the ground. Streams, ridge lines and paths can all be used to set the map correctly, making subsequent identification of features a lot easier to do. A compass can also be used, orientating the top of the map towards north.

CONTOUR INTERPRETATION

This is the single most important skill to master. It means being able to relate the contour relief on the map to that visible on the ground, and knowing what certain features are going to look like before you get there.

The contour intervals on the map will dictate how much information you can glean by reading the contours, but maps with 10 metre (30ft) intervals are excellent for fine navigation. To practise, walk around in good visibility and when you come across a feature, such as a small bump on the ground known as a ring contour, or a V shape known as a re-entrant, take a moment to study its shape in relation to the relevant contours on the map. By doing this, you will be able to remember a host of different landform shapes, making it much easier to recognize these features when you come across similar ones in poor visibility.

BASIC COMPASS SKILLS

Although using the map efficiently is such a huge part of navigation, being able to use a compass is also a very important skill that should become second nature. When using a compass, make sure that there are no metal objects near it, such as an ice axe or camera, that could affect the magnetic field, causing the needle to waver from its true position.

GRID AND MAGNETIC BEARINGS

Due to changes in the positioning of the magnetic poles, in some areas of the world there is a difference between grid north, where the map says north is, and magnetic north, the direction that your compass needle points. This difference can be quite marked and change from year to year, so it is important to check in the area where you are operating as to whether this is a consideration or not. This information is usually supplied as printed text in the map key. If it is so, you will either have to add or subtract the difference between grid and magnetic north each time you take a bearing from or to the map. To ignore the difference between the two norths can leave you considerably off target after having walked on an uncorrected bearing for even a short distance.

TAKING A BEARING FROM THE MAP

This is made far easier if the map that you are using has a series of grid lines on it. Not all maps, especially those for remote areas, have these, so it's worth checking out what is available.

Place either the edge of the compass, or better still one of the long lines on the baseplate, between where you are, A, and where you want to go, B. Ensure that the direction of travel arrow on the baseplate is pointing the right way. Now, holding the baseplate firmly on the map, rotate the housing until the lines on the base of the housing are parallel with the grid lines on the map, and the arrow on the housing is pointing north on the map. Note that the needle has nothing to do with this part of the process.

Once you have checked that A and B are still in line, you can now take the compass off the map and read the bearing from the mark at the front of the housing. This will be a 'grid' bearing and will need to be adjusted to a magnetic bearing if appropriate, as mentioned above.

PUTTING A BEARING ON TO THE MAP

If you need to find your position accurately, perhaps when on a long featureless ridge, you can use the compass to help. Identify a feature at right-angles to your ridge and take a bearing to it by pointing the direction of travel arrow at it and rotating the housing so that the north arrow lines up with the needle. If there is a difference between grid and magnetic north, you will have to adjust the housing accordingly. Now place the compass on your map with either the edge or a line on the baseplate over the feature. Rotate the entire compass, not just the housing, around this point until the lines on the base of the housing are parallel with the grid lines on the map, and the housing arrow points to the top of the map. Where the edge or line crosses the ridge is your position.

In a flat area, you could take two or more of these bearings and draw lines on the map as you go, with the point at which the lines cross being your position. This is known as a resection.

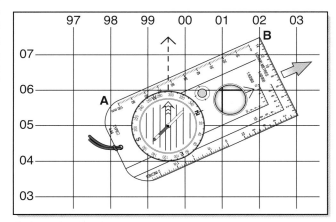

Taking a bearing from the map

WALKING ON A BEARING

This is obviously critical, as there is no point in being able to take fantastically accurate bearings if you just wander off without sticking to them. It is not possible to walk and stick to your bearing by just looking at your compass needle as you go, without using intermediate features. It is easy to drift off to one side or the other of your line and using the features will keep you on track. Although speed is usually of the essence, don't rush, as staying on the precise line is important.

FOLLOWING A BEARING

Hold the compass firmly in your hand in front of your body, making sure that there are no metal objects nearby. Rotate yourself until the needle sits in the correct manner over the arrow on the bottom of the housing, ensuring that you have the north end of the needle, often painted red, over the pointed part of the arrow. Now look along the direction of travel arrow on the front of the baseplate and note a feature along your bearing (not too far away and on your side of the objective), perhaps a rock or large clump of grass. You can now walk to that point, stop, let the compass needle settle and repeat the process. As long as you travel from point to point like this, you will always stay on your original bearing until your objective comes into view.

FOLLOWING A BEARING WHILE MOVING

This takes some practice to get right, but is useful if you need to get off the hill or from A to B with speed. Only try this method once you are completely happy with the stop-start method mentioned above.

From your starting point sight a feature as normal, and walk towards it. As you get closer let your compass needle settle into the correct position over the housing arrow, line yourself up so that the direction of travel arrow points at the feature, look beyond it and identify another. You can now ignore the first feature and move on to the second. This is repeated until you arrive at your objective.

Although a very efficient way of moving, accuracy is the important thing here, so if you need to stop to double-check a feature then do so, otherwise you could wander some way off target.

FOLLOWING A BEARING IN BLANKET SNOW

Some conditions, such as wide snow cover when the cloud is down, will stop you from identifying obvious features to walk to. If you are on your own, you may be able to discern individual ice crystals just a very short distance away, perhaps just a couple of metres, and use these. Alternatively, making a snowball and throwing it ahead so that it makes a mark on the ground will

help and you can walk to it and stand the appropriate distance one side or the other so that you are still on your bearing.

If there are two or more of you, you can use each other as markers. One of you stands at the start point whilst the other walks out ahead for an appropriate distance, most likely pacing (covered below). Once they have stopped they turn round and use you as the marker point. To do this, they hold their compass back to front so that it is 180 degrees out, and line themselves up with you by moving left or right, keeping the north end of the needle over the south end of the arrow on the housing, and using the direction of travel arrow to line up on you. They do not change the bearing at all, but simply rotate the compass in their hands. Once they are happy that you are both lined up they can give you a wave and you can join them.

This process is quite slow but it is the only option when there is limited visibility and no ground features can be seen. The advantage is that there are two of you checking each other's bearings and pacing distances, making it quite accurate.

As soon as ground features are seen you should use them, as this will speed things up considerably.

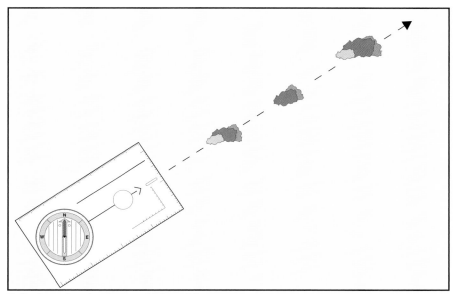

Following a bearing from point to point

CALCULATING DISTANCE

This skill is important in poor visibility or when an objective is not obvious.

In poor visibility, keep a constant check on your position

MEASURING ON A MAP

There are various ways of doing this, but it is probably easiest by using the compass. Most designs will have a scale printed on the base-plate as well as inches or millimetres along the side, and these can be related to the printed map scale and used to calculate distance quite accurately.

TIMING

Knowing your speed across certain types of terrain is important when estimating distance travelled, and a good guideline is to use an average person's walking speed. This is obviously subjective, but can be tweaked to suit most people and terrain.

An average person walks at five kilometres (three miles) per hour. This can be further subdivided into how long it takes to walk 100 metres, for example, and this takes 1.2 minutes. Thus, if you had to walk for 500 metres on the flat, it would take you six minutes to complete the distance.

There is also ascent to consider. A reasonable pace would be to ascend a 10 metre (30ft) contour line every 30 seconds. Thus, if you had to walk 500 metres along and up 60 metres, the time taken would be 6 minutes plus 6 x 30 seconds = 3 minutes, thus 9 minutes overall. Note that taken over a full day, one minute per 10 metre contour line may be more accurate.

Contours in descent are generally ignored unless the going gets steep, requiring you to zigzag down, and you might then add 20 seconds per contour depending upon conditions.

Obviously, all this will change when a variety of other factors are introduced. Terrain, weather, load carried, using crampons, tiredness and the state of the rest of the group will all have relevance.

You may find that, on a good day when not carrying much, you can move along at six kilometres per hour. Another time, with a heavy load, going uphill in snow at the end of a long day, you may be down to two kilometres per hour. Knowing what speed you are moving at is the key to getting the final calculation correct. The diagram below sets out speed in kilometres against distance, with the result in minutes. This is a useful thing to copy out, laminate and have with you to avoid needing to do calculations on the move when you also have to concentrate on other things.

PACING

This is having a known amount of double paces for 100 metres, or 100 yards. If you know how many you take on the flat – for most people this will be between 60 and 70 – if you have to walk, say, 600 metres in poor visibility then you will always know where you are.

Measure out a 100-metre, or yard, line on the flat somewhere handy. A 50-metre climbing rope could be handy for this. Now,

Speed k.p.h. / Distance m	2	3	4	5	6
50	1.5	1	45 secs.	36 secs.	0.5
100	3	2	1.5	1.2	1
200	6	4	3	2.4	2
500	15	10	7.5	6	5
1000	30	20	15	12	10

A timing chart

starting with your left foot, walk along it at a normal, relaxed walking pace and count every time your right foot hits the ground. The total will be your control number for that distance. Obviously, this will change when adding various factors such as terrain, up or downhill or snow underfoot, so you need to find out how this will affect you. There is no equation for working out the difference when walking uphill for example, as some people who take 65 paces on the flat may only increase slightly to 70, others may double to 130.

When you are walking more than 100 metres or yards, always count to your maximum number, 65 for example, and then start at 0 again. Don't be tempted to keep counting into the hundreds or you will lose count. This is where the counter on your compass, or toggles on your lanyard, will come in handy. At the end of each 100 metre or yard section, click the counter up one, or pull a toggle down, and start at zero again. You can then check the counter display, or count the toggles, to check how far you have travelled.

Accurate navigation is important in the mountains

NAVIGATION TECHNIQUES

There are a number of techniques that are useful to know, any of which could be used to help you accurately arrive at your destination. Like anything else, they will need practice but are relatively simple things to carry out.

TICK-OFF FEATURES

These are features that you pass on your way from the start of the navigational leg to arrival at your objective, and mentally tick off as you go. They could be crags, streams, a change in contours, in fact anything that is noteworthy and will tell you whether you are on the right course. Have a look at the map before you start walking to see what features will be on your route. If you expect to have to step over a stream, for instance, after 300 metres, and you do so, you can be fairly confident that you are on the right track. If you do not, however, this should serve as a warning and if it does not appear soon afterwards, you will need to set about relocating yourself.

It is also important to look at what features you might find beyond your objective in case you overshoot, and use these as a collecting feature (see p. 18).

AIMING OFF

If you are aiming for a stream junction, for example, in poor visibility, there is a good chance that you will end up one side or other of it and be unsure in which direction to head to reach the point. When you aim off you purposely add a few degrees to your bearing so that you arrive a little on the upslope side of the objective. When this section of the stream is reached, you then know in which direction to turn to follow it to the junction.

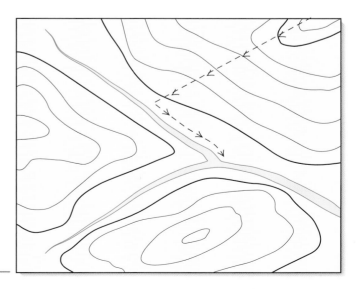

Aiming off

Boxing around an obstruction

A dog leg

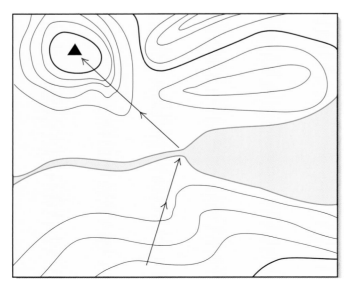

An attack point

BOXING A FEATURE

This is useful if you find an obstacle in the way of your bearing, such as a gully cutting into a cliff-top. When you reach it, turn out at 90 degrees to your original bearing and pace out until you are beyond the obstacle. Now turn 90 degrees again back on your original bearing and pacing count until clear. You now come back in on yourself with another 90-degree turn, pacing back by the same amount that you originally deviated. A final 90-degree turn brings you back on your original bearing.

DOG-LEG

This is a way of avoiding features in poor visibility, such as a steep cliff edge, by walking on two separate bearings to reach your objective. The point at which you turn may not even be a feature but could just be a point printed on the map, such as the corner of a grid square, to which you can take a bearing and a distance. Your pacing will need to be accurate, otherwise the second section of the process could cause you to over- or undershoot the objective.

It is commonly used for finding a ridge and getting off a mountain if handrailing (see below) is not appropriate due to a cornice hazard.

ATTACK POINT

This is a feature close to your objective, but one that is more obvious or pronounced. For instance, if you were trying to get to a re-entrant where you have left your tent, but there was also a large lake nearby, the lake would be an easier feature to find. You could then use the lake as the attack point to find your tent, as the margin for error would be that much less as it is closer than your original starting point.

HANDRAILING

This simple technique allows ground to be covered rapidly. It is when you follow an obvious feature, such as river or cliff edge, that leads you towards your objective. You could get to this by aiming off, the feature is then handrailed, and an attack point, such as a stream junction or gully, used to reach your final objective.

COLLECTING FEATURE

This is an obvious feature a short distance behind your objective, which will indicate that you have overshot your target. It could be a change in slope, the edge of a cliff (obviously taking care in winter or in poor visibility), a river or anything else obvious. You could then handrail this to an attack point and come back towards your objective from there.

ASPECT OF SLOPE

This can be used as an aid to location in poor visibility. Its main property is to tell you where you are not, rather than where you are, but this may also have benefits.

Keeping the compass baseplate horizontal, you need to take a bearing directly up or down the slope, and correct the bearing for any magnetic deviation from the map. Now place the compass on the map in the area you estimate that you are, keeping the arrow in the housing parallel with grid north on the map. Move your compass across the map, maintaining north to north, and where the lines on the baseplate of the compass cross the contours of the slope at exactly 90 degrees will indicate a possibility as to your location.

Even if this is accurate, you will still have to find out how far up the slope you are. It is also difficult assessing an exact 90-degree angle on a slope in cloud or bad weather, as all perspective is lost. However, it is a useful technique to know, and it can be used along with other information to help identify your position, and will certainly indicate which side of the hill you are on.

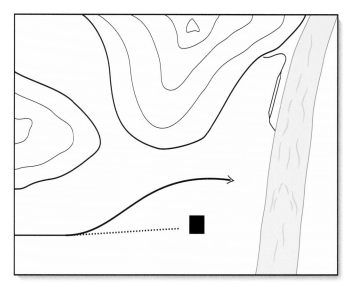

A collecting feature

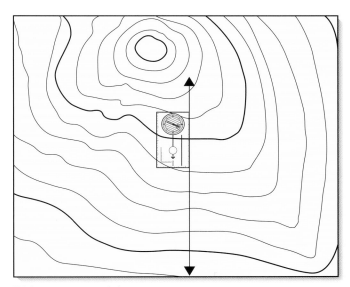

Taking an aspect of slope

Easy enough to find in good weather, accurate navigation will be needed to find your tent in poor visibility

WINTER CONSIDERATIONS

Navigation comes into its own in the winter, particularly if the cloud is down and the wind is blowing, creating poor visibility. Having a pair of ski goggles to hand is a very good idea, as trying to walk into driving snow at the same time as peering ahead to locate features is almost impossible.

Left: Poor visibility in full winter conditions

TAKING A GRID REFERENCE

Most maps that have grid lines on them also have accompanying numbers for each line. This allows you to come up with a grid reference, useful for identifying objectives to other group members, or when notifying the emergency services of the location of an accident.

Start by reading along the numbers at the bottom of the map, then the ones up the side. If you remember 'along the hall then up the stairs', this may help. The diagram shows the hatched box as being 9704. If the squares on the map are one kilometre across, the location will have the accuracy of one square kilometre. However, to get even greater accuracy, each of the grid boxes could then be subdivided into 100 imaginary squares. Stating these, such as 975043 in the diagram, will give a 100-metre area of accuracy. For even greater detail, this could even be subdivided further to give a 10-metre pinpoint. A GPS (global positioning unit, the use of which is outside the bounds of this book) will give you a 10-figure grid reference, refining the reference point to a 1 metre square.

If using the grid reference for rescue purposes, for example, and as each number is repeated every 100km, prefix the number with the map sheet number, or the unique letters designated to that section of the map. These will be found in the key that is printed down the side.

Having a companion walking ahead to sight on when using a bearing has already been mentioned. Be careful that you do not get too far apart though as it would be very easy to lose sight of each other after just a few paces. Also, take care when navigating in an area where there are edges. Roping up would be a good precaution, and as you know how long your climbing rope is, this may help you when calculating distance travelled. For instance, 6 legs using a 50-metre rope will be 300 metres travelled.

A true whiteout is where ground, horizon and sky merge into one grey mass, and a problem here is that your eyes have nothing to focus on, giving rise to headaches after a while, as well as difficult navigation. If caught out like this, making a snowball and throwing it ahead will make marks in the snow and give you something to lock on to, and could also be used as a point to walk to when on a bearing.

A snowball is also useful when trying to work out if any hazard may be ahead. Throwing one in front will indicate if the ground is flat or sloping, and this can

help to identify steep drops. Be careful if near corniced edges though, as you could walk onto a cornice next to a snowball mark, only to find yourself standing on unsupported ground.

Hand-railing is a useful technique for getting off the hill, and it can make travel very quick. Be very careful if hand-railing a cliff edge, as the entire group could be caught out, either by suddenly sloping and icy ground, or by cornice formation. To hand-rail safely in these conditions, use a rope and tie one person on to the end. They will be the one hand-railing, so they need to know what they are doing. The other group members, preferably at least two, tie on to the rope around ten metres away and walk on a line parallel to the edge, guided by their companion. If the latter should be unlucky enough to fall through a cornice, for example, they will be counterbalanced by the others who can then help retrieve them.

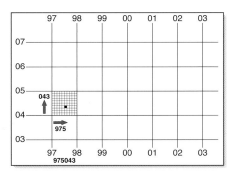

Taking a grid reference

Using the rope for security when handrailing

TECHNICAL EQUIPMENT

Fundamental to any climbing or mountaineering trip is to have good quality, functional equipment. Shops and Internet sites are full of wonderful things, all designed to do a variety of jobs in interesting ways. The trick that we have to learn as consumers is how to tell what is the good gear amongst the poorer quality clones, and which piece of kit is appropriate for the task that we are going to undertake.

There are a number of basic items of gear that are worth mentioning, and these are outlined below. Kit that is more specific to a certain type of environment, ice axes for winter climbing for instance, is covered in the relevant chapter.

Helmets are lightweight and strong

HELMET

This is a very important piece of equipment, although many climbers will choose not to wear one when sport climbing or bouldering. It helps to protect your head from the effect of a fall, as well as giving protection from any debris such as rocks or ice that may fall from above.

The best helmets are lightweight and easy to adjust, and they should have a mechanism for holding a head torch if this is going to be necessary, for instance when winter or Alpine mountaineering.

When you go to the shop to choose one, take a hat with you and make sure that the helmet fits securely both with and without it on, as this will increase its usefulness to year-round.

HARNESS

There are many different types of harness, and if you are going to be an all-round mountaineer or climber then it will be tricky finding one that does all of the jobs well within all disciplines, from summer sport climbing to Alpine mountaineering. One of the most important considerations will be the provision of an abseil loop, the sewn loop at the front that connects the leg loops and waist section. Personally, I wouldn't buy a harness without an abseil loop as it can be used for many jobs other than abseiling.

For traditional and sport climbing in good weather, a harness with fixed size leg loops would be fine, as these tend to be a little lighter than their adjustable counterparts, with fewer straps to get in the way. Padding is a good idea, especially if you are going to be sitting in it for a long time or taking a number of falls whilst attempting hard routes. The gear racking system is very important, and personally I like to have a number of gear loops with a couple quite far forwards on each side so that I can access my gear easily.

If you are going to be climbing in winter, it would be a good idea to opt for a harness with adjustable leg loops. These will allow you to put it on over bulky clothing and crampons, and still have the ability to tighten them in for the good weather when less clothing is worn. Having a good range of adjustment at the waist helps as well, as you can then centre the harness appropriately to suit your preference for gear loop positioning.

Alpine and expedition harnesses tend to be cut down to save weight, and will often have minimal padding. This is because you will most likely be wearing a lot of clothing which provides the padding for you. A consideration may also be the ability to disconnect the leg loops whilst still being safely attached to the waist belt, in order to answer calls of nature.

ROCK BOOTS

The choice of rock boot comes down very much to your style of climbing. Many manufacturers design boots with specific disciplines in mind, such as bouldering, smearing, edging and cold-weather boots.

Generally speaking, comfort is an important issue. Unless you are going to be climbing at the highest grades, don't go for a boot that is three sizes too small. Get a fit that feels quite snug in the shop and, by the time the lining has softened a little, they should be feeling fine for extended use. If you are going to climb a lot of multi-pitch mountain routes, having a slightly larger fit, but without excessive movement, may be necessary, to give you the comfort to last the day. Cold-weather rock boots, designed for use in cold climates, are a specialist item and the padding in them will help the fit.

Boots come with a choice of fastenings, with a lacing system being preferred by many as it gives the ability to adjust the fit of the boot around their foot. However, Velcro straps are popular with climbers who are wearing very tight, technical boots. This gives little room for infinite adjustment, but does make the boots very quick to put on and, more importantly, to take off again after a route has been completed.

It is worth leaving boots on for a while when buying them from a shop, to allow your feet to swell a little, as they would do in use. Try using the edge of the boot on any small holds that are provided, even the top of a skirting board will do. Also, make sure that the heel section will not pull off when heel-hooking, as this can be a problem with some Velcro-fastening types.

Lace-up rock boots, top, and Velcro-fastening, bottom

ROPES

These come in a huge range of sizes, colours and types, and every climber will have their own opinion as to what type suits them best for any given job. There are two basic types of construction, dynamic and static or, more correctly, low-stretch. The first is the only type that should be used when protecting a climber in a lead situation, as it is designed to elongate when loaded, thus absorbing energy and reducing the impact force on the falling climber and the belay system (see Appendix II). Low-stretch ropes should never be used where a lead fall is a possibility, and they tend to be reserved for abseiling, rigging and used as fixed ropes.

Dynamic ropes are divided into categories of use, relevant to their strength when tested. This means that they will be designated as a 'half' rope or a 'full weight' rope, and these properties are denoted on the packaging and rope ends with a ½ in a circle and a 1 in a circle. This is important information as it tells us that a ½ rope should only be used in tandem with another of the same or higher rating, such as can be seen when using double or twin rope techniques (see 'Climbing Rope Systems'). A full weight rope has been tested and passed to be used on its own, as is commonly seen with single rope methods.

Bear in mind that a rope with a ½ should never be used to hold a fall without being used alongside another rope, but conversely one with a 1 in a circle can also be used in tandem with another for twin or double roping. As full weight ropes are now manufactured down to a diameter of 8.4mm or even less, many climbers are choosing to use these and benefiting from the extra security, along with the knowledge that they can use them singly for lightweight climbs or paired up for extra security.

A dynamic rope that is suitable as an all-round bit of kit could be something like a full weight rope of 60 metres length and 10.5 or 10.2mm diameter. This will do well for rock climbing in all its forms, as well as for use during the winter. More specialist ropes, such as 70 metres of 8.5mm or less are useful for Alpine climbing, where double rope techniques will often be employed.

Many ropes are available with a dry treatment having been applied to them. This stops the ingress of water and thus not only keeps the ropes light in inclement conditions, but also helps them not to freeze in winter or at altitude. For the little extra money that it costs to buy one with a dry treatment, it is well worth doing.

Low-stretch ropes, particularly those that are going to be used for fixed ropes on expeditions, can be bought in a range of lengths including reels of, commonly, 200 metres. These come in a variety of diameters, with 9 to 10mm often being the choice of anyone intending to fix ropes. Obviously, the thinner the rope the more prone it is to wear and tear, so make sure that you err on the side of caution. Fixed ropes for short use on a simple snow slope can be thinner than those rigged for a long time on rock buttresses.

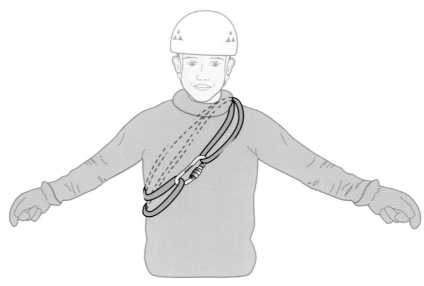
Carrying a 120cm (8ft) sling around the body

SLINGS

These are very useful items of equipment and come in a variety of lengths and widths. They are generally sold in metric sizes with their lengths measured when they are doubled and flat, but many countries still refer to their circumference size in feet.

The thinner slings are made from Dyneema, a very strong, lightweight fabric. It is easy to tie knots in but, being thin, it has a low melting point and can be easily damaged if abused. The wider slings are made from strong nylon webbing, they are a little heavier than the Dyneema but equally strong. They can be more awkward to tie knots in, being wider, but have better abrasion properties. Slings are best equipped with a screwgate karabiner as standard, as this makes them both easy to carry and ready to use.

Dyneema 60cm (4ft) slings are very useful as extenders for off-line protection. They can be equipped with two snapgate karabiners and live on your harness ready to use, with the thin fabric making them easy to handle. To carry them neatly, thread one karabiner through the other and clip it into the remaining sling loops. When needed for use, simply unclip any two sections of the sling and the karabiners will slide to either end, ready to be clipped to the protection and rope.

Slings of 120cm (8ft) are handy for all sorts of jobs, such as equalizing anchors, making thread belays and the like. They can be of either fabric, and I would suggest that you have a couple of lightweight ones for mountain routes and a couple of thicker versions for day-to-day use, where they will be more resilient than thinner slings to frequent handling.

To carry a sling of this length, double it, pass it over your shoulder and under your arm and then clip it into itself. This makes it easy to take it off with one hand, something that is not possible if you just wrap a couple of loops over your head.

You may even want to consider carrying a 240cm (16ft) sling, particularly on technical multi-pitch routes. Choosing one of Dyneema means that you can tie knots in it easily when equalizing anchors, and its large size lets it sit comfortably over a range of spike anchors. To carry it, double it, clip it into itself, then treat it like a 120cm (8ft) sling by taking it over one shoulder and under the other arm.

SNAPGATE KARABINERS

These are commonly used when leading routes as they allow quick clipping of any gear being placed for protection, and most of the separate items of kit on the leader's rack of gear will have a snapgate attached.

Available in a huge range of shapes and sizes, there are two main categories, those with solid gates and those that have wire gates.

Solid gate karabiners have been around for many years, but for many climbers, wire gates are taking over as their first choice. This is for three main reasons. Firstly, wire gates weigh less, an important consideration if a number are to be carried.

Secondly, the gate is sprung closed by the positioning of the attachment points of the gate itself, thus there are no moving parts to break, jam or freeze up, unlike the solid gate which will generally have an internal spring.

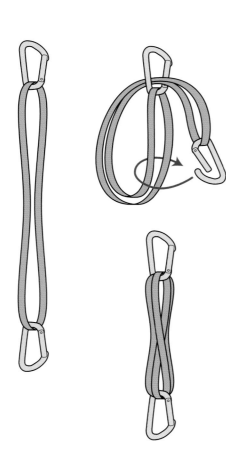
Looping a 60cm (4ft) sling through itself for carrying

Thirdly, and of a great deal of importance, is the mass of the gate. When a rope runs through a karabiner with any speed and force, such as when a fall is occurring, it sets up vibration. This has been shown to cause a solid gate, with its high mass, to open and close very rapidly. If the moment of full loading on the karabiner, which is the stage at which the fall stops and the climber's weight comes on to the rope, coincides with the gate being open, its strength is dramatically reduced. A wire gate, however, as it has far less mass, is less affected by the vibration and therefore is very unlikely to be in the open position when the fall stops.

A simple test here is to knock a solid gate and a wire gate against the palm of your hand. You will most likely hear the solid gate click each time, with no noise coming from the wire one. This is exactly the same effect as in a fall.

Snapgate karabiners are also available with two different gate shapes, straight and bent. A bent gate karabiner allows you to clip the rope in a lot more easily, ideal for desperate or hard to reach clips. However, there is also a slight increase in the chance of the rope unclipping itself in a fall situation, particularly if the rope has been clipped in incorrectly (see 'Sport Climbing'). Take care when using bent gates, and if climbing mountain routes I always substitute my bent gates for straight ones, as the chance of accidental unclipping on long-extended runners is then reduced.

Bent gate karabiners should always be used on the rope end of the system and never clipped in to the placement, as they could twist themselves off in some circumstances, such as if they were flicked and inverted by the rope.

Solid gate and wire gate snap karabiners

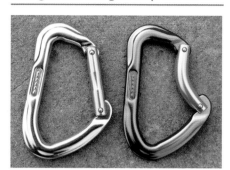

A straight and a bent gate snap karabiner

Snapgate karabiners are used to carry the gear on your harness

SCREWGATE KARABINERS

These differ from snapgates in that they have a sleeve device that can be fastened to prevent accidental opening. This is obviously important whenever they are being used as part of an anchor system or if used to connect a belay or abseil device to you. Although there are various sizes, they are generally categorized into two main types, D shape and HMS, or pear shape.

The greatest line of strength of a karabiner is when the load is pulling along the line of the back bar, that is the side away from the opening gate, and D shape karabiners will automatically align the rope or other attachments into this position. An HMS karabiner does not have such a tight bend at either end of its back bar, thus any load could be some distance from it. This makes the overall strength of the karabiner a bit less than that of a D. However, you will be unlikely to notice this difference in strength on a day-to-day basis, and it is only when the equipment is misused, such as being loaded incorrectly or excessively, that it will become apparent. 'Cross' or 'sideways' loading, where the load is taken at the middle of the back bar and across the gate, dramatically reduces the strength of any karabiner and should be avoided at all costs.

An HMS karabiner is ideal for clipping big knots into, and it is first choice for use with a variety of belay and abseil devices. One huge advantage is that it is ideal, indeed designed, for use with an Italian hitch when belaying or abseiling, as the lack of tight curve at the end of the back bar allows the hitch to rotate freely. If you tried using an Italian hitch with a D shape karabiner, it would easily jam under load when being reversed, as it will squash itself against the tight curve by the back bar and refuse to move.

There are also different mechanisms that lock the gate. The commonest is a rotating sleeve that you screw up shut to prevent accidental opening. Don't be tempted to over-tighten it, otherwise it could become jammed and be difficult to release.

The other style has an automatic locking system, consisting of a one- or two-stage function. A single-stage means that you simply have to either rotate or pull back on the sleeve, and the gate can be opened. A two-stage auto-locking karabiner involves either rotating the sleeve then pulling it back, or depressing a button then rotating the sleeve. The two-stage system is generally thought of as being the safer of the two automatic styles, although many

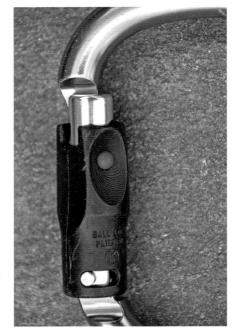

This style of two-stage karabiner requires the green button to be depressed and the sleeve then rotated in order to open the gate

climbers have an inherent distrust of this type of locking karabiner and always choose a normal screwgate design instead.

BELAY DEVICES

This is an essential piece of gear for most climbing and mountaineering situations, and it will have to perform well in a variety of roles, such as belaying both leader and second, and as an abseil device. There are a vast number of styles available, and the selection of a device suitable for your needs should be made carefully and after due consideration.

Belay devices can be roughly categorized into three types, and these are slick, stiff and grabbing. Multi-purpose self-locking devices are another sub-category. These terms describe how efficient each is when used to manipulate a rope and the characteristics of their holding power.

Slick devices generally consist of a plate or tube with two large diameter slots through which one or two bights of rope are threaded. Quite safe in experienced hands, these devices can be difficult to brake with, thus be 'slick' when used with ropes of diameters less than 10mm and practice is needed to hold a fall safely. However, a slick device is very useful if you are belaying when using snow or ice anchors, or a rock anchor that is not as sound as you would like. As shock-loading must be avoided, so that you do not run the risk of your anchor failing, a slick device allows some dynamic

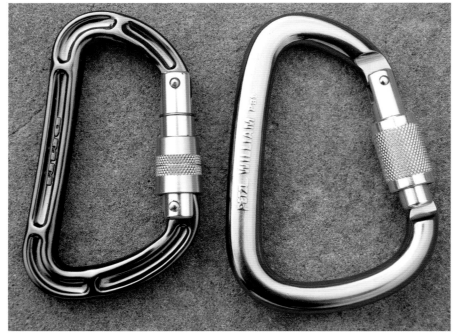

A D shape and an HMS karabiner

A variety of belay devices, slick on the left, stiff in the middle and grabbing on the right

Types of extender

braking to take place, where slippage of the rope through the device is permitted as a fall is arrested. This consequently reduces the loading at the anchor and allows a gradual absorption of energy into the system. This is also a technique used to reduce the loading on running belays in the event of a leader fall, where the runners may be poor placements and a shock load could cause them to fail. Allowing gradual braking through a slick device will help to lessen the chance of this happening.

The second type, a stiff belay device, most often describes one that has a controlling groove next to each of the rope slots, which helps you when holding a fall or abseiling by providing extra friction to the braking hand holding the dead rope. These slots often have ribs in them which helps with the braking. An advantage of this type of device is that it may be turned round so that the slots are not used, allowing it to function in the same way as a slick device. This is useful if using thick ropes, or ropes that are starting to freeze.

A grabbing device describes the action whereby the rope is held firm immediately the device is loaded, such as in the event of a fall or when abseiling, and can be further split into active and passive systems. An active device, also known as an active self-locking belay device, will generally incorporate moving parts and, in the event of loading, it reacts in a manner very like some automotive seat belt systems, whereby the weight of the climber on the rope pushes a camming mechanism into a position where the rope is held firm with little slippage. To release the rope, a lever

on the outside of the device is pressed which then moves the cam away from the rope, thus allowing you to pay out as required. These types of devices are very popular on sport climbs, where the strength of the anchors and bolts is usually high and a dynamic braking effect is not always needed.

A passive system, also known as a passive self-locking belay device, applies to a device that has no moving parts but that relies just on the loading of the rope to lock itself off. In this case, it is held in position by a retaining karabiner clipped into a loop of rope at the back of the device, which in turn will most commonly be used on a direct belay system. These devices are very popular with instructors, who can bring two clients up on two separate ropes at one time. However, they are very difficult to release under load and should not be used if there is the possibility when your partner cannot get their weight off the rope to help. Some designs incorporate a ribbed section that makes the task a little easier, others have a handle to do a similar job. They are still notoriously difficult to release, however, and a way out of this problem can be found in the 'Emergency Procedures' section.

EXTENDERS

Also known as quick-draws or tie-offs, these will make up a very important part of your rack. They are typically made from a short length of sling material, often Dyneema, and will have a snapgate karabiner clipped into each end. The length of the extenders is very much up to the style of climbing

that you are doing, but generally speaking those being used on sport routes can be quite short, about 15cm (6in), and those used on other rock climbs can vary from 15cm (6in) to 30cm (12in). This variation allows runners off to one side or other of the line of the rope to be clipped without causing rope drag.

They are best bought ready sewn, as this is a specialist job, and you can add your own karabiners to suit your style of climbing. Alternatively, many manufacturers offer a full extender set-up, including tape with one bent gate and one straight gate karabiner attached. Buying multiple sets will often work out cheaper than buying individually, and if you think that a basic rock climbing rack will typically have at least eight extenders on it, which makes 16 karabiners, price may well become a consideration.

Some extenders are small open loops, others are sewn along their length and are quite stiff, with the karabiner at the rope end either being in a very tight loop, or supplied with a rubber device that keeps the karabiner hanging in the correct orientation for clipping. Generally speaking, sport route climbers like short, rigid extenders, whilst those taking part in general mountaineering like the extenders to be a bit looser, giving more flexibility in the karabiner position.

WIRES

These are the staple of most climbers' racks, and although they can be very small they are an essential component of the safety chain. They are made from different sized wedges of metal that are attached to the end of a swaged wire loop, and although they look simple they are actually very technical pieces of kit. They have been designed to rigorous standards and are of a very high strength, able to repeatedly hold the weight of a falling climber.

A large size choice is available and these can range from just a couple of millimetres (3/32in) in width to 2cm (3/4in) or more, with the strength rating running from around 2kN on the smallest up to 12kN or so on the larger sizes (see Appendix II).

Most rock climbers find that a rack of wires made up from two sets of 1–10, with each size being doubled up, covers most eventualities. Often they will double up the sizes from two different manufacturers, so as to get a variation in the head shape, thus allowing more flexibility in placement. Winter climbers may carry far fewer wires, and sport climbers none at all, or maybe just a small selection for areas of rock where bolts are missing.

Small wires, known as micro-wires, are also handy for some styles of climbing, and they may sometimes provide the only protection on routes with very thin cracks.

How to carry wires is up to personal preference. It would be very difficult to manipulate a whole double set, twenty or more, on one karabiner. Add to this the disastrous consequences of dropping the karabiner with the wires on when halfway up a route, and you can see that splitting them on to two or more karabiners would be a good idea. Having 1-5 on one krab

A selection of chocks on both rope and slings

and 6-10 on the other is one way, although some climbers will prefer to have a full set on each karabiner. In this way, if you drop one krab at least you have a full range of wires left on the other. If you were carrying a lot of wires, then micros and size 1s on one krab, 2-6 on another and 7-10 on a third would be a good compromise.

CHOCKS

This is a generic name given to a variety of alloy wedges that are attached to wire or, more commonly, rope or sewn slings. Often called 'nuts', 'stoppers' or 'hexes', they come in a variety of shapes and sizes, and climbers will have their favourites.

It is worth having a logical size progression throughout your protection equipment, so the smallest chock should start up where the largest wire left off.

CAMMING DEVICES

Also known as spring-loaded camming devices or SLCDs, cams, as they are more popularly known, are a key item in a climber's arsenal. Running from around a tiny 12mm (1/2in) through to a huge 150mm (6in) or even more, these

A double set of wires on two karabiners

A set of micro-wires

A three- and a four-cam unit

A range of SLCDs

extremely useful bits of kit are key to the problem of protecting many climbs that offer little more than parallel-sided cracks for placements. They also fit well into pockets and flutings, and can even cope with cracks that flare slightly outwards.

They come in rigid and flexible stem options, with the flexible stem being a firm favourite with most users. This is because it increases the range of placements that can be made, such as horizontal cracks and pockets, where a rigid-stemmed cam would not do such a good job.

Also, they come in three- or four-cam units, with the latter being most people's preference. However, the advantage of a three-cam unit is that it can be manufactured quite narrow, obviously having less width than a four-cam unit, so it can be placed into smaller cracks and pockets. Climbers will often have a couple of small three-cam SLCDs, then continue up the size range with four-cam units.

Some SLCDs require you to clip an extender on to them, others have a sewn sling already attached. These are my personal favourite, and I have a number of the type that allows the sling to be easily extended if the cam is going to be placed a little off line.

NUT KEY

This is an invaluable tool, and certainly will constitute the best money that you have ever spent on a piece of gear! Generally made from a long flat bar with a hook at one end and a hole for a carrying karabiner or cord at the other, it is ideal for tweaking out stubborn-to-remove wires and other protection. Carried as standard by the second person on a climb, leaders will also find having one to be useful, as it can help pull slings through awkward threads, remove wires that didn't quite fit right and for cleaning cracks of mud and debris, a useful thing to do on multi-pitch routes, particularly in the mountains.

PRUSIK LOOPS

These are extremely useful, light and cheap items of kit, and you would normally carry two for most climbing and mountaineering situations. You can protect an abseil with them, set up a hoisting system, and they can even be unpicked to use in an Abalakov thread as abseil tat on ice.

The loops need to be in the region of 40cm (20in), measured end to end when laid flat, once they are tied with a double fisherman's knot. The commonest material to use is 6mm (1/4 in) climbing accessory cord, which can be purchased straight from a reel at a climbing shop.

A prusik loop, tied with a double fisherman's knot

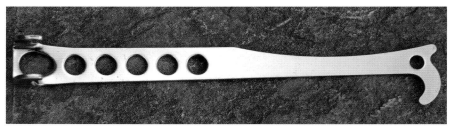

A nut key

GEAR PLACEMENT

Being swiftly able to identify and utilize an appropriate gear placement, as well as the relevant piece of kit, is fundamental to being safe on crags, hills and mountains throughout the world. Practice is always the key, and you should take every opportunity to learn as much as you can about the correct use of any protection equipment that you may buy. Remember that good gear placement can save your life, or that of your partner, and if you approach the task with that in mind it helps to put it all into perspective. You may be the greatest climber in the world, but if you cannot place gear swiftly and soundly, it will all mean nothing in the end.

Efficiently placing wires on the lead

Gear placements occur on the lead, at anchors and when constructing a sound system to abseil from. Because of this, it is a good idea to have some mental check as to how good you think each placement will be. A standard method is to use a scale of 1 to 5, where 1 is poor and 5 is as good as it gets. If you are leading and can rate all of your gear as a 4 or 5, then things are looking up!

When dealing with anchors, work on a total of 10. This means that, if you have placed two wires, for example, that you rate a 3 and a 4, you will need another of at least a 3 rating to give an overall anchor rating of 10. This is, of course, an ideal situation, and it must be said that in some situations, particularly on long, hard winter routes, you would be lucky to find anything at all! However, having a basic system to work to makes things easier to understand, and puts the security of your various systems into context.

A spike runner with the sling shortened using an overhand knot

SLINGS

These are undoubtedly the easiest gear placements that we use, as they can be dropped over spikes or threaded through holes. It is easy to see how well they are placed, and the resulting placement tends to be very strong.

Take care if using a spike runner or anchor, as the sling can lift off the rock if moved by the run of the rope. Either use a longer sling, which will often solve the problem, or weigh it down with a couple of bits of kit to make it less likely to rise up.

If you are using a thread, pay attention when placing, and in particular when retrieving, the sling, as it may get stuck in the confines of the crack. When used as an anchor, and if the crack between boulders is very tight, it may be a good idea to pack it out at the back with some small rocks, grass or even a pair of gloves, to ensure that the sling does not become irretrievably snagged when placed under load.

You can also use a thread around a tree root, trunk or branch. Don't larksfoot the sling when you wrap it round as this makes it quite a weak knot, and could also cause the sling to tighten and jam. Instead, clip the two ends together with a karabiner.

Slings can be shortened by tying an overhand knot in them, and the karabiner can be clipped in above that. Alternatively, they can be wrapped twice around a small spike and both loops clipped.

When you place a sling on the lead, it may be worth shutting the screwgate, just to provide a bit of extra security. If you are climbing in winter and are worried that the gate might freeze shut, don't bother, but for other times a couple of seconds to do it up may be time well spent.

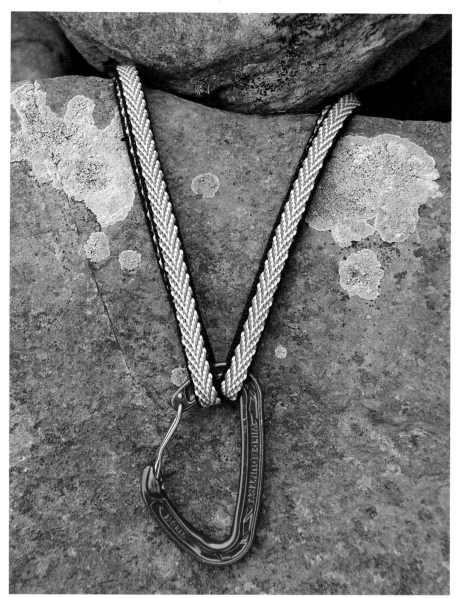
A thread runner clipped correctly

WIRES

Due to the curved head-section of most styles of wire these days, they fit well into a variety of placements and are generally very stable. The concave/convex head shape means that they only need three points of contact to function correctly, allowing them to be placed securely into near parallel-sided cracks and fissures.

They can be placed into either vertical or horizontal cracks. Ideally, the best placements will be where a vertical crack is wide at the top and tapers in towards the bottom, with the rear of the crack being a little wider than the outside edge. This shape will allow a wire to be placed in a very strong position, able to sustain a high load in the event of a fall without pulling through, and also be less likely to be flicked out by the movement of the rope.

A well placed wire in a vertical crack

A wire threaded through a gap

Having selected the appropriate wire to use, don't unclip it from its carrying krab but place it into the crack with the head of the wire sitting in the correct orientation that will allow any load to be pulled evenly down the line of the wire loop to the karabiner. Now use the other wires still on the karabiner to help seat it by giving them a smart tug downwards two or three times.

This is purely to help the wire seat itself snugly into the crack, and not to see if it will pull out when loaded, as if the latter is a concern then you have chosen the wrong crack or wire in the first place. Always hold on tight to the rock with your other hand when seating a wire, as if it should ping out when tugged you could be thrown off balance and fall. Never seat a wire by pulling with two hands for exactly that reason. However, don't be tempted to seat the wire too aggressively, as your second will have to remove it, which can often prove to be a harder challenge than positioning it in the first place.

Another placement that works well is to thread a wire down through a natural gap in the rock or in the space between two boulders. Unclip the wire from the karabiner and push the wire loop down and through, clipping it with a karabiner where it emerges. The head of the wire may rattle about a bit, but will never pull out. Make sure that you tell your second how it went in, otherwise they will be spending hours trying to work out how to retrieve it!

Wires with a concave/convex section also work well in many horizontal placements. Initially, place the wire with its rounded side downmost, as this allows the head to rock when under load, causing it to jam tighter into the placement.

Many micro-wires have a complicated, uneven trapezoid cross-section, which fits well into a variety of slim cracks and splits in the rock. Some manipulating may be needed to get it into the optimum position, but this is the only option if you are climbing otherwise blank sections of ground.

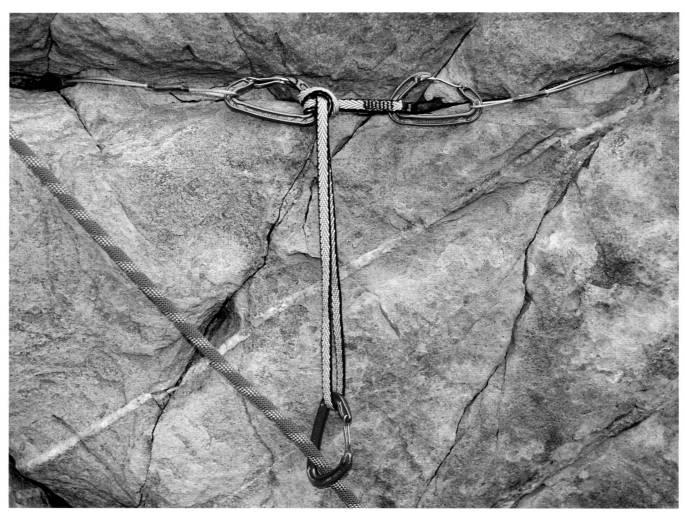

Two wires placed in opposition. The connecting sling has been tied off around one with a clove hitch

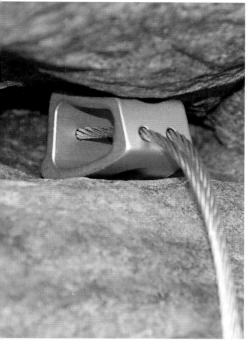

A chock being used between two sections of rock, loose but safe

A chock efficiently placed in a tapering crack

A chock being used end-on in a tapering crack

A wire placed into a horizontal crack with the convex side of the head downmost

When a wire is placed on the lead, you will most likely be clipping an extender to it. This straightens out the line that the rope takes up the route, and reduces the chance of the wire lifting out. For this reason, make sure that the extender is long enough, and on some routes, particularly in winter where you may be zigzagging around a lot, you may find that you have to use long slings to straighten the line and reduce rope drag. If you are placing a wire immediately after leaving the ground or a ledge, you could just clip a single karabiner straight on to the wire instead of using an extender. This gives you a little more height advantage should you slip, and subsequent wires can then be clipped as normal.

When you are using wires as part of an anchor system, for instance when setting up a belay or abseil point, a screwgate karabiner should be used on each wire to provide maximum security. Never be tempted to just pass a sling or rope directly through the wire loop and use that as an anchor or running belay, as the wire can easily cut through the material if loaded.

Very occasionally, it may be useful to place two wires in opposition, so that they pull towards each other when loaded as opposed to pulling outwards. This could be handy on a section of traverse where an otherwise well-placed wire will be pulled sideways and outwards by the rope tugging on the extender, and placing another wire in the opposite direction will keep it in place. There are a number of ways of doing this, but the most efficient for the majority of

cases will be to run a short sling from one wire, clove hitch it on to the karabiner of the other, and use the remaining tail as the extender.

CHOCKS

The majority of modern chocks rely on a differential in the side sizes to provide a rotating and thus camming action when loaded. They are best placed with the narrowest plane to the rock, and can be used in both vertical and horizontal cracks. If being used horizontally, and the style of chock has one section of rounded face, place this downmost, as you would for a wire.

Another common and useful placement is where the head of the chock is placed behind a constriction, such as two boulders that are nearly touching, so that it is not camming in the conventional sense but will still not pull through when loaded.

As with wires, most chocks can be used in the sideways plane if necessary, and this allows a far greater size range of cracks to be exploited.

A chock being used in a horizontal crack

CAMMING DEVICES

These very useful pieces of protection equipment are also often the least understood and, unfortunately, the most abused part of a rack as well. If they are not placed properly they can fail under load, jam irretrievably in a crack or 'walk' in and become wedged, making recovery difficult.

Most styles require a hypodermic syringe type movement to operate, with your thumb on a central bar or loop and two fingers on another bar or loop. Squeezing your fingers together causes the cams to retract.

Cams should be placed into a crack that covers around their mid-70 per cent size range. Anything smaller and they have a chance of jamming in, any wider and the cams may be too open to grip under load. To place one, retract the cams and present it to the crack. There should be a little play either side, so if both sets of cams are touching rock as this stage then you need to go for a smaller size. Align the unit so that the stem will be in line with the possible direction of loading, and release the trigger so that the individual cams touch the rock. If they open out to anything approaching 90 degrees from the stem, then that is too wide and the unit needs to be replaced with a bigger size.

If you think that the unit is the correct size but it doesn't seem to seat too well, take it out and turn it round 180 degrees, then try again. As the individual cams are wider on one side than the other, obviously more so with three-cam units, this may do the trick.

Cams, particularly those with flexible stems, can be placed in horizontal cracks. Initially, position them with the wider cams downmost, as this will make the placement more stable. However, you may find that in some cases they sit in a better position the other way up. They do not need to be pushed far into the crack, and make sure that the flexible part of the stem is running over the appropriate part of the crack edge. Be very wary of using rigid-stemmed cams in horizontal placements, as falling on to a rigid stem, particularly one that is protruding for any distance will almost certainly cause it to bend or even break.

One thing that affects most cams is 'walking'. As each of the three or four individual cam segments is sprung independently, any side-to-side movement of the rope could cause the unit to walk deeper into the crack, or pop out of the top if the crack is not capped. To avoid this, make sure that the rope will run freely and it won't tug on the unit, and use an extender or sling if this is going to help the cam remain motionless.

A number of units have stops built into the sides of each individual cam section. This allows them to be placed wide-open,

A camming device correctly positioned in a vertical crack

in much the same manner as a passive nut. You will need to be fairly desperate to do this, as other possibilities for placements may well exist, but it is worth knowing that the option is there, should you need it to protect a section of ground.

Note that the use of camming devices as part of an anchor system is not to be recommended. As they tend to walk, the orientation of the anchor rope, or the vectoring angles if more than one is being used, can change (see Appendix II). If you have one very sound anchor you may choose to use a cam to bring you into line, but don't use them where failure would be catastrophic.

A cam in a horizontal placement

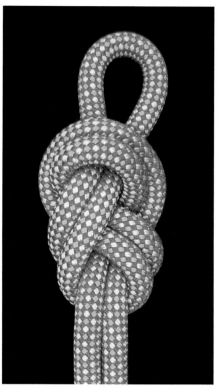

The basic figure of eight knot

KNOTS

There are a number of knots that are very useful, if not essential, to know for climbing and mountaineering purposes. Although knowing two or three basic types will do for most situations, having the ability to use knots to equalize anchors and arrange emergency systems will require you to have a little extra knowledge. However, the task is not huge, the main consideration being to assess which knot is suitable in which situation. A little forethought and prior practice will soon sort this out.

FIGURE OF EIGHT

This is an essential knot, and it can be tied in a number of ways. It is the main method that many people use when tying on to a harness, and when tied slightly differently it is a quick and effective method of tying on to anchors.

Its simplest form is a basic figure of eight, tied on a bight, or loop, of the rope. It is often used when tying a loop in the end of the rope, and this will subsequently be used to attach the rope to a harness with either one or two screwgate karabiners.

This method of connection is frequently seen being used by climbers who are lowering from a sport route, after rigging the rope appropriately at the lower-off point. It is also used in a bottom rope situation, but should never, however, be used by anyone leading a climb, as the connecting karabiners introduce a weak and vulnerable link into the safety chain, with the possibility of cross-loading and a huge reduction in their rated strength in the event of a fall.

The rewoven version is a very good way to tie on to a harness, and it has the added advantage of being a recognizable shape when fully tied, useful when checking the attachment of others. Once the knot is completed, the loop created by the rope needs to end up roughly the same size as the abseil loop on the harness. If your harness does not have an abseil loop, making the rope loop just under fist size will be about right.

Once the figure of eight is completed, secure the end with a stopper knot, the best being half a double fisherman's knot. This is to ensure that there is no way that the figure of eight can loosen whilst you are climbing or belaying. The tail left over when the stopper knot is completed should be about 5cm (2in) long.

Another version, the figure of eight on the bight, is ideal for use when constructing belays, and it is relevant for all rock, snow and ice situations. A huge advantage of this knot, apart from the ease with which it can be tied, is that if it is shock-loaded it will tighten within itself and absorb part of the load, thus reducing a percentage of

Starting the figure of eight rewoven

**The finished knot – it must now be
tightened and have a stopper knot tied**

The figure of eight on the bight

the force transmitted through the anchor system holding a fall, especially that of a leader.

When you tie the knot, start with a bight of around 60cm (24in) and pass it through the tie-in loop of your harness. This means that when the knot is completed the tail that is left over will be around 30cm (12in) in length, and this is important as it ensures that the knot does not loosen and undo. Once the knot is complete, pull all four sections of rope to make it snug.

A final version is the double figure of eight. This is also referred to as bunny's ears, and can be used for connection on to two anchors if a sling is not being used to equalize them. This is because each loop can easily be lengthened independently of the other, allowing for varying distances between attachment points to be reached. It is also handy when rigging a bottom rope climbing session, as the knot is easy

The knot tied on to a harness

to undo after it has been loaded (see 'Top and bottom roping').

If you are using it to equalize two sides of an anchor system, the knot should be tied loosely and each of the loops adjusted to the required length before the knot is finally pulled tight. Further adjustment is still possible if need be. It is important, however that both of the loops are clipped into with a karabiner, as there is a chance, if the loops are short, that one could pull through if the other is loaded.

DOUBLE BOWLINE

This is a useful knot to know, and it has a number of uses. Its overriding property is that it can be released easily once it has been subjected to considerable loading and, because of this, is often the first choice of those climbing hard routes and taking a number of falls. It is also a popular choice on indoor climbing walls for the same reason. It is also easy to tie around your waist if you are not using a harness, and can be used to anchor the rope to a tree, for instance, when arranging an abseil. It has recently taken precedence over the single bowline, where the tail of the rope only went through one wrap of the main rope instead of two, which many climbers have used quite satisfactorily for years.

The only drawback is the ease with which it can undo if not tied or completed

Starting the double figure of eight

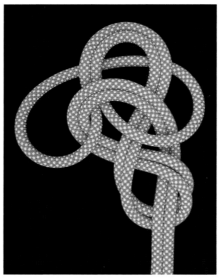

Fold the bight of rope over the back

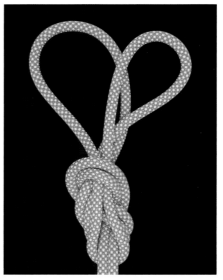

The completed knot

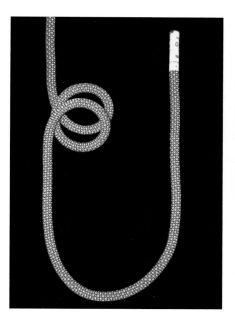

Starting the double bowline

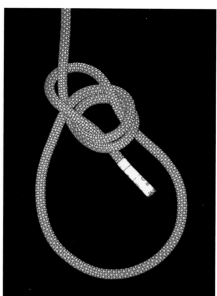

The completed double bowline shape, before being tightened

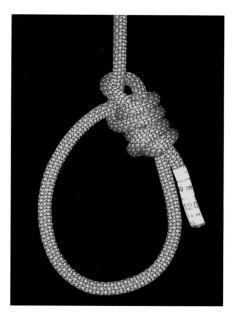

The double bowline with stopper knot

correctly, so it is essential that you tie a half a double fisherman's stopper knot to secure the tail end of rope. Make sure, once this is tied, that it is butted up tight to the main knot.

DOUBLE FISHERMAN'S KNOT

This is useful for joining two lengths of rope together, such as when setting up an Abalakov thread, making up equipment like a prusik loop, or for tying two climbing ropes together prior to an abseil.

A common use is half of the knot used as a stopper knot to tie off the rope end, after connecting yourself to a harness.

The double bowline tied on to a harness

An exploded view of the double fisherman's knot

The completed double fisherman's knot

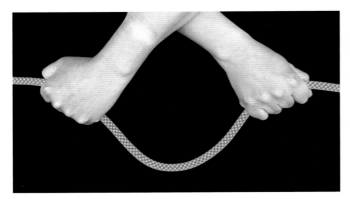

Starting a clove hitch

Uncross your hands

Place one loop behind the other without twisting

CLOVE HITCH

This is an extremely useful knot, and it is used throughout all areas of mountaineering. Its simplicity of tying, allied with its ease of adjustment, make it ideal to secure yourself to an anchor system. It can also be tied with one hand, a useful property when needing to arrange an anchor whilst holding on to the rock or an ice axe for security.

It will be best clipped in to an HMS karabiner. It can be put into a D shape but, if so, make sure that the knot is sitting in the correct manner and hasn't crossed over itself, making it harder to adjust and not being quite as secure.

The load rope of a clove hitch should, in theory, be on the side of the rope that is closest to the back bar of the karabiner, as this is obviously where the strength of the karabiner lies. In practice, don't worry too much about this, as you will be hard pushed to create enough force under normal conditions to make a big difference to the strength of the system. However, do bear this in mind if you are tempted to clip more than one clove hitch into the same karabiner, as the load rope could now be quite some distance from the back bar, resulting in a levering effect on the gate side of the karabiner in some circumstances.

Inverting a clove hitch is a common way of getting it to grip tightly in situations where it is not tied in to a karabiner, such as around the shaft of an ice axe in the winter, or on an in-situ anchor such as a metal stake. Once the hitch has been placed around the object, simply take one side of it and wrap it once around the back, swivelling the hitch away from the load side.

The completed clove hitch

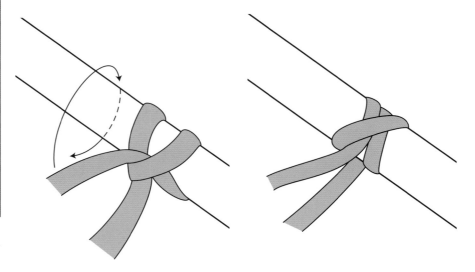

Inverting a clove hitch

Tying it with one hand takes a few moments of practice, but can be useful. It is all in the twist of your hand, and the photographs show the sequence.

Adjusting a clove hitch is quite simple. Decide which section of rope needs to be taken in, trace it through the karabiner, and, using the karabiner as a pulley, pull on the rope on the opposite side. Once you are tight on the anchor, pull the slack through on the dead rope side to make it all tight.

Rotate your hand and grasp the rope

Straighten your hand to make a loop

Starting to tie an Italian hitch

Fold your hand together to complete the hitch

ITALIAN HITCH
Also known as the Münter hitch, this knot has a variety of uses, and can help you to belay, abseil and safeguard emergency systems. Once you have tied it, it will look a bit like the clove hitch but will not lock itself off automatically when loaded. It is very important that the hitch is always clipped into an HMS karabiner, so that there is no chance of it jamming during operation.

When being used to belay your partner, with the hitch often being directly clipped on to an anchor, the maximum braking effect is achieved with the live and dead ropes being held parallel. Because of

Clip the loop in to make the clove hitch

Uncross your hands

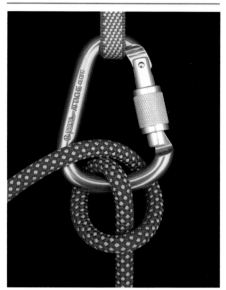

The completed hitch on a karabiner

this, the hitch should be placed behind or upslope of whoever is belaying. One of the advantages of this method is that your second, when they reach the stance, can continue a bit behind you and still be protected, an advantage when using small ledges on steep technical ground. A further plus point is that it can be easily locked off, even when under load, and this property makes for a slick change-over at stances. A locked off hitch can be used as a secure back-up on emergency systems, as if it is backing up a French prusik that slips, the complete system can ultimately still be released.

It can also be used as an abseil method, very useful if you have inadvertently dropped your belay or abseil device. It will tend to twist the ropes a bit over a long distance, but as long as you take a moment to let the ropes unravel this should not be a problem.

As with the clove hitch, it can be tied with one hand with a little practice, leaving out the final twist (see above). However, as you will most likely be using it when secured to an anchor or on the flat, the reasons for tying it with just one hand are few and far between.

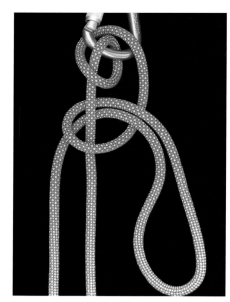

Tying a slippery hitch

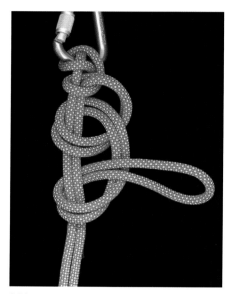

Add two half hitches

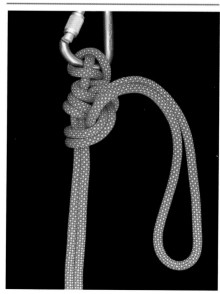

The fully locked off Italian hitch

LOCKING OFF THE ITALIAN HITCH

It is worth becoming adept in locking off the Italian hitch, as there are a number of reasons for doing so. Try doing it with the system loaded and unloaded for both locking off and releasing, as this could be the case in an emergency. If you are securing your second at a stance on a multi-pitch route after belaying them up using the Italian hitch, they can be safely locked off whilst you swap gear, or they could remain at the stance whilst you climb the next pitch.

It will be best to start with the hitch orientated on to the paying-out side of the karabiner, as this stops any slight chance of a jam occurring. Start by tying a slippery hitch, with approximately 60cm (24in) of bight being used. This should be slid up tight to the HMS before being secured with two half hitches that are also pulled up snug, this time to the slippery hitch. Once the process has been completed, make sure that you have an end of rope left over of approximately 30cm (12in) in length, as this will ensure that the knot has no chance of unravelling.

FRENCH PRUSIK

This knot can be used in a variety of situations, such as abseiling and during emergency procedures. A very important property is its ability to be released when under load, and this sets it apart from most of the other knots that are tied using a prusik loop.

The number of turns around the rope depends on a number of factors, such as the thickness of the rope, whether it is wet or dry, old or new, etc. Make sure that the knotted section of the prusik loop isn't part of the wrapping, as this will stop it gripping quite so efficiently. Remember that it is possible to put on too many wraps, which will cause the knot to be very awkward to move, as well as not putting on enough, which will stop it from gripping properly.

Although a very good knot in its own right, if it is being used as part of an emergency system it is important that it is backed up by a tied-off Italian hitch, just in case it starts to slip. Never shock-load a French prusik, or any similar knot for that matter, as if it slips down the rope the thin cord from which it is made could melt through in about a metre (36in), or severely damage the main climbing rope, perhaps stripping right through the sheath.

A klemheist

KLEMHEIST

This is useful for hauling and hoisting rigs, as well as ascending the rope and escaping the system. There is some similarity with the French prusik, but the one major difference is that, whereas the French Prusik can be released when it is loaded, the klemheist cannot. Also, the klemheist works when pulled in one direction; the French prusik, being symmetrical, works in both directions.

Start to tie the klemheist knot from the top downwards. Hold a small eye of the prusik loop against the climbing rope and wrap the rest of the loop neatly around

A French prusik

the rope. A sling could also be used, particularly if escaping the system with the anchor points out of reach, with Dyneema being particularly good at gripping. As for the French prusik, the number of wraps depends upon a variety of factors, such as the thickness of the rope. It will also not be a good idea to have too many wraps, as this will cause it to be very difficult to move. Bring the long tail end of the prusik loop up and through the smaller eye and back down again along the line of the rope in the direction that it is to be loaded. A karabiner can be attached to this loop for connection to whatever system you are rigging.

Pulling down on, or loading, the karabiner causes it to pull down the longer loop, which pulls the coils tight via the shorter loop. If you are using it to prusik up a rope, for example, pushing the small top loop a little when the knot is unweighted will make it easier to slide up the rope.

PRUSIK KNOT

This is the original 'gripping' knot, but as it does its job so well it has been superseded in many cases by the French prusik and the klemheist. It is a little easier to tie with one hand than the others, so has its place in some emergency situations. It is also symmetrical, taking a pull from either direction.

The prusik loop is wrapped through itself a number of times, with the number

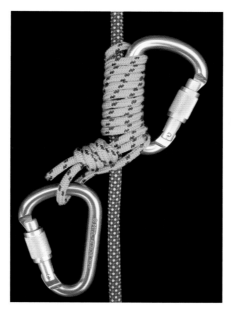

The Bachmann knot

An Alpine clutch

of wraps dictating how tight it will grip the rope, with more than three often being excessive. A karabiner is clipped into the resulting loop of cord and the attachment made at that point.

BACHMANN

The Bachmann knot is similar in design to the French prusik and the klemheist, except that it uses a karabiner in the system to provide a handle that can make moving the knot a bit easier, especially when wearing thick gloves. The main disadvantage is that it is very poor at gripping on icy ropes as it can sometimes slip a little due to the back bar of the karabiner touching the main climbing rope.

Clip a prusik loop into a karabiner and, holding the back bar against the rope, wrap the loop around the bar and rope a number of times. Attachment is made to the loop that will subsequently be hanging from the bottom of the karabiner.

ALPINE CLUTCH

This can be used in a number of situations, for instance as an alternative to a jamming knot such as the klemheist or mechanical device like an ascender. It works by two karabiners butting against each other when loaded, causing them to grip the climbing rope. However, it only works in one direction and cannot be released under load, so it should not be used where having to pay out slack is a possibility.

If it is used as part of a hauling system, the friction created will take away some of the mechanical advantage of the system, although this may be repaid by the ease

with which it locks off. It is best to use two matching HMS karabiners, as you may sometimes find that other types tend to jam when taking the rope in.

REEF KNOT

This is useful for joining two ropes together when organizing an abseil (see 'Abseiling'). It is also useful for securing the ends of the rope around you for carrying, once it has been coiled at the end of a route (see 'Coiling a rope'). When tying, if you remember 'right over left, left over right', you will end up with the correct knot.

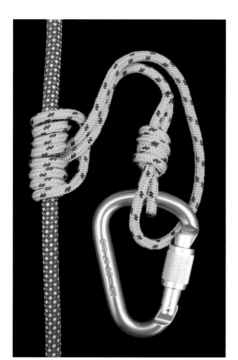

The prusik knot

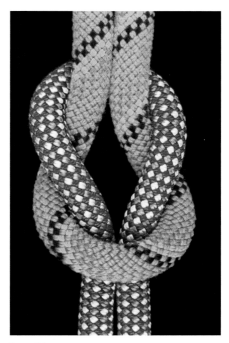

A reef knot

Starting the Alpine butterfly

Having pulled the end loop to your thumb, pull the new end loop over the rest

Tuck it underneath and pull it through

The completed Alpine butterfly

ALPINE BUTTERFLY

This comes in very handy, both when rigging fixed ropes and for tying on to the middle of the rope if moving together. Its main advantage is that it can be pulled from either end without distorting. It is quite simple to tie, but many will feel that a simple overhand knot on the bight will do the same job, particularly when tying on a middle-man.

LARKSFOOT

This is a weak knot that does not perform well under load tests. However, there are two common uses that it can be put to. The first is to join two slings together without using a karabiner. It is important that the knot sits neatly and looks like a reef knot once it is completed.

The other very common use is for attaching a cowstail to a harness. This is employed in abseiling and sport climbing, amongst other uses, and it provides a quick and secure attachment.

LOCKING OFF A BELAY DEVICE

This is an important skill to learn, and will come into its own when you are running one of the emergency procedure systems. It is basically the same as locking off an Italian hitch, as it uses a slippery hitch followed by two half hitches. The difference is that it is tied around the back bar of the belay device karabiner, not in front. It is possible to both tie and untie it when loaded, and it helps to keep a hand clamped around the device, holding the dead rope in place, when doing this.

Start with a bight of rope about 60cm (24in) long, as this will leave you with a 30cm (12in) tail once the knot is completed. At each stage, pull the rope towards the belay device so that all of the knots sit snugly against each other.

Two slings joined with a larksfoot, arranged to sit like a reef knot

A larksfoot on a harness

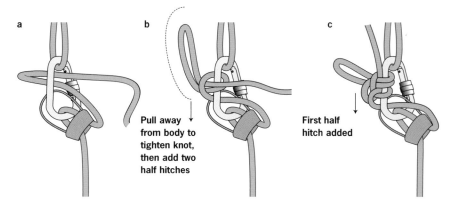

a

b

Pull away from body to tighten knot, then add two half hitches

c

First half hitch added

Locking off a belay device

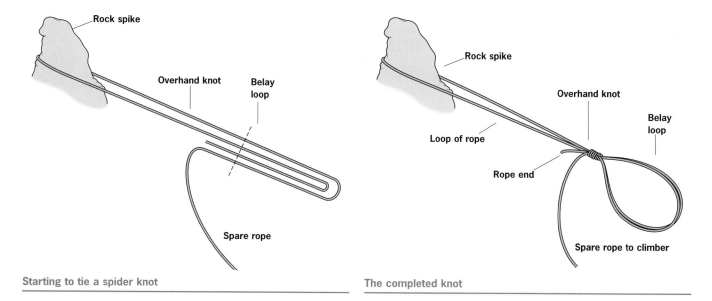

Starting to tie a spider knot

The completed knot

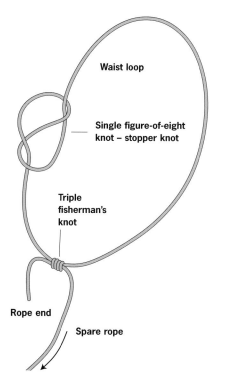

The punter knot

PUNTER KNOT

If you have a number of people who are not using harnesses but who you need to bring up a short section of ground, this is a very handy method of attaching them. It is basically a single figure of eight on the rope, along with a triple fisherman's, which is tied in the same manner as a double but with one extra turn. The function of the figure of eight is to stop the fisherman's from sliding too tight around the person's waist when the rope is loaded, and it can be adjusted for each user if need be. Once the main rope is loaded, the knot will stay secure around their waists.

SPIDER KNOT

This is a quick way to tie on to a single point anchor like a spike or thread, and is commonly used when no other equipment is to hand, such as when scrambling with just a rope and maybe a sling or two. It secures you to the anchor quickly and accurately, making placing yourself at the correct belay point very easy. It does use up a lot of rope, so is not appropriate if the anchor is a long way back from the belay point.

PARISIAN BAUDRIER

This is a method of improvising a chest harness, and is particularly useful in an emergency situation. Tied with a sling of the appropriate length, either one at 240cm (16ft) or two 120cm (8ft) joined with a larksfoot, it is important that it cannot tighten around the person's chest, otherwise it could suffocate them.

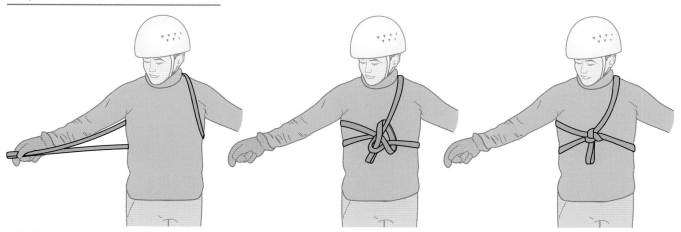

A Parisian baudrier

Load ⟶

◄— **Anchor**

The basic Tyrolean tensioning system

Load ⟶

◄— **Anchor**

The improved Tyrolean tensioning system

A rope bag opened out and being used

A SIMPLE TYROLEAN RIG

Although not strictly a knot, this is a method of securing the rope for a traverse and as such is appropriate here. This technique could be used for gaining dry access to a sea stack, for example, when passing between two rock peaks, or as a method for ferrying loads above a river. It will be best set up with low-stretch rope, although a dynamic rope can be used if it is the only one to hand.

The simplest version is shown in the photograph above. This will cover most eventualities, is the easiest to remember and the quickest to set up. The tail end of the rope can be secured with an Italian hitch locked off, which allows the system to be collapsed once it is finished with.

To get even greater tension on the crossing rope, the system in the next photograph will be appropriate.

When crossing, you should secure yourself with a screwgate karabiner at the very least, with a pulley backed up by a screwgate being better. If a pulley with a locking mechanism is available that will be best of all, as it will stop you from sliding back along the rope as you near the far end, where the going will be steeper due to rope sag.

COILING A ROPE

To carry your rope, the best ways would be to either flake it or use a rope bag. Although we generally talk about 'coiling' a rope, this is not very good for the rope itself, as the fibres can become unnaturally

Starting to flake the rope by laying it across your hand

Wrap a few turns of rope around the flakes

Pull a loop through the top and place this over the flakes and pull the ends snug

twisted, causing it to kink over time, apart from being quite awkward to undo and rather prone to knotting.

A rope bag is a purpose-made piece of gear, looking to all intents and purposes like a small rucksack. Inside will be a mat made from a waterproof fabric some 2m x 2m (78in x 78in) square, on which the rope lies ready for use. Opposite corners of this fabric have tabs sewn in, on to which the ends of the rope can be tied. To use it, one end of the rope is fixed to a tab and the rest of the rope is run through into a pile on the mat. The other end is fixed to the second tab. The mat is now rolled up with the rope inside, and placed into the carrying bag, which is secured. When the rope is needed, undo the carrying bag, unroll the mat, undo the top end of rope and you are ready to go. There is no need to run the rope through to check for knots, as this will have been done in order to put it away in the first place.

The other method is to wrap the rope up by flaking. This has the advantage over the older coiling method that the rope sits how it wants to and you are not introducing any twists into it. It will also not knot itself when being undone. To start, lay the centre of the rope over your left hand, hanging down. Now flake the rope across your hand backwards and forwards, alternating the direction each time. When you have only a couple of metres (78in) left, wrap a few coils tight around the main flakes near the top. Now push a loop through the hole where your left hand is, and put this loop

The rope being carried on the climber's back

A correctly flaked rope will not kink or knot when it is uncoiled

over and down around the flakes, pulling the ends to secure it.

To unwrap the rope, simply take off the final top loop and pull it back through, undo the small wraps, isolate an end and place the rest on the ground. Now you can run the rope through just to check that there are no kinks or knots in it, which, if it was flaked correctly, there won't be.

If you want to carry the rope, say, down from the top of a crag, perhaps during an abseil, you can carry it around your body a bit like a rucksack. Just leave longer ends when flaking it, put the finished rope behind your back and run the tails over your shoulder, cross them over behind the rope and bring them back to the front, securing them with a reef knot.

Safely clipped in to an anchor system

ANCHORS

To be able to select and construct a sound, appropriate anchor is a fundamental skill as far as any branch of climbing and mountaineering is concerned, and crucial for the safety of both yourself and anyone else in your party. This selection may be as simple as making a judgment about the solidity of a single boulder, or the construction of a complicated multi-point equalized system on a steep technical route at altitude.

One of the basics to understand is the ABC of climbing. Here, A is the anchor, B is the belayer and C is the climber. Firstly, it is very important that the anchor, belayer and climber are all in a straight line. With the belayer positioned to one side of the line between the climber and anchor, if the climber falls, thereby loading the system, there is a high probability that the belayer will be pulled sideways from their stance, more so if they are standing up. The ABC

is also relevant in a vertical plane, as well as horizontal.

Secondly, the belayer must be tight on their anchor. If they allow slack to appear between them and the anchor, any loading of the system will cause them to be pulled forwards. This may result in them losing control of the belay device as they could be pulled over the edge of the crag from their stance, or be pulled forwards and off balance if they are standing up.

SELECTING A SOLID ANCHOR

There is a progression that is worth going through when selecting either a spike or thread anchor. Start with a visual check of where the boulder has come from; is it well seated or has it just rolled into place, ready to roll further downhill when touched? Next, put a hand on it and give it a tap and a bit of a wobble. Make sure at this point that you are not down-slope of it, and neither is anyone else in your party, just in case it moves. Next, try to pull it away from its seat or give it a kick or two, and finally give it a really good thumping with your feet in the direction that it will potentially be loaded in. If, at any stage during this series of tests, it does not feel steady, abandon it and find an alternative.

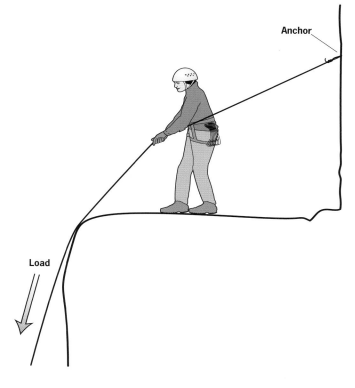

Anchor

Load

Correct ABC

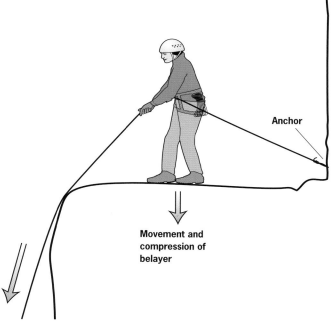

Anchor

Movement and
compression of
belayer

ABC off line vertically

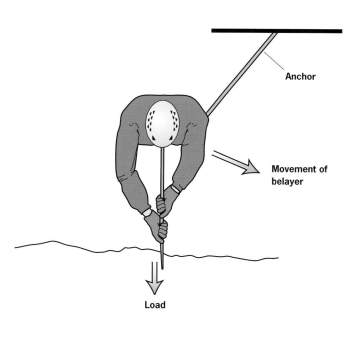

Anchor

Movement of
belayer

Load

ABC off line horizontally

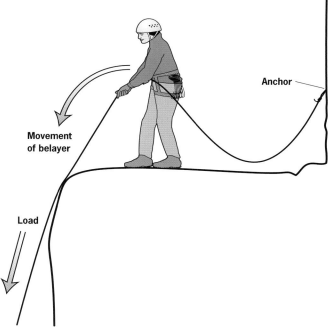

Anchor

Movement
of belayer

Load

ABC slack

A spike anchor

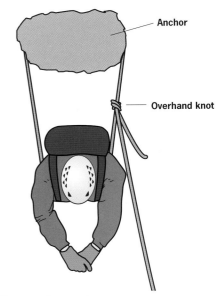

Anchor

Overhand knot

The open loop system

SPIKE ANCHOR

This is exactly as it sounds, a spike of rock over which a sling or the rope can be placed to provide an anchor or running belay. In firm conditions, there may be areas of hard snow or ice that can be used in a similar fashion. As spikes tend to stand proud of the surrounding ground, they will need careful testing before use, to make sure that they are secure.

THREAD ANCHOR

This is where the sling or rope has to be threaded around or through the rock or ice in order to make the attachment. A classic thread will be something like a jammed block in a chimney, well seated in place and ideal as an anchor. Two large boulders butted against each other would also be an example, as would passing a sling around the trunk of a tree, as obviously the branches would prevent it being used as a spike.

Ice threads exist in a number of forms, but they will typically be a natural thread, where a column of ice is well attached to the ground, and a manufactured one, such as the Abalakov thread (see 'Using ice protection').

Threads are best done with a sling of the appropriate length. Simply pass the sling around the object and clip the ends together with a karabiner. If there is a chance that the sling will bite in to the constricted part of the thread and be difficult to remove once it has been loaded, try to pack out the back of it using small pieces of rock, twigs or anything else to hand. Avoid the temptation to use a larksfoot knot when linking the ends of the sling, as when loaded it will place a high degree of constricting pressure on to the placement.

TYING ON TO ANCHORS WITH THE ROPE

If you are not using a harness, as when scrambling on easy snow slopes, there are a variety of options open to you. The spider knot, detailed in the 'Knots' section, would be appropriate. Other options would be to tie a loop in the end of the rope and fix this to the anchor, making a second loop further down to fix around your waist, or to have the end tied around you and make a loop an appropriate distance along the rope and this then goes to the anchor.

Another option is the open loop system. The main criteria here are that you must be seated when belaying, and the ABC is critical. However, it does make a very solid anchor, which is easily adjustable to get the distance from your anchor correct. It must only be tied with an overhand knot, which makes adjusting the size of the loop simple to do, and never a figure of eight, which is prone to slippage in this situation.

Most of the time, however, you will be using a harness. The aim here is to be able to use a clove hitch and figure of eight on the bight to create a safe and effective anchor system. Once you have understood the basics, you will be able to tie on to any number of anchor points very quickly and with ease, creating a safe system that has extremely good shock-absorbing properties.

There are two basic categories of anchor that we are going to look at, those where the karabiner at the anchor is in reach and those where it is out of reach. This means that you either can or cannot easily reach the karabiner from your final belaying position.

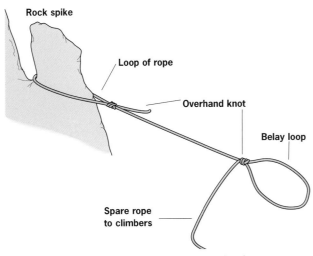

Rock spike

Loop of rope

Overhand knot

Belay loop

Spare rope to climbers

A spike anchor with the end of the rope fixed to it

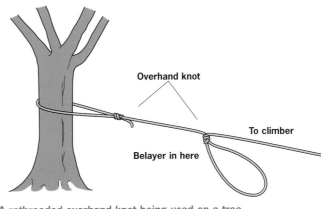

Overhand knot

To climber

Belayer in here

A rethreaded overhand knot being used on a tree

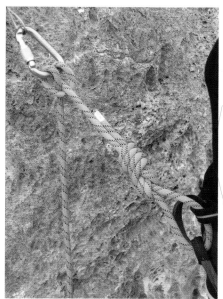

A clove hitch on a single anchor point within reach

A figure of eight on the bight used for a single anchor point out of reach

If you are using a single anchor point, and it is within reach, then all you need to do is to clip into it with a clove hitch. This can easily be adjusted to get the tension between yourself and the anchor just right.

If you are using a single anchor point out of reach, you have a couple of options. The simplest would be to use a figure of eight on the bight, which is tied around the central rope tie-in loop at your harness. This knot has an advantage over the next method in that it possesses dynamic properties that let it absorb a quantity of any shock-load taken by the belayer, and subsequently the anchors.

The other option is to clip the rope into the anchor, bring it back to your tie-in loop and clip it in to a karabiner with a clove hitch. This obviously makes an out of reach anchor into a within reach one. Only use one clove hitch on the karabiner as using two would change its loading characteristics, as well as being very awkward to adjust.

The next option will be tying on to two anchors, and in the first example they are within

reach. From your harness, clip into the first anchor with a clove hitch. Leave a bit of slack and clip into the second anchor with another clove hitch. Take the rope back to your harness and tie on around your tie-in loop with a figure of eight on the bight. Any adjustment that needs to be made can easily be done by moving the rope in or out of the clove hitches.

For two anchors that are out of reach, two separate figure of eights on the bight are the best option. Each needs to be tied via its respective anchor with exactly the same tension as the other, so that the load is shared, and you must be tight on the anchor when finished, remembering the ABC of climbing.

To start the system off, it may be a good idea to clip the rope into each of the anchors and then pull the rope with you as you make your way to the stance. This will save you having to get up again to

Tying on to two anchors within reach using clove hitches

A clove hitch clipped back in to the harness tie-in loop

Tying on to two anchors out of reach

One anchor in reach, one out of reach

retrieve the rope from the second anchor. Watch out for your safety whilst doing this though, and use a different method if there is any chance that you could slip before being secured. Although your belayer may still have you on belay, you will have a lot of rope pulled through the system if you slip from near the stance.

If the system is set up so that one anchor is in reach and the other out of reach, clip into the furthest one with a figure of eight on the bight to your harness tie-in loop, and using the rope coming from the back of the knot you can then clip into the nearer anchor with a clove hitch.

Once you have the idea of using a mixture of figure of eights on the bight and clove hitches, you will be able to tie on to any number of anchors. Just a little practice will be needed to get the whole thing set up quickly and efficiently.

EQUALIZING ANCHORS

It is very important, with multiple-point anchors, that each part of the system is loaded equally. If the anchor is just one single point, such as a spike or thread, this is not a problem, but if two or more attachment points are being used then you need to ensure that the placements are sharing the load evenly. This means that, should one of the anchor points fail, those remaining are not shock-loaded.

You may well have tied on to each of the anchors independently, using the rope and a sequence of clove hitches and figure of eights on the bight. However, in some circumstances, tying on with just the rope may not be the best option. For instance, if you were going to use a direct belay system, having all the anchors brought down to one point would be a huge advantage. Also, if you were going to lead all of the pitches on a multi-pitch route and your partner was just going to belay, having the ability to easily clip in and out of a sling would greatly speed up the climb.

A sewn sling of 120cm (8ft) will hopefully do for most circumstances where the

placements are close together, although one of 240cm (16ft) will allow a bit more leeway in the position of the anchors. Make sure that the sewn section is always away from any knot that you are tying, and this can be simply done by shuffling the sling around a bit before securing it. There are a number of ways in which a sling can be used to bring the anchors to one point and we will go through some of them here. The first two are the commonest and easiest to tie, with the other versions being useful options to know about. Here, we will assume that we have two anchor points, and both have screwgates on, which will be secured once the sling has been clipped in.

Clip the sling into both of the screwgates and, holding on to both sections of the sling between the placements, pull it in the direction that the load will be taken. Now tie an overhand knot on the bight (or a figure of eight if you have enough slack) to create a small loop. This will be the attachment point, and you can clip one or more karabiners into it depending on what you are going to use the set-up for.

The second method is handy if the

The second method is handy if the anchors are a bit further apart, as it uses up less sling length. It does look a little strange once tied, but it is completely secure!

Clip one end of the sling into an anchor, and tie an overhand knot loosely part way along it, before clipping the other end on to the second anchor. This knot can be moved along the sling, if need be to the point of loading, and then pulled tight. A screwgate karabiner is then clipped into each of the two individual loops that you have created.

Although the above two techniques should do you for just about every situation involving two anchors, the following few will be worth remembering in case they prove to be better under some circumstances.

Using clove hitches on a sling, especially one of a thin construction, makes adjustment a bit fiddly. However, adjust it you can, and that is the advantage of the following method. Tie a clove hitch in the sling and clip it to the karabiner in the first anchor point. Leaving a bit of slack, tie a second clove hitch and clip this into the other anchor. Leaving slack between the anchors allows you to adjust the clove hitches if need be. At the point of the sling where any loading will occur, tie either an

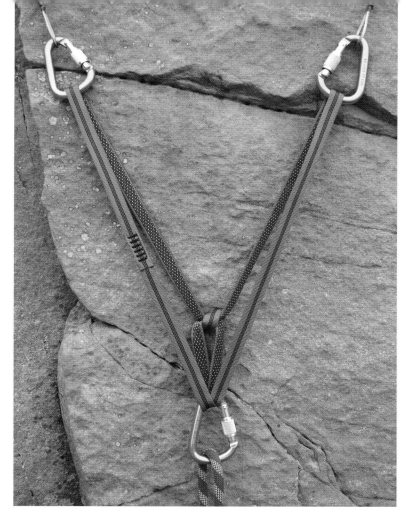

Equalizing anchors using the overhand knot method

Equalizing anchors using a loop on a bight

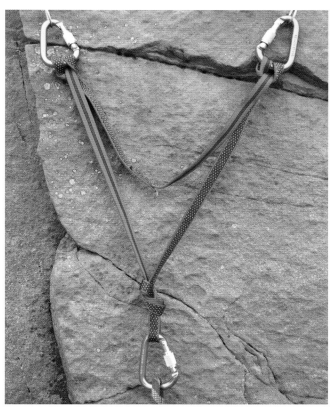

Equalizing anchors using the clove hitch method

A self-equalizing sling, restricted with overhand knots

Equalizing anchors using two separate slings tied together

An equalizing system where one sling is shortened and clipped to the other

overhand knot on the bight, or a figure of eight, and clip your attachment karabiner in to here.

A self-equalizing method exists, where the load point can be moved during use and the karabiner travels along the sling, still safely clipped into both anchors. This may sound good, but the drawback here is that, should one anchor point fail, the second will be shock-loaded by however much slack has been introduced into the system. A variation, the one shown above, incorporates a couple of extra knots to lessen the chance of this shock being so severe.

Estimate the load point of the sling, and tie two overhand knots, each a few centimetres (2in or so) either side. Once you have done this, clip the sling into both of the anchors. On the short section of sling between the two overhand knots, cross the sling over itself and clip a karabiner in. This will slide from side to side a short way, inhibited by the knots which can be moved in or out if need be, letting the sling self-equalize.

If you only have two short slings, or the anchor points are some distance away from each other, you can use these together to bring them down to a single point by a couple of methods.

Firstly, you could clip a sling into each anchor and tie them both together at the required height, using an overhand knot. Now clip through each of the slings above this with your attachment karabiner.

Secondly, if one of the slings is the correct length and the other a bit too long, shorten the latter with an overhand knot at the appropriate point and clip the two together with a screwgate.

If you are faced with three anchor points, quite likely on some multi-pitch routes or when rigging an abseil point, you can use a system very similar to the first method that we looked at. Using a long sling, clip it into all three of the anchors. Hold each of the lengths of sling from between all of the anchors, and pull these down to one point. Now tie an overhand knot into them, creating the attachment point.

Sometimes, when you are rigging a fixed rope, perhaps for ascending or for an abseil, you can use a double figure of eight for the attachment. This is adjustable, quick to tie and needs no extra kit, such as slings, which you may need elsewhere on the route.

Bringing three anchor points down to one

An anchor equalized using a double figure of eight knot

GROUND ANCHORS

There are a number of considerations as to whether ground anchors are appropriate to be used and, in most cases, you will probably find that they are. Differing weights between climber and belayer, the availability of anchor points and the state of the ground at the base of the climb will all go some way towards you making the decision to anchor or not. The effect of a fall on your belayer will often be the overriding factor, and if there were any chance that they will be pulled up and into the rock, possibly injuring themselves and dropping as well, anchoring them would be a good idea.

Ground anchors are often used on single-pitch climbs, so that your belayer is secured and safe from being pulled upwards and inwards in the event of them holding a fall. On multi-pitch climbs your belayer will normally be anchored anyway, but if you have taken an intermediate stance on a very large ledge and elected not to rig an anchor system, a ground anchor would be very appropriate here as well.

In most situations when using ground anchors, you will have your belayer tied securely to the ground. However, it has been found that the ability for the belayer to be lifted about a metre (39in) from the ground does a great deal to reduce the impact force on the system, consequently lessening the chance of a runner pulling out or some other part of the system failing. This is particularly important in situations where the runners are not as good as they might be, such as gear in poor placements on rock, or when using ice screws.

If your belayer is going to be tight to the anchor with no slack in the system, it is important that the rope is used for the connection, as opposed to a sling. The rope, having dynamic properties, will make holding a fall a better experience for the belayer, as well as reducing impact force a little throughout the system. As a sling does not stretch, there will be no give between the belayer and the anchor, thus transmitting forces directly through to it.

The ABC is relevant, even though the belayer is on the ground, as you will be pulled forward with more force at the base of a climb when holding a leader fall than you would be as a leader belaying a second and just holding their weight.

Think carefully about where the best place will be to belay from. It is important that the belayer is not positioned too far from the base of the climb, as a fall from the leader may cause the rope to lift most of the downwards-orientated runners up and out of their placements, leaving the climber vulnerable to a fall to the ground. They should be positioned close in so that the rope runs up the route in as straight a line as possible. If this cannot happen, perhaps due to the nature of the ground at the bottom of the cliff, then make sure that the first runner on the route is placed to take an upwards pull, as this will have the effect of aligning the rope straight up through the rest of the gear.

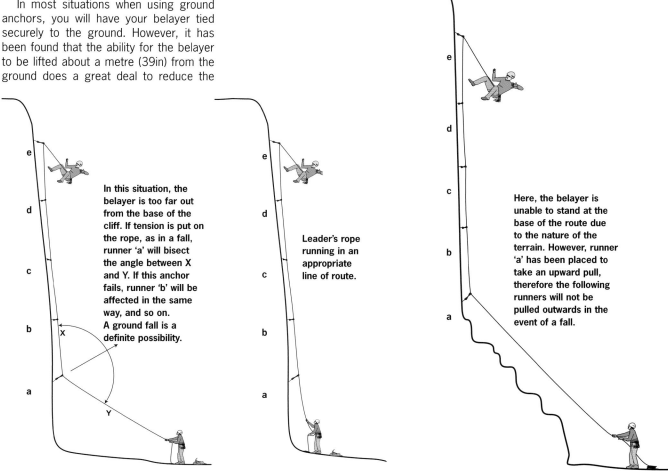

In this situation, the belayer is too far out from the base of the cliff. If tension is put on the rope, as in a fall, runner 'a' will bisect the angle between X and Y. If this anchor fails, runner 'b' will be affected in the same way, and so on. A ground fall is a definite possibility.

Leader's rope running in an appropriate line of route.

Here, the belayer is unable to stand at the base of the route due to the nature of the terrain. However, runner 'a' has been placed to take an upward pull, therefore the following runners will not be pulled outwards in the event of a fall.

Belayer too far from the bottom of the climb | Belayer in the correct position | Bottom runner redirecting the rope

Attentive belaying is important, even on the steepest of routes

BELAYING

There are three main categories of belay system: indirect, semi-direct and direct. Within these types there are many variations, and the skill is to know which one is relevant in what situation and why. The 'direct' part on the name indicates how the load will be passed through to the anchor. A direct belay, therefore, has 100 per cent of the load taken by the anchor, indirect perhaps only around 40 per cent, and semi-direct something between 60 and 100 per cent.

INDIRECT

An indirect belay is commonly a waist belay, with the shoulder belay being in the same category. Here your body provides the friction needed to make the rope controllable. To obtain this effect, the live rope comes from the climber, passes around your back (making sure that it is on top of, not underneath any anchor ropes, and that it is well down if a rucksack is being worn), and out on the opposite side

The indirect belay is often used in winter

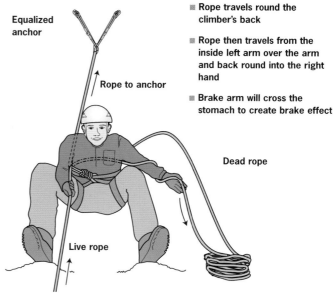

- Rope travels round the climber's back
- Rope then travels from the inside left arm over the arm and back round into the right hand
- Brake arm will cross the stomach to create brake effect

Equalized anchor

Rope to anchor

Dead rope

Live rope

A waist belay

with a twist of the dead rope being taken around the arm. It can be used either left- or right-handed.

To create the brake, the arm holding the dead rope is brought across in front of your body and you also grip with that hand. This maximizes the friction and you will be able to hold a fall. A very important trait of the waist belay is that it is quite hard to hold any but the shortest of falls without letting some of the rope slip through your hands and around your body. This has the important effect of reducing the amount of load that is transferred through to the anchor system, making it a good belay method if your anchor system is of questionable quality, such as when using ice screws or poor rock protection. The system is versatile, and can be used to belay a leader or a second, and also as part of a lower. However, because it can be very uncomfortable to hold a fall, certainly a leader fall of any distance, if the anchors are good quality many climbers will opt for a semi-direct system instead.

Your hand that holds the dead rope must never let go, as it is this that provides the control and security. The following method will be for if you are holding the dead rope in your right hand, but it is important to be ambidextrous, so simply reverse the process if you are going to use your left hand. It is important that gloves and long sleeves are worn, otherwise just a short distance of rope slippage could burn your skin.

To bring the rope up towards you, as if belaying a climber coming up a route, have your left hand extended and holding the rope, with your right arm bent and hand close to your body, a twist of rope around the lower forearm. Pull the rope up with your left hand at the same time as pushing out with the right, making sure that you are co-ordinated and there is no slack rope running around your back.

Release the grip of your left hand slightly and slide it down the dead rope until it is a little further down than your right hand. Using thumb and forefinger, grip the rope below your right hand, relax the right-hand grip a little and slide it back up towards your body before holding the rope tight again. The rope being held between your left thumb and forefinger can now be dropped, and that is you back to the start.

The ABC check is essential when using a harness with a waist tie-in point. If you have the anchor rope running down to your left-hand side, the climber's live rope is on your right, and in the event of them falling you will be twisted round, possibly losing control or injuring yourself. Make sure that the anchor rope and rope to the climber are in a straight line at all times. If you are not using a harness, however, and are simply tied on around your waist, as the attachment point will be at your back there should be less of a problem.

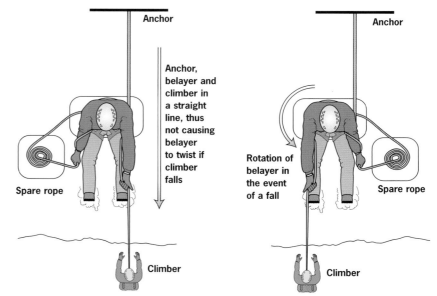

Anchor

Anchor

Anchor, belayer and climber in a straight line, thus not causing belayer to twist if climber falls

Rotation of belayer in the event of a fall

Spare rope

Spare rope

Climber

Climber

The correct (left) and incorrect (right) orientation of the rope when using a harness and a waist belay

T044573

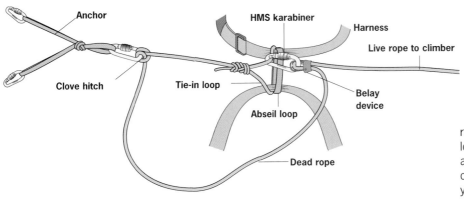

Anchor

HMS karabiner

Harness

Live rope to climber

Clove hitch

Tie-in loop

Abseil loop

Belay device

Dead rope

A semi-direct belay

SEMI-DIRECT

This is perhaps the commonest style of belay, used by most people who are climbing with harnesses and have sound anchor systems. With this belay, you make up a small percentage of the belay system, with the rest being passed through to the anchor. You will be anchored, the device is clipped in to your rope loop created by tying on and any load created by your partner is thus directed via the tie-in loop to the anchor system.

The semi-direct belay is quick to set up, the device is in front of you and thus easy to operate, and it is possible to provide a helpful pull or two to a second that needs it by giving a tight rope. Once again, the ABC is critical.

It is important that you have the orientation of the device correct, as this helps any load pass through to the anchor system, bypassing your harness. It also greatly reduces the chance of jams occurring in the device itself.

If you are tied on to the end of the rope, clip the belay device on to the rope loop created by tying on. This point of attachment is much better than simply clipping straight on to the abseil loop of your harness, as it directly transfers the load to the anchor point, stops you being compressed slightly in your harness and makes techniques such as escaping the system a lot easier to complete.

If you are belaying a leader, the karabiner holding your belay device should be clipped on to the top of the rope tie-in loop, meaning that the dead rope will be coming out from the bottom of the device. If you have led a route and are belaying your second, then clip the device to the bottom of your tie-in loop, having the dead rope coming out from its top. Make sure that you can operate smoothly with your braking hand, and that you are not going to be restricted by bulges of rock or ice.

Belaying a leader, with the device clipped in to the top of the tie-in loop

Belaying a second, with the device clipped in to the bottom of the tie-in loop

DIRECT

This means that 100 per cent of the load that is created by a falling climber is taken solely by the anchor. This term can be applied to a number of situations, such as running a rope around a rock and you taking it in hand over hand as a climber comes up towards you, an Italian hitch on a snow belay when lowering, a complicated hoisting set-up where you are not part of the system, and many more. It can be quick to set up, essential when moving together on Alpine terrain, and is very comfortable to belay with, as you are not going to be affected by any loading and are free to move around the stance within reason.

The direct belay should normally only be used when a static load would be taken, such as when holding the weight of a second or in the case of a lower. If you are on a multi-pitch route and need to belay a leader, it would be better to use an indirect or semi-direct system, as there will be more control and they are designed to cope with the extra shock-load created by a fall. Obviously, belaying a leader on a direct belay from a spike anchor, where there is a chance that the rope will be pulled upwards and off the spike, thus causing the anchor to fail, should not be contemplated.

The other important factor with the direct belay is that you must be totally confident that your anchor, be it snow, ice, rock or even a tree, is utterly sound and its integrity is beyond question. Take great pains when selecting an anchor to use, as to get one that is not 100 per cent solid opens both the belayed climber, plus other group members, to great danger.

DIRECT BELAYS ON ROCK

Competent use of these leads to swift and efficient movement in Alpine or high mountain terrain, and they are excellent if you need to protect your second and subsequent climbers, although they should not be used for belaying a leader.

The most basic type of direct belay on rock will be exactly that, where the rope is managed around a suitable rock spike or boulder. It can be used for bringing up a second and subsequent climbers, for protecting a down-climb or for lowering. In any of these cases, your body position and that of your hands controlling the rope are important, as it is from here that you will safeguard your partner. Always hold the rope with both hands, letting go only to put one hand over the other for taking in.

For lowering, simply shuffle the rope out with neither of your hands letting go of the

rope at any time. Don't let the rope slide, as you will lose control.

Another simple method is to use an Italian hitch on a direct belay. In its purest form, this will be a sling over a rock, with an Italian hitch clipped into an HMS karabiner. Look after your own security as well, and you can also clip into the sling if need be.

This can be used for all of the above applications, with the advantage that you will have a lot more control over the rope and be able to feed it out or take in smoothly as you are not relying on the friction of the rock. It is also a lot easier to lock it off once your companion arrives, and to swap leads.

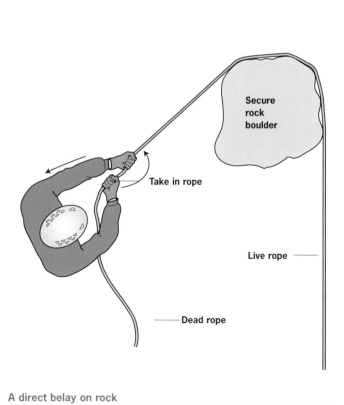

A direct belay on rock

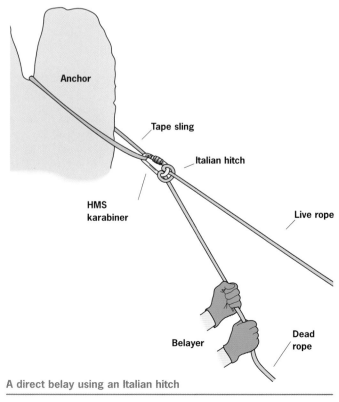

A direct belay using an Italian hitch

Using an overhand knot in the rope to create a clip-in point

rope is secured in some way. If you are not tied on, either tie it to part of the anchor or, at the very least, put a couple of knots in it near the end so that there is no chance that you will let it run through your hands by mistake.

DIRECT BELAYS ON SNOW AND ICE

There is no reason why you should not be able to arrange direct belays when using snow and ice anchors, but the strength of the system will only ever be as good as the material into which the belay has been constructed. Even the best constructed anchor will be worthless if the snow or ice it has been built into is rotten.

A snow bollard is a very useful tool to use as a direct belay anchor, and its construction is covered in the 'Winter' section. It should never be used with the rope moving around it, as this could easily cut through the snow and cause complete failure. To set the system up once the bollard has been constructed, tie a loop of rope around it and secure it with a suitable knot such as a bowline, to make something akin to a large sling. A sling can be used if it is of a suitable length. Either the end of the rope or a section from part way along can be used, depending upon the situation and what is to hand. Now clip an HMS karabiner into the rope loop (or sling), and put the Italian hitch on to this. Watch out for your own security at all times, and if you are not already protected by the bollard, clip yourself on with a cowstail or a clove hitch into a spare section of the rope.

You can use just about any standard snow or ice anchor to set up a direct belay, as long as it is solid enough. You may need to extend the sling on, say, a buried axe or deadman anchor to ensure that any load is pulling directly through the snow pack and not upwards. At the end of the sling, at the point that you have clipped an HMS karabiner, dig a small ledge in the snow so that the Italian hitch can operate uninterrupted. If it lies flat on the snow and is subsequently loaded, there is a chance that it could dig into the ground and jam. Once again, look after your own security with a cowstail or spare rope to a karabiner on the sling.

Be careful if using ice screws as a direct anchor, as ice is more prone to shattering than snow, and the quality of it can be harder to assess. Use at least two screws and equalize them to ensure a constantly shared load.

Another quick way to set this up when tied on to the end of the rope, useful if you need to be some distance away from the anchor, is as follows. Having secured yourself on to the anchor and positioned yourself at the stance, tie an overhand knot on the bight on the ropes between yourself and the anchor, a short distance behind you. You thus remain attached to the end of the rope, but can belay easily, along with the advantage that you can untie and escape should you have to whilst the system is loaded.

When setting up a direct belay, perhaps on a lower, make sure that the end of the

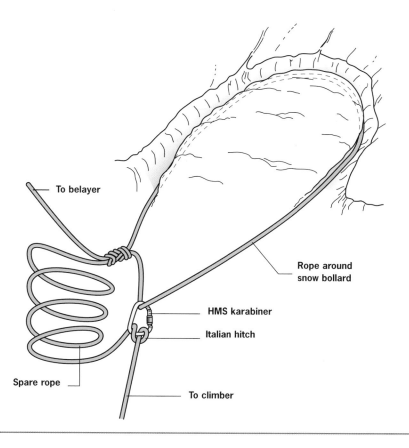

To belayer

Rope around
snow bollard

HMS karabiner

Italian hitch

Spare rope

To climber

The direct belay bollard set-up

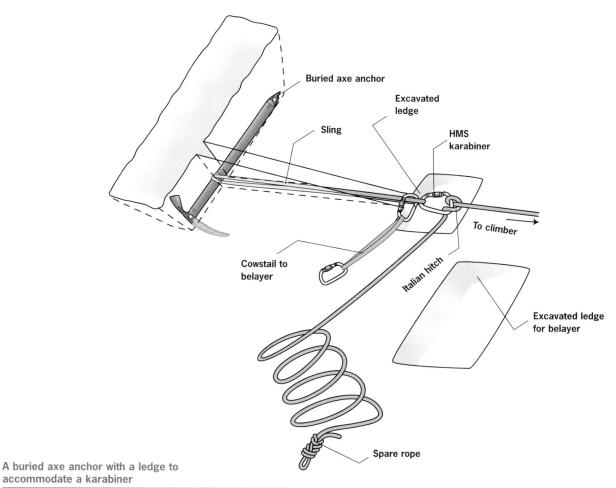

Buried axe anchor

Excavated
ledge

Sling

HMS
karabiner

Cowstail to
belayer

To climber

Italian hitch

Excavated ledge
for belayer

Spare rope

**A buried axe anchor with a ledge to
accommodate a karabiner**

Using a single rope system in winter

CLIMBING ROPE SYSTEMS

There are three generally accepted methods with which you can control the ropework when climbing on technical ground, and these are classified as single, double and twin. Each have their own advantages and benefits to give to differing situations, and the choice as to which one you select will have to do with the type of route you are going to climb, how long it is, the availability and positioning of protection, and whether you will need to abseil from the top, amongst others.

SINGLE ROPE TECHNIQUE

This is the simplest of the systems to operate as a belayer and manage on the lead, and is very commonly seen from local crag through to the high mountains. It is where one full-weight rope is used and clipped into each protection point. Its advantages are, apart from the simplicity of use, that it is lighter to carry, lighter in use than systems using two ropes, and it is possible to belay with an active self-locking belay device that only admits one rope, such as frequently used in sport climbing. The disadvantages include lack of abseil length if needed, a chance of rope drag if the route zigzags, increased risk of falling a distance if poor protection is clipped above head height, and reduced usefulness if the rope is damaged by a rock fall or other means.

DOUBLE ROPE TECHNIQUE

This is relevant in a variety of situations, from low-level technical routes right the way through to long mountain ascents. It is where two ropes, either rated as a half rope or, more commonly these days, two thin full-weight ropes, are clipped into runners in an appropriate order, but just with one rope into each.

The advantages are the reduction in rope drag, flexibility for belaying at stances, usefulness if abseil descents have to be made, the ability to have two climbers follow you with one on each rope, and giving less of a problem in the mountains if one is damaged by rock fall. However, one of the biggest advantages is the way in which runners can be clipped with each piece of rope in a manner that reduces the possibility of a long fall, a problem with single rope techniques. As an example, if you have placed a good piece of protection at waist level, and then place a potentially poor runner at above head height and are using a single rope, you would have no option but to clip into the higher runner. If you should then slip off and the higher runner pulls out, you would

fall the total length of the rope run out from your harness, up to the higher placement and down to the good waist-high runner. However, if you used double ropes in this instance, one rope would be in the good runner at waist height and the other clipped into the higher runner. Now if you slipped and the top piece of gear came out, you'd fall a far shorter distance, being held by the rope through the lower runner.

Disadvantages include the extra weight to carry to the climb and for a leader to tow up the route, a higher chance of tangling if stance management is not slick and tidy, and the much harder job of the second who is belaying. This final point is one that often leads to very poor belaying, as the person below has to control two sections of rope, which every now and then may need one paying out whilst the other is taken in. This can occur when the leader has clipped into a high runner and moves up to it, so the rope through the lower runner has to be paid out but the rope to the higher one has to be taken in. This all takes some practice, but will become possible with time.

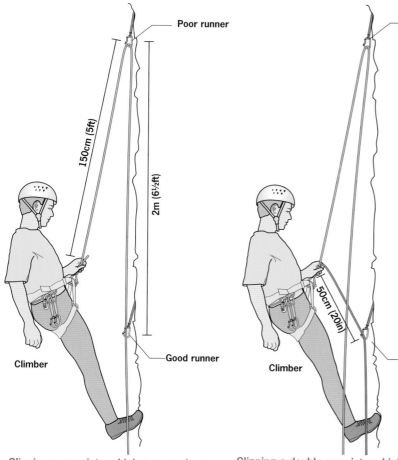

150cm (5ft)

2m (6½ft)

Poor runner

Climber

Good runner

Clipping a rope into a high runner when using single rope techniques

50cm (20in)

Poor runner

Climber

Good runner

Clipping a double rope into a high runner, thus reducing the potential fall distance

TWIN ROPE TECHNIQUE

This is sometimes mistaken for the double rope system, with the main difference being that in twin rope technique both ropes are clipped into all of the runners, with a consequent loss of ability to reduce the rope drag. It has its place where thin half-weight ropes are being used, as in tandem they will be rated the same as a full-weight one. Its other advantages are the same as for double ropes, with the addition of a far simpler task for the belayer. However, as the ropes are both clipped into each runner there is the problem of what to do if there is a poor higher runner, akin to using a single rope. Using a single strand in a double rope-type mode to clip into the high runner, and clipping the second rope in as soon as they draw near, is not to be recommended, because a fall would mean the ropes would move at different speeds through the lower karabiner, with possible consequent rope damage through friction.

This style of ropework is sometimes used on Alpine climbs, where the route is straight and the ability to abseil long distances is important, but since the advent of very thin and strong single weight ropes

that lend themselves to double roping, this latter form has become more popular. Care should also be taken if choosing to twin rope, as in the event of a fall the two ropes may move through a karabiner at different speeds, causing heat damage to the rope sheath and possibly even failure. If thick ropes are used, there is also the concern that there will be extra outward pressure on the gate side of a karabiner when it is loaded, causing failure at a lower than rated strength.

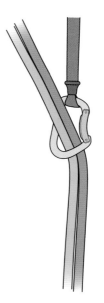

Twin ropes running through one karabiner

TOP AND BOTTOM ROPING

Both top and bottom roping are used extensively in climbing scenarios in all disciplines, including icefall climbing. The main attraction for many is that it takes away the seriousness of the climbing in that it will not be necessary to lead a route, thus allowing the climbers to concentrate purely on the technical side of getting up the climb. For this reason people sometimes use it for working out moves on very particularly hard climbs, as well as a convenient method of training.

The difference between the two styles is that with top roping the belayer is at the top of the route, with bottom roping they are at the base. There are advantages and disadvantages to both, although bottom roping is often chosen, as it is more of a social activity, where the belayer and climber can see each other and easily talk through the moves and sequences.

A TOP ROPE RIG

This is very similar to a leader belaying their second (see 'Belaying'), as all the controlling of the rope happens from the top of the crag. The advantage with this method is that the climbers can top out safely, protected by the rope all the way to the top of the cliff.

A difference is that a direct belay system will often be chosen over a semi-direct one, so that the belayer is not being pulled around by the climber if they fall off. An Italian hitch is quite appropriate here, as would be an active self-locking belay device. Because of this, a single anchor point, or several that have been equalized and brought down to one, would be the best choice. Both the belay method and the cowstail to the belayer can be clipped in to here, and the entire system is easy to run and quick to set up.

A BOTTOM ROPE RIG

The end result with this set-up is commonly for the climber to get to the top karabiners and then be lowered off. If they want to top out, they will be in a lead situation for a while, as they pass the karabiners and get to the top of the cliff. This may not be appropriate for beginners or on very hard ground, as a slip could result in them falling some distance.

There is a bit of work to do to set up a good bottom rope rig, as well as the need for two ropes, one to rig with and one to climb on. An extra piece of kit that is useful is a rope protector, and this can be as simple as an offcut of carpet.

We will assume that two anchors are being used. With the rope that you are going to rig with (preferably a low-stretch type, although this is not essential), tie a double figure of eight knot at an appropriate point, most likely at its centre. A little up from this tie an overhand knot (a figure of eight is also fine, and may be easier to untie after prolonged use) to bring the two ropes together before they go over the edge of the crag. Each side of the rigging rope is clipped in to an anchor point, with clove hitches being useful, as you can fine tune the rig's position later if need be. Into the double figure of eight go two screwgate karabiners, facing opposite directions and orientated so that the gates open at the bottom. This ensures that any vibration set up by the rope running through causes the locking sleeve to stay shut and not vibrate open. The climbing rope goes through these karabiners, with both ends being lowered down the cliff, with due care given to anyone that may be below. Place the protective matting at the cliff edge, and at any other rub points, and secure it if necessary with a short length of accessory cord. This matting is not only to protect the rope, but also to help stop erosion of the rock at the cliff edge. That is the rig complete.

You may find that it is helpful to drop the climbing rope down the route before clipping the rigging rope to the anchors, as this will help to get the distances right. Also, watch out for your own personal safety when setting the system up, and clip in to an anchor whilst you are working, if necessary.

The rope will be easy to control from the bottom of the route, with a variety of belay techniques being appropriate, such as a belay device to your harness or an Italian hitch to a solid ground anchor.

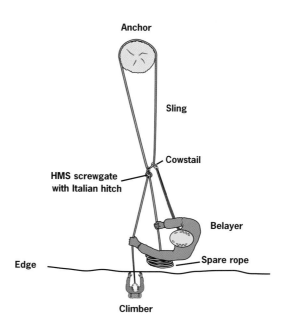

A direct belay system being used when top roping

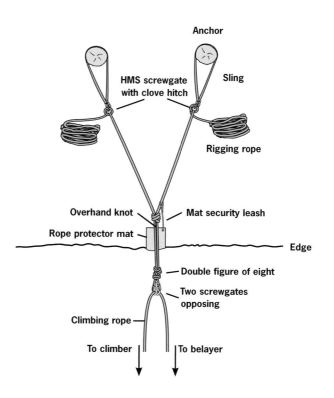

The bottom rope rig set-up

2: TECHNICAL SKILLS

ABSEILING

There are many reasons why you may have to abseil. Retrieving gear, getting to the base of a climb, descending after calling a halt to a climb part way through or going down to assist an injured person are but a few.

There are many things to be considered before starting down, such as the equipment to hand, the availability of anchors, the length of the rope in relation to the distance to descend and the ability to retrieve the rope once you are down. There are many more factors, and all are important. Abseiling is one of the most dangerous things that we do in the mountains, and we need to think through all the relevant points particularly carefully before committing ourselves to a descent.

A classic abseil

An abseil using the rope doubled

ABSEILING WITHOUT A HARNESS

This may be necessary if you are on the hill with just a length of rope and perhaps a sling or two, such as when making your way up easy scrambles, or along snow-covered ridges. Although simply sliding down with the rope running through your hands will often do the trick, there are two methods that give a lot more control. The first can be useful if the rope is tied off at an anchor and just one strand is to be used. However, it cannot be recommended as being particularly comfortable!

The description that follows is for a right-handed abseiler, and this can obviously be altered to suit you if you are left-handed. This method is generally known as the 'classic' abseil.

Face the anchor and step over the rope, and pick it up from behind you. Bring it in front of your right hip, across your chest, over your left shoulder and diagonally down across your back under your right arm, taking a wrap around your arm as you do so, and then hold it in your right hand. Put your left hand on to the rope where it disappears under your crotch, as this will help to keep you in balance.

Turning your body sideways with the right shoulder down-slope helps with comfort and to see where you are going, and descent is made by allowing the rope to run slowly through your right hand. It is very important that you wear gloves and have long sleeves for this method, as the twist of rope around the arm could very easily cause a burn.

If your rope is doubled, as would be the norm in order to allow the rope to be pulled down once you have descended, a slightly different method can be used.

Step between the ropes and pick them up, holding one in each hand. Cross them over behind your back and bring your hands forwards at each side.

There is a loop of rope running down from each hand. Step the left leg over the left loop and the right leg over the right loop, and grasp both ropes together with one hand behind you once you have done so. Holding the ropes together, bring them up to the right-hand side of the body if you wish to control the descent with the right hand, or to the left-hand side if you prefer that side. These will be best held palm up, with no twist needed around the arm.

To descend, feed the ropes through with the hand holding them. Your other hand is not needed for control, so it can loosely hold one of the sections of rope above you if you feel the need to do so.

ABSEILING WITH A HARNESS

This will be the commonest way to descend, as it gives comfort and security. The abseil loop at the front of the harness, a sewn section of tape, is where the attachment of any device will usually be made.

Most belay devices also double up as tools for abseiling, which saves you having to carry two pieces of kit. Group abseilers will often use a large figure of eight abseil device. This is designed to dissipate heat quickly through its large surface area, and is very good at its job. However, they are heavy to carry so are not frequently seen on the harnesses of technical climbers unless they are also being used as belay devices. Some mechanical devices such as the Grigri and the Italian hitch can also be used.

It is important to get your body position right when abseiling. Let the harness take

Protecting an abseil

Abseiling above the sea can be particularly impressive

all of the weight, with your hand simply controlling the rate of descent. Face the rock with your legs straight and feet around hip width apart. Your upper body should be relaxed, in an upright position and not leaning forward.

PROTECTING AN ABSEIL

Although simply sliding down the rope with just an abseil device attached is quick, it can also be very risky, particularly if control is lost. Protecting an abseil is very easy to do, and should be considered for all but the simplest of descents.

Clip your abseil device to the abseil loop on your harness, by extending it away from you by around 20cm (8in). This can be done by using an extender with screwgate karabiners replacing the normal snapgates, or by threading a 60cm (24in)

sling through the harness next to the abseil loop and clipping the ends together.

Tie a French prusik around the dead rope and clip this to the bottom of your abseil loop, using a separate karabiner. Quite how many turns you take with this prusik depends on whether one or two ropes are being used, fewer turns for two ropes (around four wraps should do), more for just one. It is important that the prusik loop is short enough that it will not reach the top of the abseil device when loaded.

Step over the rope, and prepare to abseil with one leg either side. One hand holds the French prusik in the released position whilst your other hand controls the descent by gripping the dead rope. If you need to stop, the French prusik can be released and will travel a short way up the rope, tightening as it does so

Protecting an abseil with the prusik attached to a leg loop

A sling being used as a cowstail

and stopping any more abseil rope from running through.

A useful technique is to clip the abseil device to your harness using a 120cm (48in) sling divided into thirds. The first third is used to extend the abseil device away from your harness, the other section can be used as a cowstail that can be clipped into the next belay point when it is reached. This is very handy for protecting yourself on multiple abseils, as you can be constantly connected to either the abseil rope or the anchor. A useful place to clip the end karabiner is onto one of the two ropes above the abseil device. This then works as a reminder as to which side to pull during retrieval.

Another place that the French prusik can be attached is your leg loop, with the rope running to your side. For this method, the abseil device is usually attached directly to the abseil loop with a karabiner and not extended. Although this method will be quite adequate under most circumstances, be very aware that any sideways motion that you may make when it is locked off, such as reaching over to retrieve a piece of jammed gear, could cause your leg to lift, consequently allowing the prusik to touch the top of the abseil device and release. Only use this method for uncomplicated, straight-down abseils.

ABSEILING WITH AN ITALIAN HITCH

It is quite possible to use an Italian hitch for an abseil. Although you may not choose to do this as a matter of course, if you have dropped your abseil device down the cliff, for example, there may be few other options.

It is important that an HMS karabiner is used. Assuming that doubled ropes are going to be descended, which will most often be the case, one large Italian hitch is tied and clipped in to the HMS.

Be very careful that there is no chance that the dead rope of the hitch can run across the gate of the karabiner, possibly unscrewing the sleeve and causing it to open. To prevent this, have the back bar of the karabiner on the side of your controlling hand, and make sure that the wide end is away from you.

Although maximum braking effect with an Italian hitch is when both the live and

Using an Italian hitch to abseil with

dead ropes are held parallel to each other, in an abseiling situation this is quite difficult to achieve. Simply keeping a tight hold on the dead rope should give sufficient friction for a controlled descent to take place.

Abseiling using the Italian hitch can cause the rope to become a bit twisted, and this can consequently make it difficult to retrieve. If you clip a free-running karabiner on to one of the abseil ropes before descending, you can use this to overcome the problem. When you arrive at the base of the abseil, uncross the ropes as much as is necessary so that the karabiner slides down to you. When it reaches you, there will be no more twists in the rope and it can be pulled through as normal.

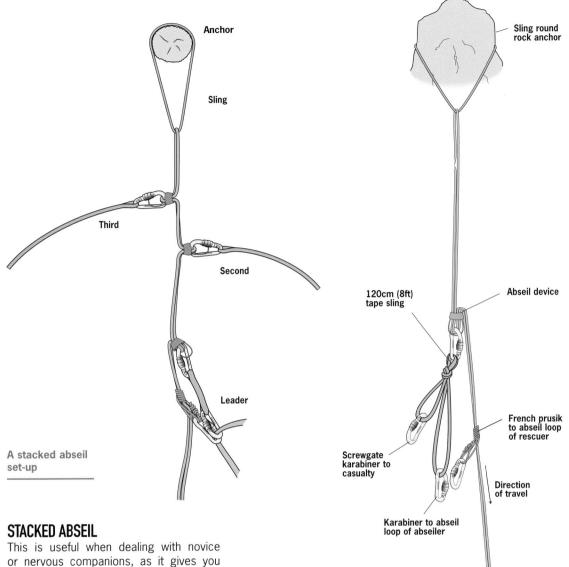

A stacked abseil
set-up

Anchor

Sling

Third

Second

Leader

**Sling round
rock anchor**

**120cm (8ft)
tape sling**

Abseil device

**French prusik
to abseil loop
of rescuer**

**Direction
of travel**

**Screwgate
karabiner to
casualty**

**Karabiner to abseil
loop of abseiler**

A 'Y' hang being used on an accompanied abseil rig

STACKED ABSEIL

This is useful when dealing with novice or nervous companions, as it gives you complete control over them once they are attached to the rope. You can then safeguard them from below during their descent by pulling on the abseil rope as required, to either slow them down or stop them altogether.

Attach your companions to the abseil rope with an abseil device extended to their harness with a doubled 60cm (4ft) sling. This stops them from being pulled around as you descend. Connect yourself as normal to the abseil rope and position everyone in line, with them sitting down if the anchor is low.

As soon as you start abseiling they are unable to move and will remain safe, as the rope will be pulled tight in their abseil devices. Once you reach the ground, the next person can descend, with you holding the abseil rope as a back-up, and their weight stops the third person from being able to move. The process is then repeated for any subsequent people.

A 'Y' HANG AND ACCOMPANIED ABSEIL

This is used when two people have to abseil together on one abseil device, and is most likely to be used during an emergency procedure, or when dealing with a very nervous or inexperienced person. In the latter case the stacked abseil will usually be a better option, but this is a useful alternative.

Tie an overhand knot near the middle of a 120cm (8ft) sling and attach one end of the sling to the abseil loop of your harness with a screwgate or a larksfoot. Now clip in your abseil device. Place this on the rope, along with a usual French prusik back-up, and clip a screwgate karabiner

into the other end of the sling. This will be the connecting point for the other person, and you can knot the sling as appropriate if you want to vary their height in relation to yourself. Depending on the situation, you may decide to make the 'victim's' part of the sling a little shorter than yours, as it makes placing your feet when abseiling down the cliff a bit easier.

If the other person is unconscious, you will find that it is easier to have them at 90 degrees to yourself, across the line of the cliff. A Parisian baudrier (see 'Knots' section) may have to be tied around them in order that they stay upright.

DEPLOYING THE ABSEIL ROPE

There is a variety of ways in which the rope can be deployed down the cliff or snow slope. If the weather is calm and you are abseiling directly downwards, there should be little problem in letting the rope snake out from your hand, checking for kinks as you go.

Having the middle of the rope marked is very useful, not just for quickly locating the centre when abseiling but also for coiling the rope after use. This mark will often have been made by the manufacturer with either tape or coloured ink marking. If you want to do it yourself, purchase a specially formulated rope marking ink. You could also use coloured tape as the marker, but take care that the adhesive used on the tape will not react with the rope.

Throwing the rope overhand will be the best option in many cases, particularly if it is a bit windy. Don't be tempted to coil it, as this is guaranteed to result in a tangle when you throw it. Flake the rope from the anchor end of the system across your hand, and once all of the rope has been flaked, divide it into two sections, one part in each hand. Throw the flakes incorporating the free end towards the target, allowing for the effect of the wind. The weight of this section of rope will then pull the flakes off from the other hand, allowing the rope to run free to the objective.

Another method that works well when deploying the rope on steep slabs or snow slopes is the rope bomb. Wrap the rope around your hand a few times, slip it off and make a few more wraps around the initial coils. The angle of coiling is then changed again and the wrapping continued. The finished article will resemble a large ball of knitting wool, and will roll down the crag when deployed with a good deal of accuracy and little chance of knotting.

Make sure that, if there is a chance of other people being below you when deploying the rope using any of the above methods, that you shout 'Rope below' to warn them.

It is a good idea to tie a knot in the end of the rope, to stop any chance of you abseiling off it. If the rope easily reaches the ground or a large ledge then you will probably not bother. However, on a multi-pitch abseil to small or non-existent ledges, knotting it would be a sensible precaution. The best way is to tie a single overhand knot into each of the ends. Any kinks in either side of the rope can twist themselves out as you go down, and there is still no chance of you abseiling off the end.

Preparing the rope in flakes for throwing

Preparing the rope bomb

A double fisherman's knot with a reef knot, used to join two ropes together

JOINING THE ROPES

If you need to join two ropes together, a very good method is to use a double fisherman's knot. To stop the knot from becoming awkward to untie once you have descended, a reef knot can be tied prior to tying the double fisherman's.

This does, however, result in a fairly bulky knot that has a chance of catching on uneven ground when pulling the rope down. If this is a concern, it may be a good idea to tie the ropes together using a double overhand knot. When the rope is pulled for retrieval, this knot will present its flat side to any obstruction and reduce the chance of the rope becoming stuck. When tied, the overhand knot should have tail ends of at least 30cm (12in), and pull it fully tight before using it.

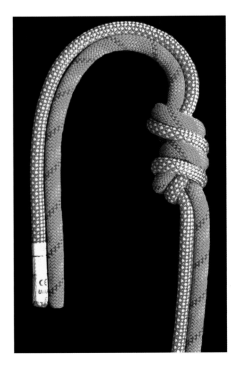

A double overhand knot joining two ropes

RETRIEVING THE ROPE

Being able to retrieve the rope is generally very important, unless it has been tied off at the top and will thus be left in place for the day. Routes that include abseils as a planned part of the climb will frequently have dedicated abseil stations in place, and these will vary from a collection of short sections of rope and old slings left by previous climbers, through to modern bolted and chained abseil points.

Purpose-made stations make life very simple, as you just thread the rope through the appropriate part of the system and go down. Retrieval of your rope from here should therefore be quite straightforward.

Take care if you need to abseil from a collection of old slings that have accumulated over the years. Slings and offcuts of rope can deteriorate fast and thus lose their strength very quickly, due to factors such as ultraviolet degradation, exposure to the elements and by burning through caused by rope retrieval. If you have any doubt whatsoever as to the integrity of the anchor, then it needs to be reinforced. Carrying lengths of tape or spare slings, along with a small knife, would be a good idea if you suspect that you will need to abseil.

Very frequently, however, the rigging of the abseil point will be something that you will have to do yourself. This may mean that you have to abandon gear, but rather than take a risk with a sub-standard set-up. However, many anchors can be rigged just with a sling or off-cut section of rope, and if so the abseil rope could be run directly through it without the need for a karabiner to be left behind. Pulling a rope down, causing it to run through the sling, generates sufficient heat to melt it. However, as the rope would most likely be doubled for the abseil, it would be static for the descent. It is only when you have finished the abseil and the rope is pulled through that there would be a chance of the

sling being damaged, but by that time you have finished with the system. However, never be tempted to re-use slings that have been used in this way, as they could have been severely weakened by the action of pulling the rope through. If you are going to use the anchor again, if making frequent abseils on a sea cliff when climbing a number of routes for example, always use a karabiner to protect the sling.

It is important that the rope is pulled from a sling anchor in a direction that will not cause it to jam by introducing unwanted friction into the system. Make sure that you pull on the rope on the side of the sling closest to the anchor, as this action will lift the sling slightly away from the anchor, allowing the rope to run smoothly.

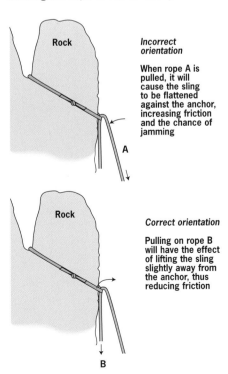

Incorrect orientation

When rope A is pulled, it will cause the sling to be flattened against the anchor, increasing friction and the chance of jamming

Correct orientation

Pulling on rope B will have the effect of lifting the sling slightly away from the anchor, thus reducing friction

Pulling the correct direction on a sling anchor

In high mountain ranges, you may only have one full-weight rope but still need to abseil as far as you can each time. It is possible to do this, with the use of a length of accessory cord, thin and light but with a high strength rating. Kevlar is good for this, and the cord should be the same length as the main climbing rope.

Tie a figure of eight knot on the end of the abseil rope and also on the accessory cord, and connect them together with a screwgate karabiner. Place the main rope into the anchor, which should be made small enough (using a small karabiner or sling tied with an overhand knot) so that there is no chance of this knot being pulled through, thus making retrieving the rope impossible.

The screwgate connecting the two ropes is also clipped into the main abseil rope below the anchor. You can now go down on the main rope, and once the ground or next stance has been reached,

the accessory cord is pulled down and the abseil rope will be retrieved.

The above method can also be used for setting up an abseil when using a device that only works on a single strand of rope. Alternatively, if the descent is not too long, such as on a single-pitch crag, and your rope easily reaches the ground when doubled, a similar system can be used.

Clip the abseil rope into the anchor, again making sure that the section that it is clipped through is not of such a large diameter that any subsequent knots could jam in it. Tie a figure of eight knot on one side of the anchor, and use a screwgate karabiner to clip this across to the rope coming from the other side of the anchor.

You can now abseil on the rope that does not have the knot on it. When you have reached the ground and taken the device off, pull on the other rope and it can be retrieved.

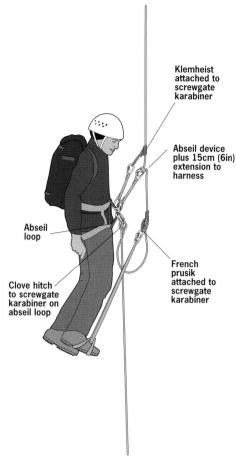

Re-ascending the rope after an abseil

The rig for a retrievable abseil rope with accessory cord puller

A B S E I L   S I D E ↓

Using a single rope to abseil on and then be retrieved

CHANGING FROM ABSEIL TO ASCENT OF THE ROPE

This may have to happen if you make a long abseil, for example, on a remote mountain crag, only to find that the rope does not end up anywhere near the ground or a suitable ledge, and re-ascending is the only option.

Once you have stopped abseiling, clip a clove hitch into an HMS karabiner on your abseil loop to act as a back-up. Attach a second prusik loop or small ascender to the rope above the abseil device, extended appropriately, and also clip this to your abseil loop. Now abseil again until your weight is taken by the new attachment above the device. The abseil device can now be removed.

Use a sling to connect the French prusik to your foot, and now take the prusik off the karabiner connecting it to your harness. You can now ascend the rope (see 'Prusiking' below), taking in the slack through the clove hitch as a back-up every so often.

Falling isn't necessarily dangerous

PRUSIKING

This is very useful in situations such as crevasse rescue, where it may be quicker to prusik out of a crevasse rather than wait for your companions to effect a rescue with a hoisting system or similar rig. It also has its place in other scenarios, such as abseiling too far down an overhanging cliff and having to climb back up to regain a suitable ledge.

The simplest method is to have a French prusik on the rope, along with a sling, to create a foot loop. It would be worth taking a couple of wraps of the sling around your boot to keep your foot in place, as well as shortening it to the correct length. A klemheist then goes straight from the rope to your abseil loop via a screwgate karabiner.

To go up, stand up on the sling and slide the klemheist upwards, then sit back in your harness and slide the French prusik up. Stand up on the sling again and repeat the process. When you have ascended a short distance, clip a clove hitch, tied on the rope from just below the French prusik, into an HMS karabiner clipped in to your abseil loop. This will act as a back-up in the event of the klemheist slipping, and it can be adjusted after every few movements upwards.

Obviously, having too few turns on the French prusik and klemheist is no good, but having too many is also very awkward, to the extent that you may not be able to move at all. Practise this skill well before it is needed, and take note of how many wraps for each knot are appropriate.

EMERGENCY PROCEDURES

There are a number of emergency procedures that all climbers and mountaineers should know. At the very least, to able to set up an assisted and unassisted hoist, along with the ability to escape the system safely from a variety of belay set-ups, should be learned early on in your climbing career. They are quite simple to do and to understand; the main issue will be deciding which technique is most appropriate in any given situation.

As with any new procedure, get some practice in a safe environment before trying the skill out for real on a high mountain crag. Most of the techniques can even be walked through at home, and this will help you become a lot slicker when out on the crag.

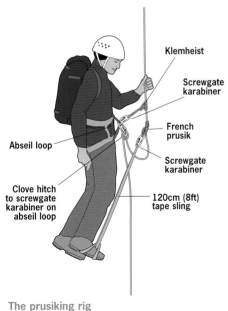

The prusiking rig

ASSISTED HOIST

This is the most basic of all the emergency procedures, and can be used in a variety of situations from rock climbing to crevasse rescue. It is useful, for example, when a second is unable to complete a pitch, either due to tiredness or perhaps because the section is too hard or overhanging. It comes into its own when there is no chance of the second being lowered to the ground, such as when you are on a multi-pitch route, or climbing over the sea. For the following, we will assume that the second is not too far below the belayer and directly underneath them, and they are belayed with a semi-direct system.

First, the belay device needs to be locked off (see 'Knots' section), to give the opportunity to work hands-free. A French prusik is then attached to the live rope directly in front of the belay device, with plenty of turns so that it can hold the weight of the climber. In this situation it is fine to clip the French prusik directly into the belay device karabiner using a separate screwgate. Once the French prusik is attached, push it as far as possible down the rope until it is snug.

Taking a bight of rope from the dead rope side of the locked off device, either lower or carefully throw this down to your second, who then needs to clip it into their abseil loop with a screwgate karabiner. Make sure that the rope is running smoothly at this stage and that there are no twists in it, otherwise the friction created will make the hoisting trickier to manage.

Now carefully untie the locked off belay device, pulling through the slack rope as you do so, and still holding on to the rope now coming up from the second. Care should be taken to not shock-load the French prusik, otherwise it could slip and cause you problems. Clamp one hand around the outside of the belay device as you pull the rope through the slippery hitch, squeezing the dead rope in the locked off position. This will make the final part of untying much easier.

Now that the system is rigged, the second pulls down on one side of the loop of rope that you lowered to them, and you pull up on the other. This gives a mechanical advantage that allows you to hoist them up with surprising ease. As you pull the rope in, the French prusik will travel up and sit against the belay device loosened off. Should the effort of holding your second whilst they take out a piece of gear mean that you need to stop hoisting,

push the French prusik down the rope as far as it will go, then slowly release the load on to it. It is very important that you do not let go of the rope completely, as you are acting as a back-up in case the prusik slips.

This system works for the best when both the belayer and second are coordinating their efforts and pulling together.

If you are climbing with a double or twin rope system, a very simple form of assisted ascent requires the second to pull up on one of the ropes whilst you take the other one in tight. This technique obviously

requires a good deal of strength on the part of the second, and the more purchase they are able to get with their feet the easier the process will be. The rope that the second is pulling on can be locked off at the belay device by simply tying a large overhand knot on the bight on the dead side, and this leaves you free to pull on the other one. Once the section of hard ground is overcome, the second is held on the second rope whilst the first is unlocked and taken in.

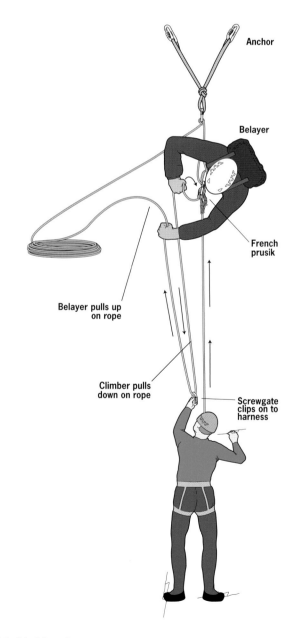

Anchor

Belayer

French prusik

Belayer pulls up on rope

Climber pulls down on rope

Screwgate clips on to harness

The assisted hoist system

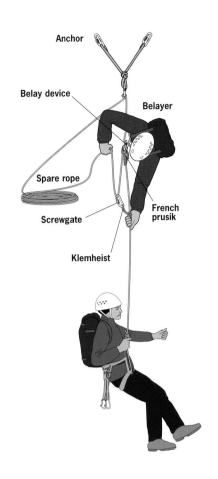

The unassisted hoist

UNASSISTED HOIST

This is useful if a problem occurs on a multi-pitch route where your second is unable to make their way up to you for some reason, and is also unable to help the leader with an assisted hoist. This may be because they are injured, or simply because they are more than a third of a rope length away and thus there would not be enough rope to lower a loop down to them.

This system is far easier to operate if you are able to escape the system before starting. We will assume the same anchor and belay set-up as for the assisted hoist.

The first few things that you have to do are the same as for the assisted hoist. Lock off the belay device, attach a French prusik and clip it to your belay device karabiner. Now, instead of lowering a loop of rope down to your second (as they obviously can't reach it), tie a klemheist on to the live rope, below the French prusik, orientated so that it will lock when taking a pull upwards. Clip a loop of rope from the

dead rope side of the belay device into the klemheist, using a screwgate karabiner, and push these both as far down the live rope as possible.

Take a couple of wraps of the dead rope around your wrist so that it does not get dropped, untie the locked off belay device and pull the slack rope through. Make sure, once again, that the French prusik is not shock-loaded at any point.

To hoist your second up, pull on the dead rope and this then loads the klemheist that consequently locks around the live rope, pulling it up. After a few pulls, the klemheist will have lifted to just below the French prusik. Now, push the French prusik down the rope and gently release the load with the dead rope so that it grips, keeping a loose hold of it yourself. The klemheist, which will now be loose, can be released and slid back down the live rope as far as possible. Keep this sequence up until the required distance has been gained.

It is possible to increase the mechanical advantage by introducing an extra karabiner and another prusik loop. The first section of the system is set up as previously detailed, but now clip either the end of the rope, or a suitably slack section, to the anchor. The rope that you would have pulled with the above technique has a klemheist put on to it with a screwgate. This karabiner is now

clipped in to the rope that you have just secured to the anchor.

Pulling on the slack side of this rope allows the klemheist to grip the original pulling rope, which will in turn grip the live rope, and the climber can be pulled up.

Carefully lower their weight on to the French prusik as required to allow the various knots to be repositioned.

Note that there is a point where you start to lose the mechanical advantage gained through the use of extra pulling mechanisms, as the friction created by the system increases. Doubling up karabiners will go some way to help, in order to give a larger radius for the rope to run round, and the use of pulleys will make things a lot easier, although these might only be carried as standard in a glacier travel situation.

ESCAPING THE SYSTEM

Escaping the system is a technique that is easily learnt, even by practising indoors at home, and it can change a potential epic into something more manageable. There are many reasons why you may need to escape, such as injury to your climbing partner or a jam in the ropework system.

To make things interesting, we will assume that there is a leader belaying a second who has got him or herself into difficulty, and the system is loaded with their bodyweight. The anchor, in this case, has been equalized to one attachment point. It is essential, in all of the following cases, that you are able to lock off the belay device efficiently.

The very simplest solution will be to lock off the belay device and step out of your harness. No great length of time is needed, or any particular equipment. However, you must be sure that you are completely safe moving about without a harness on and, if not, you will need to come up with a way of securing yourself.

If the situation is more serious, such as being on a small ledge in the mountains, where stepping out of your harness is not an option, the following system would be appropriate. The anchor point here is within easy reach of the belay stance.

Once the belay device is locked off, attach a sling to the anchor and adjust it so that when a screwgate is clipped in it will be just in front of the belay device. Simply tying an overhand knot in the sling to shorten it will be fine. Put a French prusik on to the live rope directly in front of the belay device, with plenty of turns so that it can hold the weight of the climber. This is now clipped into the sling you have just placed.

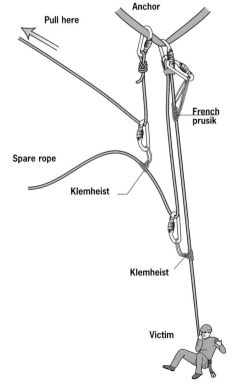

An improved unassisted hoist

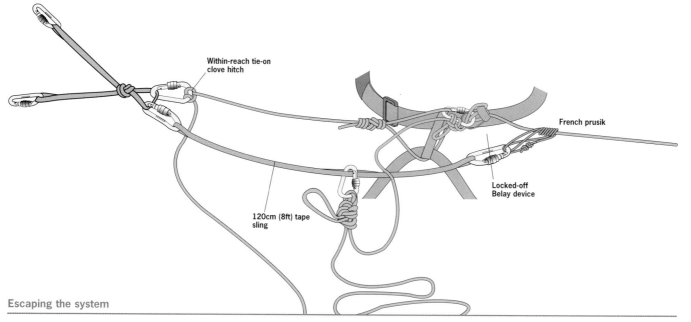

Within-reach tie-on
clove hitch

French prusik

Locked-off
Belay device

120cm (8ft) tape
sling

Escaping the system

Also on to this sling goes an HMS karabiner. Into here, clip an Italian hitch and lock it off, using rope taken from a section of the dead rope coming from the back of the belay device lock off knot. This will be used as a back-up, just in case the French prusik slips.

Push the prusik as far as possible down the live rope so that it is tight all the way through the sling to the anchor. Now unlock the belay device, taking care that you don't accidentally shock-load the prusik, and gently let the weight of your second go on to the new rig. By unlocking the belay device you will have introduced slack into the system, so now take this up via the Italian hitch, unlocking it to do so and locking it off again afterwards.

You can now take your belay device off the rope, and are free to move about as required, taking great care again with your own personal safety. Having a cowstail

clipped in to the anchor would be a good idea at this point.

If you cannot reach the anchor point, you will need to do things slightly differently to the methods above. First, lock off the belay device as before. You now need to create a new anchor point, and this can be done by using just a sling, or a prusik loop with a sling to extend it. It should be tied around the anchor rope using a klemheist with plenty of turns, so that the knot cannot slip. The other end of the sling should be adjusted so that it sits just in front of the belay device. Now continue as for the previous process.

Once you have got out of the system, knots should be tied into any slack or loose ends of rope to ensure that there is no chance that the klemheist can slide off.

It is possible, but quite tricky, to escape the system when an indirect belay has

been taken. This type of belay normally means that you are part of the anchor and, as such, will probably find it very awkward to manoeuvre.

For the process below, we will assume that you are using a waist belay and a bucket seat, with a reinforced axe belay at the top of a winter climb. The system is loaded, although some of the load is taken from you due to the friction created by the rope cutting into the snow. The karabiner on the sling from the axe anchor can be reached at the back of the bucket seat.

Turn slightly sideways so that you can reach up to the screwgate behind you more easily. Loop a sling through the karabiner and clip both ends together. Alternatively, you could larksfoot the sling around the karabiner, shortening it with an overhand knot if it is too long. Whichever option you decide on, it is important that the end of the sling finishes just in front of you at your

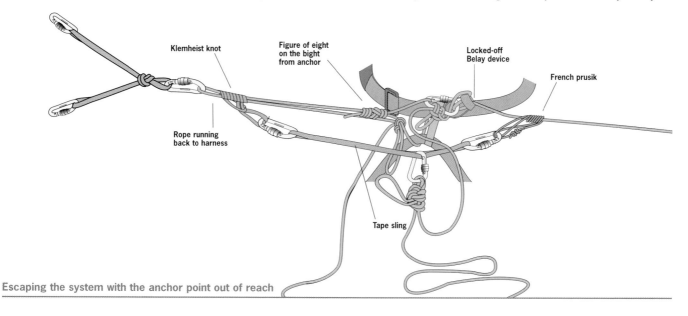

Klemheist knot

Figure of eight
on the bight
from anchor

Locked-off
Belay device

French prusik

Rope running
back to harness

Tape sling

Escaping the system with the anchor point out of reach

side. Clip a screwgate karabiner into the sling, and onto this attach a French prusik (a klemheist would also do, but of course cannot be released under load), that is tied around the live rope. This will all be made simpler if you are in a position to use the fingers of the hand that is still holding the dead rope.

You can now slacken the load a little, so that the prusik takes some of the weight, which will allow you to move a little more easily. It is essential that you do not undo the waist belay at this point. Straight away, use a bight of rope coming out of your live rope side and back up the prusik knot with a locked off Italian hitch. You can now carefully release the weight on to the system and finally take off the waist belay.

Make sure that the anchor has the correct loading maintained on it throughout this procedure and that you don't alter the line when shifting around at the stance.

If the anchor karabiner is out of reach, it would make escaping the system as above a very difficult task. An easier option would be to clip the prusik to the harness central tie-in loop, backing it up with a karabiner at the same point, and then take the harness off. This would mean that your harness is left attached to the anchor, so it could not be used if needed for descent or other types of personal security.

You will have noticed that I have suggested using a tied off Italian hitch as the back-up knot for the above systems.

Although other knots could be used, the advantage of the Italian is that, should the prusik knot slip or fail, the climbing rope can still be released under load. This would be a very difficult thing to do with any other type of knot used in its place.

COUNTERBALANCE ABSEIL

This is the logical progression after escaping the system. It is a very technical procedure and right at the top end of what we would ever want to do, but it is worth knowing as it may just be useful one day. It allows you to abseil to your companion if they were injured, for instance, connect them to you and continue on down to the ground or a suitable stance, using just the one rope.

To start, escape the system, taking care with your own personal safety by the use of a cowstail, and place a screwgate on to the anchor. Take the rope from the dead rope side of the Italian hitch, through this karabiner and then deploy it down the crag. Connect yourself to the rope, ideally with a 'Y' hang rig and French prusik back-up (see 'Abseiling' section), and move the device as close to the anchor as you can.

Now undo the Italian hitch, salvaging the karabiner it was clipped to, and feed the rope through your abseil device to make sure that you are still up close to the anchor. Next, you need to lean out from the anchor with all your weight, reaching down at the same time to release the French prusik placed when escaping the system. You are now counterbalancing your companion, so keep tension on the rope at all times by leaning back. Any spare karabiners and slings can be removed from the anchor, and you can undo your safety cowstail and abseil.

On the way down, strip out any running belays that you pass, as they will not only be useful later but will also help the run of the rope and decrease the friction in the system. Once you arrive next to your companion, connect them to you not only with the appropriate section of the 'Y' hang but also with a short sling, giving you more control over their position as you descend. If they are injured, you may need to rig a Parisian baudrier (see 'Knots' section) to help keep them upright.

Remember that the rope will be running over the edge of the stance, so take care that it cannot jam or become damaged when in use. You may need to sacrifice some gear to pad the edge out, but better this than ending up irretrievably jammed some distance above the ground. Also bear in mind that you can only descend a maximum of half a rope length each time,

so you will need plenty of gear for building intermediate stances on the way down.

Finally, remember that it may simply be quicker to hoist your companion up to the ledge that you are on, particularly if they need first aid attention.

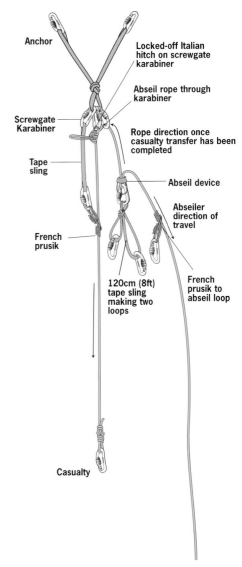

Anchor

Locked-off Italian hitch on screwgate karabiner

Abseil rope through karabiner

Screwgate Karabiner

Rope direction once casualty transfer has been completed

Tape sling

Abseil device

French prusik

Abseiler direction of travel

120cm (8ft) tape sling making two loops

French prusik to abseil loop

Casualty

The rig for a counterbalance abseil

Buried axe anchor

Screwgates (x3)

Extension sling

Bucket seat

Rope ledge

Locked off Italian hitch

Spare rope

French prusik

To victim

An indirect belay system escaped

ABSEILING PAST A KNOT

Although this scenario is quite unlikely, there may be a time where you have joined two ropes together and are going to descend in one long abseil with the rope tied off at the top anchor. Obviously it is then abandoned. Alternatively, there may have been damage to the rope and you have tied a knot in it to isolate that section, or perhaps two ropes of unequal length have been joined and are being used doubled during descent.

If you can get your weight off the abseil rope easily, such as on a snow slope, there should be little problem. Look after your own personal safety when doing so, often best done with a clove hitch from below the knot on to your harness, and move the abseil device to below the obstruction. With large figure of eight abseil devices on fixed ropes, you may find that a little pushing lets the knot pass through the device when it is not under tension.

If you are hanging free or are otherwise unable to get your weight off the rope, you will need to be a bit more technical in your approach. As you get near the knot, stop about 60cm (24in) above it. Pull some rope up from below and clip this in to your abseil loop as a clove hitch to provide a back-up. Now place a French prusik on the abseil rope above your abseil device, clipping it into your harness with a sling adjusted to give you about 50cm (20in) of distance.

Next, lower yourself so that this new French prusik holds your bodyweight when your abseil device and back-up French prusik are approximately 30cm (12in) above the knot in the abseil rope. Now take off your abseil device and back-up French prusik, replacing them snugly against the underside of the knot.

Pull down on the top of the upper French prusik, the one above the knot, so that your weight is lowered on to the abseil device once more. It is here that practice will pay off, as you should know how many wraps of the prusik loop makes a secure knot but one that can be released under your body weight. Once it is slack, undo it and retrieve the gear. After you have undone the clove hitch at your harness, you can continue the descent.

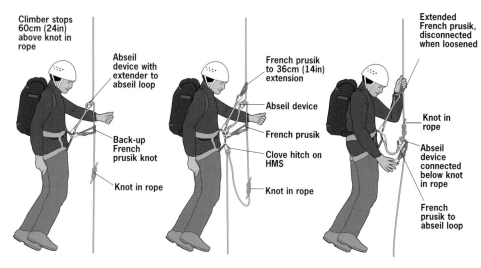

Abseiling past a knot

A LEADER FALL ON A TRAVERSE

This problem occurs on high, overhanging terrain, where lowering the leader to the ground is not an option. It would be very difficult for the leader to ascend the rope and make their way back to the stance, so bringing them in by another method will most likely prove to be a lot quicker.

Assuming that you are belaying, lower the leader until they are just below the height of the stance and lock off the belay device (see 'Knots'). Throw a loop of rope from the anchor end of the system to the leader. They clip this in to their abseil loop with a screwgate karabiner, and you secure the free side to the anchor with an Italian hitch.

You now need to pull in as much rope as you can between the two of you, so that the leader moves towards the stance. Now lock off the Italian hitch, undo the belay device and let them down a little further. Lock off the belay device again, undo the locked off Italian hitch and pull them further towards you.

Repeating this process allows them to swing in to just below the stance, and for the final section they will be protected above by the rope to the Italian hitch as they climb up to join you.

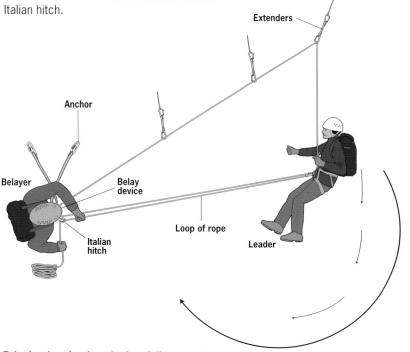

Bringing in a leader who has fallen on a traverse

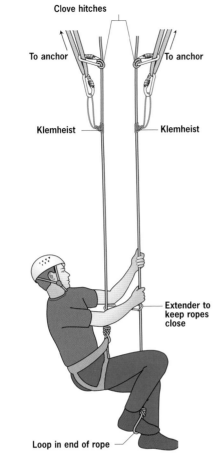

Clove hitches

To anchor — — To anchor

Klemheist — — Klemheist

Extender to keep ropes close

Loop in end of rope

The stirrup hoist

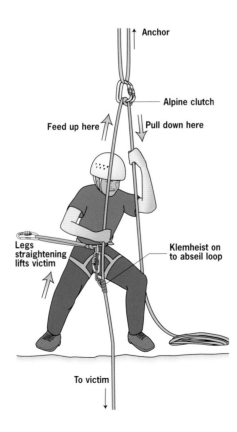

Anchor

Alpine clutch

Feed up here — Pull down here

Legs straightening lifts victim

Klemheist on to abseil loop

To victim

The hip hoist

STIRRUP HOIST

This is a technique by which your second, who is hanging on the end of the rope, can get themselves up to you, partly with your assistance but mainly under their own power. This is useful in situations where there isn't enough rope to organize any other hoisting system.

As you need a free end of rope, it can be the end of a spare rope if you have one, or the original rope if you have escaped the system. Lower the free end of the rope, with a loop tied in it, to the level of your second. Secure this to the anchor with a klemheist and back it up with a clove hitch. Now connect the original climbing rope in the same way. Exactly how you do this depends on the belay, but it will normally be done with a klemheist and the back-up clove hitch clipped in once a little slack has been introduced into the system. Arrange the ropes so that they are hanging as close as possible to each other, as this will help your second to get up. It may be worth having your second clip the ropes close together with an extender running free.

Placing their foot in the loop on the second rope, the stranded climber pulls so that they are standing up. At this point, you take in the slack on the original climbing rope, securing it with the klemheist.

The second sits back in their harness and takes their weight off the second rope. At the stance, you now take in the second rope through the klemheist. Take in as much as is needed to make the foot loop a suitable height for your second to use.

Your second can now repeat the pull up on this rope. Continue this process as often as is necessary for them to arrive at the stance, taking in through the back-up clove hitches at appropriate times.

HIP HOIST

Of use if you have rigged a stance with a high anchor point, this is a method of raising a stranded second using your leg muscles. It works well if your second is lighter than you, but becomes a bit like hard work if it's the other way round! You may need to escape the system, as this will make the whole operation much easier.

The climbing rope needs to be attached to the anchor in a way that will allow it to be taken through and then automatically locked off. There is a variety of ways of doing this, and consider if you may need to introduce slack into the system at any point. A useful knot is the Alpine clutch, and even though it cannot be released under load, it is very suitable for this job. A mechanical device, such as an ascender or small rope clamp would also be appropriate.

You now need a method of gripping the climbing rope, arranged from your harness abseil loop on to the live rope to your second. Most often achieved using a klemheist or French prusik, an ascender or rope clamp would also be quite appropriate here if available.

Bend your knees and slide the knot or ascender down the live rope. Now stand up straight, at the same time as pulling on the dead rope coming down to you from the anchor to take in any slack. Once upright, and with the load taken by the Alpine clutch or device on the anchor, you can bend your knees again, slide the knot or ascender back down the rope, and repeat the process.

HANGING HOIST

This is a useful skill to learn and is fairly simple to operate, where a climber who is hanging on the end of their rope is taken from it and transferred to another system, most often a 'Y' hang abseil (see 'Abseiling'). This could be necessary because their rope is jammed in a crack and cannot be paid out or taken in, for example.

Abseil to the climber, stopping a short distance above them so that you are not in danger of overshooting. Place a klemheist on their rope about half a metre (18in) above their tie-in point and clip a screwgate in to it. Now clip a 120cm (48in) sling into their abseil loop and run it up through the screwgate on the klemheist.

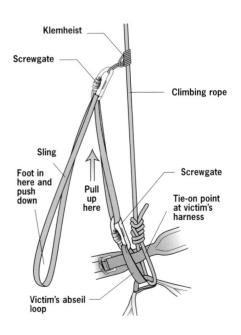

Klemheist

Screwgate

Climbing rope

Sling

Foot in here and push down

Pull up here

Screwgate

Tie-on point at victim's harness

Victim's abseil loop

The hanging hoist

To lift the victim's weight from their rope, you push down hard on the sling with your foot, using the karabiner on the klemheist as a pulley, and pull up on the climber's harness to make lifting them easier. You can now connect them to your Y' hang abseil rig or another rope, whatever is appropriate, and untie their rope knot.

RELEASING A SELF-LOCKING BELAY DEVICE

These devices are notoriously difficult to release and pay slack into when needing to lower a fallen climber, so make sure that you know how to do it before using one in anger. Some have a built-in releasing system, such as a lever that changes the orientation of the device, but those that are simpler in design need a different approach. Obviously, if the climber can regain contact with the rock or ice then it would not be such a problem to pay the rope out. However, if they are hanging free or somehow otherwise incapacitated, you will have to put a technical procedure into place. Note that this is never an easy procedure, particularly if your second is a lot heavier than yourself.

Once the device has locked itself off under load, you need to attach the dead rope to some other belay method on your harness. If there is a spare device available that would be fine, otherwise an Italian hitch will be the more likely remedy.

Either clip or loop a sling through the karabiner, providing the lock at the back of the device. This sling now runs up and through the anchor system, usually by means of a spare karabiner, and then back down to you, where you clip it in to your harness with yet another karabiner.

Hold tight to the dead rope coming from the Italian hitch on your harness and commit all of your weight to the sling. This will then cause the locking karabiner at the back of the device to rotate and be pulled in an upward direction. You should now be able to pay the climbing rope out via the Italian hitch.

Climber attaches dead rope to their harness

Fallen second

A sling is attached from belayer to the belay device, via a suitable high point

Fallen second

The belayer's weight is placed on the sling and the rope is fed through

Fallen second

Releasing the load from a self-locking belay device

ITALIAN HITCH LOWER

It is useful if you bring any multiple anchor points down to just one, preferably by equalizing them with a sling. Look out for your own security, and clip into the anchor, best done with a cowstail. Clip an HMS karabiner in to the anchor with its gate opening upwards and the wide end away. Run the rope through from end to end so that it is in a neat pile near the anchor, and the rope that is going to the person being lowered should come out of the top of the pile, as this will help to avoid tangles. You will be controlling their descent from the downslope side of the system, so make sure that you are in a suitable and safe position.

The person being lowered can either be tied in to the rope, or simply clip in to a figure of eight on the bight on the end, attached to a karabiner on their abseil loop. Get them to slowly load the system as you take their weight, and once they are on their way keep the lower reasonably slow and smooth, as they will have to find their footing on the way down.

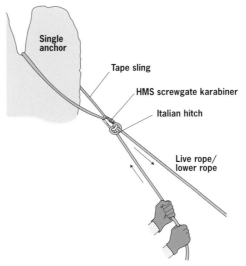

Lowering using an Italian hitch

LOWERING

This is a method of helping one or more group members descend a section of ground, and can be used in a number of situations, most commonly in the case of illness or injury. It will most usually be carried out from a direct belay, although both semi-direct and indirect systems could be used. However, the advantage of the direct rig means that you are not being pulled around by the rope when lowering your companion.

Along with the normal concerns about the solidity of the anchor, the other main thing to check is if the rope reaches safe ground at an appropriate point. To check this, you could drop the tail of the rope down as a gauge before rigging the system, but be very careful that there is no chance that the rope could get stuck as you pull it back up. Also consider how you are going to get down to join your companion. If you are lowering them a full rope length, unless you are down-climbing you will only be abseiling half a rope length, as it will most likely be doubled for retrieval. Thus, it will take you two abseils to reach them.

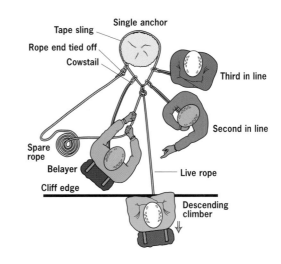

Security of the group when lowering with an Italian hitch

BELAY DEVICE LOWER

Another method for lowering is with a belay device. Although this will take a little more time to set up, its big advantage is that it will not twist the rope over long distances.

You will be in front of the device during the lower, as having it set back from the edge allows the person being lowered to weight the system before starting to descend. Thus, you need to rig the device in order that the correct friction can be applied. This is again best if the anchor is brought down to one point. With a sling on the anchor, tie an overhand knot in it about 30cm (12in) from its end, and clip the belay device to the very end. Just above the knot, clip in another screwgate and, into here, clip the dead rope from the belay device. When you are at your position in front of the rig, the extra screwgate ensures that the dead rope enters the device at the correct angle to allow for maximum braking.

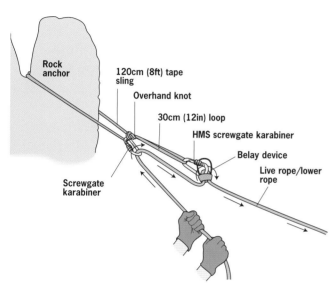

A lower using a belay device

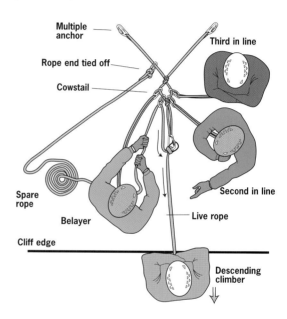

Security of the group when lowering with a belay device

LOWERING WITH A KNOT IN THE ROPE

This could occur if you were lowering an injured companion, for example, and have decided to join two ropes together to make the descent quicker than it would be if just using one rope length.

If the lower is down easy terrain, perhaps a moderately angled snow slope, it should be possible for the 'victim' to un-weight the rope, perhaps by digging a small ledge for themselves, which will let you undo the lowering device and bypass the knot. When doing this, even on very simple ground, always back the system up so that if they do slip off their ledge whilst you are rerigging the system at the top, they will not go for a long slide.

If it is not possible for them to get their weight off the system, you need to do something a bit more technical. There are many ways of rigging, but for this example we will assume that you are using a single point anchor and Italian hitches have been chosen to take the load. The anchor is equipped with two HMS karabiners and a separate screwgate with a 60cm (48in) sling and prusik loop on it.

The lower is started with an Italian hitch into one of the HMS karabiners and the prusik loop, tied as a French prusik on to the live rope, being held loose whilst the rope is moving. Once the knot to be bypassed is about 60cm (4ft) away from the Italian hitch, push the prusik down the rope and let it take the weight of the victim.

Keeping a firm hold of the lowering rope, now tie a second Italian hitch in the dead rope side and clip it into the other HMS karabiner and move the knot to be bypassed tight against it to avoid subsequent jamming in the French prusik. The first Italian hitch can now be unclipped and you can release the French prusik by pulling up on it slowly. Once it is released, it can be taken off the rope and you can continue to lower via the new Italian hitch.

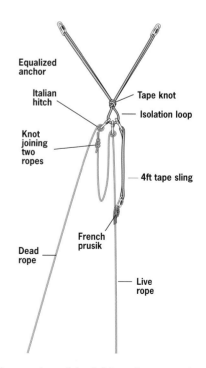

An overview of the full lowering past a knot rig, with all elements connected

Fast and light on a multi-pitch route

MULTI-PITCH CLIMBING

Multi-pitch climbing is where a single rope length is not sufficient to finish the route, or the route does not lend itself to being climbed in one go, and the team keep on leading up after taking intermediate stances until the route is completed. There are two ways in which a two-man team can approach the ropework side of a multi-pitch route. One is to do alternate leads, where one person climbs and completes a pitch, and they then anchor and bring up the second who collects gear from them and in turn becomes the leader, setting off up the subsequent pitch. This is sometimes called leading through or swinging leads.

The second style is where one person does all of the leading. This may be because their companion is a novice, the route is harder than the other person wishes to lead, or any number of other reasons. This style is often called leading on.

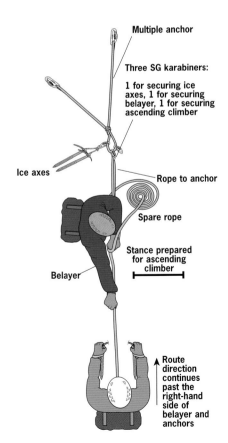

Multiple anchor

Three SG karabiners:

1 for securing ice axes, 1 for securing belayer, 1 for securing ascending climber

Ice axes

Rope to anchor

Spare rope

Stance prepared for ascending climber

Belayer

Route direction continues past the right-hand side of belayer and anchors

A basic leading through belay system

LEADING THROUGH

For leading through, the following procedure will normally be adopted. From the base of the climb, you make your way up the first pitch and belay yourself at a suitable point. In winter or on a complex mountain route, you should be aware of the direction that the next pitch takes and position yourself accordingly. You now belay the second up, who needs to be made safe when they arrive at the stance. This can be done by clipping into the anchor using a screwgate karabiner and a clove hitch taken from the rope just in front of or behind the belay device, or simply by the belayer tying a large overhand knot on the bight on the dead rope just in front of the device.

Normally, the belay device will need to be re-orientated by unclipping it and rotating it to the correct line. This means that it will have to be repositioned so that it is sitting in the right manner for the rope to run through for the next pitch. This is a step that is often overlooked, but an incorrectly orientated belay device that is then loaded has the possibility of the rope crossing over in it and jamming or becoming hard to lock off correctly. You may also find that the pile of spare rope now needs to be moved, so do this in an orderly fashion by running it through, and avoid the temptation to just pick it up and

dump it somewhere else. The equipment is passed across to the new leader and once you, as the belayer, are ready, they can unclip themselves from the anchor and continue up the route.

This is the basic method of leading through. It is possible to improve this slightly, simply by pre-placing the first piece of protection for the next pitch. By doing this, you will not only save having to re-orientate the belay device and move the rope, but will also provide a good degree of valuable protection for your anchor system.

Once you reach the stance, you anchor yourself as before. However, reaching up to the start of the next pitch you place a piece of protection, which will eventually become the first runner. You take in the rope as usual and then clip it through the protection you have just placed, and then down to your belay device. Taking a stance side-on to the rock will probably be the most comfortable when doing this. Make sure that you will not be pulled in towards the rock in the event of a fall, and that your braking hand can operate freely. When the second arrives at the stance, they make themselves safe as usual whilst the rack is sorted and swapped over. Once this has been done, the second can now become the leader and continue up the route.

The big advantage of this system is that once you have put together the anchor system, no re-orientation of the belay device, rope or other part of the system has to take place. The second simply arrives, picks up the spare kit, and climbs on. It also means that you, as belayer, have the aid of the high runner to take the weight should the second fall on the lower pitch, rather than it being taken in a downwards pull as would otherwise be the case. Having a pre-placed runner also helps to

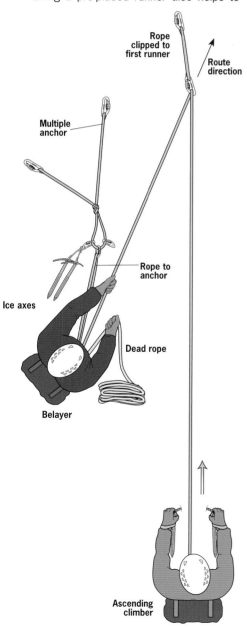

Rope clipped to first runner

Route direction

Multiple anchor

Rope to anchor

Ice axes

Dead rope

Belayer

Ascending climber

An improved set-up for leading through

dramatically reduce the possible fall factor when the next pitch is being started, an extremely important consideration.

LEADING ON

In some cases, it may be appropriate for just one person to lead all of the pitches, or maybe two or three consecutively. If so, the anchor set-up at the stance needs to be thought through before you start to rig it. By far the most efficient method is to be clipped in to one point only. This will most likely be done by equalizing any placements down to a single attachment karabiner, or may just be a sling around a spike or thread. Whatever the case, it would be beneficial not to tie in to multiple anchors with the rope, as this will make changing over a bit awkward. The process for leading on is as follows.

You arrive at the stance and set up an anchor system, clipping in to one point as soon as everything has been equalized. You then belay the second up to the stance. Once the second has arrived, they clip in to the same part of the anchor that is being used by yourself, with a separate karabiner. The rope will need to be run through, so that your end as leader is coming out from the top of the pile. The second, who now becomes the belayer, puts you on belay. You can now unclip from the anchor and continue up the route.

BELAYING TO THE SIDE

On some climbs, particularly under winter conditions or on mountain routes where there is a likelihood of steep ground being encountered, plan ahead as to where the stance will be sited as regards the subsequent pitch. It would be worth taking a stance well to the side of the fall-line that any debris might take, in order to avoid injury. On steep routes or in winter gullies,

placing the stance just below an outcrop or bulge would be a good idea, as this will give a degree of protection to the belayer.

SECURITY OF EQUIPMENT

Dropping gear from a stance is annoying at best and possibly totally disastrous. Take great care to ensure that all of your gear is clipped on to some part of the system or harness at all times. For instance, ice axes can easily be dislodged by the rope when just placed in the snow next to a stance, so clip them safely to the anchor. When passing gear over at a stance, make sure that your partner is ready and keep a good grip on the rack until they have got hold of it themselves.

PLANNING AHEAD

Think ahead and plan out what will be happening both during the climb and on your descent. If climbing a long winter or Alpine route, then you will most likely have all of the extra kit that you may need with you. However, on shorter multi-pitch routes, or ones that may take the best part of a day to complete, you have to plan what kit you may need for the following few hours. Items such as water and food become important, as does extra clothing. Perhaps a map and compass are needed for the walk-off, or a spare rope if a long abseil descent is to be undertaken. Small items, such as suncream and sunglasses, can make all the difference to your comfort when spending a long time on an exposed route.

Climbing and competing at the highest level demands years of training

3: MOVEMENT, BOULDERING AND CLIMBING WALLS

MOVING ON ROCK

Every person is different and each of us will move on rock in a different manner, even when faced with the same choice of holds as our companion. Different heights, weights and strengths will all play a part, so a problem that is solved by one person in a certain manner will probably be worked out by their partner in a totally different way. The natural ability to climb is within all of us, it is getting it out on to the surface and refining it into a useful skill that is the trick.

TRAINING FOR CLIMBING

There are various ways in which a climber can get himself or herself fit and ready to climb routes. Bouldering, climbing walls and gym workouts are all of benefit, with the latter, although being beneficial to overall fitness and general strength, being the least efficient, as it is very difficult to target the specific muscle groups used for climbing.

Bouldering is about as close to climbing a route as you can get, although long periods of time on the rock, important for developing stamina, may be difficult to do simply by the nature of the terrain. Climbing walls offer both long vertical routes and the opportunity to traverse a long way sideways, both of which are important for stamina training.

WARMING UP

Often overlooked, warming up is very important, particularly if you are going to be using a bouldering or climbing wall session in order to work hard and gain some fitness or stamina. The chance of sustaining an injury to soft body tissue, such as muscles, tendons or ligaments, is much higher if your body is not properly warmed up before making it work at a high level, like pulling hard on small holds with your fingertips. There are a number of ways of preparing yourself for climbing and a warming-up procedure should include most of the following elements.

First, do an activity that literally warms your body up, and this should last for around five minutes. Jogging or running will do the trick, perhaps even star jumps, in fact anything that gets your heart pumping and your lungs working hard. Doing this increases the blood flow to your muscles, getting them ready for use.

Next, go through a loosening-up routine. Flex all of your joints, starting with your toes and working your way upwards, working through their full range but never stretching them. Circle your ankles and hips, swing your arms around in big circles, rotate your wrists and wriggle your fingers. Do this to all parts of your body, which allows the joints to lubricate themselves, once again being beneficial in reducing the possibility of injury.

Stretching is often seen as being an important part of the warm-up procedure. However, many athletes and trainers now question its effectiveness when used extensively during a warm-up, and indeed the feeling is that it may be detrimental, serving to lengthen tendons and thus leave joints open to injury. However, a number agree that a series of very light stretches, held for 15–20 seconds, are beneficial, and this is to be recommended as part of your pre-climb session. Find yourself a large vertical hold with your right hand and lean off to the left, feeling a gentle stretch as you put weight on it. Hold this for 15–20 seconds, straighten up, swap hands and then lean over to the right. Your feet should be on the ground for all of this, so that you do not overstress any part of your body. Next, use a large hold at around or above head height and repeat the sequence, leaning back on it first with your right hand and then your left. Now use both hands on it, pulling down gently. Remember, keep it light and have your body weight supported throughout.

Other holds, such as undercuts and finger pockets, can also be used in order to stretch those parts of the body, never overdoing it. It is extremely important when stretching that you don't bounce your body, or ever stretch until it hurts, and obviously you should be warmed up properly before starting to reduce the chance of injury. Remember to gently stretch your thighs and calves as well, especially if the route is long or athletic, as this will give you more flexibility and help to avoid pulling a muscle. Stretching your legs can be done on the floor or by using a suitable boulder or section of wall, again never stretching to the point of it pulling or becoming painful.

Finally, do a little easy bouldering or climbing on big holds, concentrating on moving any body areas that still feel a little stiff. Keep it nice and simple to start with, and avoid the temptation to jump on to the local test-piece. You can build up after a while to whatever level you want to achieve for the session.

WARMING DOWN

This is also important, in particular to prevent your muscles from feeling sore the next day as well as to promote fast recuperation and strength growth. Wind down your climbing session with an easy route or a bit of bouldering, and don't be tempted to make a series of desperate technical moves your last climb of the day. A slow, easy traverse at a low grade is ideal. Rotate and flex your joints for a couple of minutes once you have finished, as this will help to prevent stiffness from occurring, and some light stretching of key areas, using a hold with your feet on the ground as before, will help with recovery and future flexibility. Pay particular attention to your forearms, wrists and fingers, and after rotating and flexing them, lightly stretch them out.

This can be done by putting your palms together in front of you at chest height, elbows out to the side, and pushing the heels of your hands lower whilst keeping your elbows in position. Alternatively, lean against a flat wall with your palms flat and fingers pointing towards the ground, dropping your body position until you feel the stretch. Remember never to overdo it, and hold each stretch for at least 15–20 seconds.

Always warm up correctly before trying any hard or fingery moves

HANDHOLDS

You will use a large variety of holds when climbing, from one-finger pockets through to huge chimneys. Some climbers often prefer to stick to specific types of hold, ones that occur frequently on their favourite rock type, perhaps finger pockets or gnarly hand jams. You should practise using lots of holds so that you get to understand the best way to use them when faced with one on a climb.

ONE-FINGER POCKET

This is a very difficult hold to utilize effectively, and it will often be used to stay in balance whilst another, better hold is found. It requires a lot of finger strength, especially if you do need to use it to move your body upwards, and a lot of pressure is placed on the finger joints. Keep your other fingers close to the one in the pocket, which will generally be either the index or middle finger. If you wrap your thumb over the top of it, it will help with support and lessen the leverage on the joints.

MULTI-FINGER POCKET

Obviously larger than a one-finger pocket, this may allow from two fingers up to a full hand to be placed in, often giving a good degree of security. If only two or three fingers fit, once again wrap your thumb over them to help them stay in place.

SMALL CRIMPS

A crimp is a small flat hold that allows you to place a couple of fingertips on it, often feeling quite secure. It is usually best to bend your fingers so that the tips are pointing downwards slightly, and bring your thumb across the top to help keep them in place.

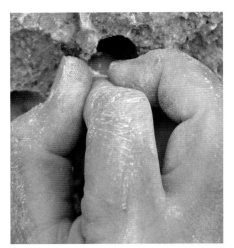

Using a one-finger pocket

A multi-finger pocket

A small crimp

LARGE CRIMPS

These will usually feel a lot more secure than their smaller relatives, and allow you to progress up and onwards with relative ease. They will typically allow all four fingers to be placed on them, and you may decide once again to bring your thumb over the top for support, although this is not always necessary.

JUGS

A jug, or jug handle as it is descriptively known, provides a good hold that you can get all of your hand around. They also rejoice in the name of a 'thank God hold', describing how relieved you often are at finding one on a particularly thin sequence of moves! They are very good for getting a rest with, as it is often possible to use both hands on the one hold, or to swap hands as needed when shaking out.

PEBBLES

These can range from the minute through to quite large, and are harder intrusions of rock that have withstood the erosion that has reduced the level of the rock surface around them. They often protrude just enough so that you can get your fingertips about them, and pinching them is often the best technique. They can sometimes be very slippery, as they are, quite literally, pebbles left behind by geological events.

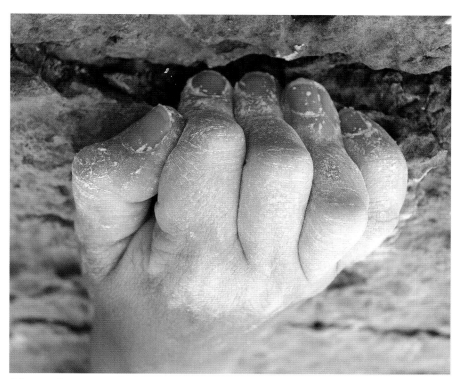

A large crimp

A good jug

Pinching a pebble

UNDERCUTS

These types of holds are often overlooked, as they may be very difficult to spot from above when searching for something to hang on to. The underside of small roofs, blocks and the top side of large pockets all have the chance of offering undercuts, and they are surprisingly secure, allowing you to remain in balance whilst working out your next move.

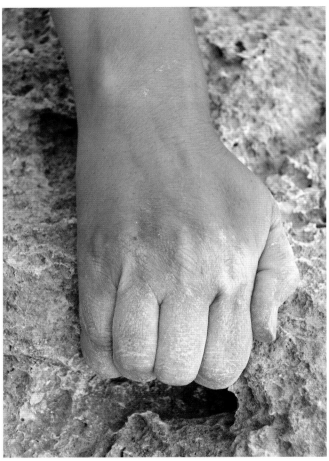

Using an undercut hold

Using a side pull

PINCHES

These are exactly as they sound, holds that you pinch to gain purchase, which are most frequently found in the vertical plane. Horizontal pinches can be quite tricky to hold on to and use to gain height.

Vertical pinches can feel very secure, using your fingers on one side and thumb on the other. If they flare out slightly towards the base, so much the better. Some routes rely almost entirely on pinches, such as those that take a line of tufa. This is a limestone feature similar in appearance to the melted wax stuck to the side of a candle.

Pinching a hold

SIDE PULLS

These are a bit like undercuts, in that they tend to be overlooked but can often prove to be the key to making a successful move or sequence. Utilizing them will normally require you to use the hold in opposition, with your body weight leaning away from the hold as you move up. They tend to be a bit like a vertical crimp, and are often quite positive. As they are frequently used to pull yourself up in balance when using your legs for support, they are usually less tiring to hold on to than normal, small crimps.

PALMING

This is a technique used where all of the more positive holds have run out and using friction is the key to progressing upwards. Maximum benefit will be found with your palms flat on the rock, fingers pointing downwards and your arm straight. Some moves, however, may be better made by palming sideways, or making the most of any scoops or undulations in the rock. Good footwork is also very important in order to maintain contact with the rock.

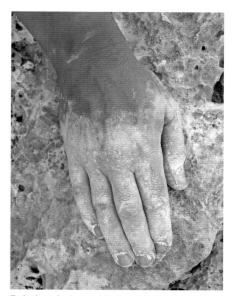

Palming during a friction move

Creating a hand jam by bringing the thumb across in front of the palm

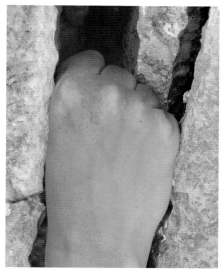

A fist jam

FIST JAM

Jamming is a very effective way of using a crack for progression. Although it may not be one of the most comfortable techniques to use, its solidity far outweighs the slight discomfort that wedging your fist into a small aperture causes. The mechanics rely on you making a fist shape that then is wedged across the internal sides of the fissure. Place your hand into the crack before making the fist, squeezing your fingers into your palm. This causes the sides of your fist to bulge out slightly, forming the jam.

HAND JAM

This differs to the fist jam in that your hand is open, and the parts in contact with the rock are the base of your thumb, fingertips and knuckles. Place your hand into the crack with all of your fingers straight, and then move your thumb across your palm, at the same time as arching your fingers. This increases the width of your palm at the base of your thumb, enabling it to be jammed into the crack.

FINGER JAM

A good technique for climbing thin cracks, finger jamming does take a little getting used to, but once it is mastered it provides a secure way of ascending awkward ground.

Although you could place your hand conventionally, with your thumb uppermost, having it downwards will give the best twisting effect, helping to keep your fingers in place. Keep your elbows low, as this will help to keep your fingers in place.

A finger jam with the thumb downwards

FOOTHOLDS

SMEARING

This is a technique where the maximum amount of boot rubber is placed in contact with the rock in order to get as much friction as possible. It is common on slab climbs, or where a move mainly requires the use of handholds with little for the feet to be placed on.

Generally, dropping your heel slightly allows the greatest amount of contact. Make the most of any imperfections in the surface, such as small scoops and bulges, as these will greatly increase traction and thus support.

Smearing by keeping as much rubber in contact with the rock as possible

EDGING

When either the inner or outer side of the boot is placed on a hold, it is known as edging. In practice, this will normally be done with the front section of the sole, and you will find that lifting your heel slightly helps to keep the edge in place. It is a very common way to use a rock boot, and anyone who is climbing a lot on rock where edging is widespread will often choose to purchase a stiffer-soled boot to help with the technique.

Edging with the inner part of the rock boot

FOOT JAMMING

This is often used in conjunction with hand or fist jams, in order to climb sections of crack to the exclusion of other holds. Place your boot into the crack with the big-toe side of your foot lifted slightly. Make sure that the sides of your boot just touch the sides of the crack, and then straighten your foot. This lets it grip and gives you enough purchase to stand on and move up.

The toe jam is a variation, and can be used with narrower cracks. The technique is just the same, except this time with less boot being in contact with the rock, and perhaps a little more pain!

A foot jam, with the big-toe side of the foot being pushed down to increase the purchase

HEEL HOOK

This is a useful method for taking weight off your arms when moving on steep ground. It is also used for negotiating technical traverses and for surmounting roofs. Whichever leg you want to move is lifted up and placed on the hold, heel first. You may have noticed that rock boots have a large patch of rubber at the back of the heel, and this is what it is designed for. Once your leg is hooked over, a lot of weight is taken from your arms and you will find it easier to pull yourself upwards. It is often worth moving your leg slightly as you ascend, in order to remain in balance and not cause too much leverage.

It can also be used around a suitable hold to help keep you in place and prevent you from pivoting off, also known as barn-dooring, a common result of using holds in opposition.

TOE HOOK

This is very helpful when trying to maintain your balance, particularly if barn-dooring is a possibility. Your toe can be hooked around the edge of a suitable piece of rock, thus using your leg muscles to keep you in place and stop you swinging out.

A toe hook

Heel hooking

SPECIFIC CLIMBING TECHNIQUES

LAYAWAY

This technique is very common on many rock types, and a whole range of variations should be practised so that you become confident in using it when and wherever necessary. It commonly uses a side pull in conjunction with reasonable footholds. A balance move, it allows you to extend yourself over blank sections of ground to reach a hold some distance above.

Having reached a blank section of ground, but with a side pull just off line, turn your body so that you are sideways on to the rock. Lift your leg on to a high foothold, using the side pull for support, so that you are now in a one-legged squat. Your other leg may have to be placed flat against the rock in front of you to stop the chance of barn-dooring off. Now pull on the hold at the same time as straightening your leg, and this will move you upwards so that you can reach for the higher hold.

A layaway

A layback

LAYBACKING

This is a series of opposition holds, linked to allow you to move up a section of ground. Laybacking will typically be used on a wide crackline or across the outer edges of a chimney, and to do it over any distance will be quite secure but become quite tiring. Technique is, however, as important as strength, although stopping to place runners becomes very difficult unless the route is bolted or there are frequent resting opportunities.

If faced with a parallel-sided crack, for instance, grip one edge with your hands, one above the other, and place your feet against the inside of the other edge. Now move one hand up a short distance, followed by the other, and then do the same with your feet. It is important to keep constantly opposing tension between the two, with your hands pulling and your feet pushing, in order to stay in contact with the rock and avoid slipping back down.

BRIDGING

This technique relies on you keeping your body weight over your feet, and is a common method for ascending chimneys and corners. Sometimes you will be relying purely on friction, but you will often be able to make the most of holds such as incuts and small ledges. You may also have to use your arms in a similar manner, pushing out and down on suitable sections of rock.

Bridging may be for just one move or for a sequence, and the ease with which it is executed depends on the frequency of good hand and foot holds.

BACK AND FOOTING

This technique for climbing wide cracks and chimneys can feel quite secure, as indeed it is. Your back is against one wall, both feet are placed on the other. To go up, bend a leg and place the sole of your boot flat on the wall underneath you. Push your body up with this, often with the flat of your hands on the wall by your sides at hip level to help, keeping some pressure from your foot on the opposite wall in order to help keep you in place. Once you have moved up a distance, place both feet on the opposite wall and walk them up slowly, still keeping pressure through your legs so that you don't slip back down. Repeat this process until another technique, perhaps bridging, becomes more appropriate.

Bridging

MANTELSHELF

This technique is used to climb on to or past a ledge or shelf that offers few other holds as alternatives. Although an ungainly belly-flop may well do the trick, having some technique will be a better way of approaching the problem, especially if the ledge is small and won't accommodate much of your body.

Back and footing

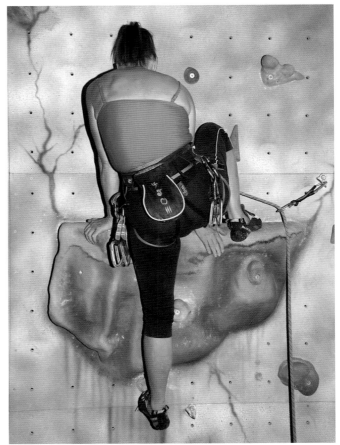

A mantelshelf

Position yourself at a point where you are supported by your arms, which will be pushing straight down on to the ledge, at or near the edge. Lift up one leg and place your foot flat on the ledge, slightly off to one side of your hands. Shift your body weight so that it is over your higher foot, and use a combination of your leg muscles and pushing down with your hands to stand up straight. After some distance, you may be able to reach up with a hand and use a higher hold, which will make the task a lot easier. If not, you will have to use a lot of balance to get it right. Turning slightly sideways will help, as this should allow you to lift your other leg on to the ledge and stand up. Using a knee will be common here, and this will certainly be effective. However, it can be painful on sharp rock, as well as making it awkward subsequently standing up, so if you can get your foot there that would be better.

It is helpful for the toe of your foot below the level of the ledge to be pushed against the rock in small dabs, as this will take some weight off the supporting leg and make the move easier.

ROCKOVER

This is a useful way of getting your body into balance, often as a preparation for a subsequent move. With your foot on a suitable hold, your body weight is rocked across so that it is in balance over the supporting foot. This will then allow you to move a hand to the next hold in the sequence, and you can stand up, often with the lower leg dabbing against the rock to help with the move.

DYNO

A dyno is one of the most impressive moves (whether it's effective or not!), but also one of the hardest to control, as well as being very aggressive on finger and arm joints and muscles. It is where you accelerate up and beyond your normal balance point, so that you can reach a higher hold.

There are three types. A first generation dyno is where you take one hand off in order to reach up to the intended hold. This will require the use of leg power to propel you upwards, arm control to keep a grip on the hold used for balance, and good technique to stop you falling off or barn-dooring. This is the most common type of dyno, and it has the advantage that, with a little practice, should you miss the higher hold you can get back down to the starting position in balance and under control.

A second generation dyno means that both hands are taken off the propelling

hold in order to catch the higher one. Missing the move often means that you fall off, as it is very difficult indeed to regain your starting position.

A third generation dyno is the most impressive, and missing the high hold will certainly result in a fall! Both hands and both feet leave the supporting holds as you drive yourself upwards, so knowing exactly where you are heading is crucial.

A very important consideration when performing any type of dyno is the dead point. This is the point at which your body stops travelling upwards, pauses for a split second, and then starts to descend through gravity. An effective dyno will be timed so that the leading hand gets on to the hold at the precise moment of the dead point, which allows for a good deal more control within the movement, as well as reducing the shock to your joints and muscles and lessening the chance of injury.

RESTING

This takes a variety of forms, and is an important part of effective climbing. Obviously, a simple rest can be taken when you come to a suitable ledge that you can stand on. However, this isn't always possible, so make the most of any small holds that allow you to stand in balance and relieve the pressure on your arms.

Hanging on a straight arm is a useful way to get temporary respite, as you will be supporting your weight mainly on bone as opposed to muscle, and this is less tiring. Swap your hands over frequently and drop the free one down by your side and give it a bit of a shake, often known as shaking out, to help get some feeling back in it.

Resting using a knee bar in a limestone pocket

In extreme circumstances, you may need to get a hands-off rest. This can be done in a variety of ways, with cunning being a handy trait when working out what to do. A crack could offer the chance of you wedging your shoulder or hips inside, thus being able to let go with your hands. For a more impressive rest, a hanging foot jam could be done, or a knee bar across a wider crack may do the trick.

Resting using a head bar on a handy projection

Bouldering at Col des Essets, Switzerland

BOULDERING

This is the climbing of short sections of rock for just a short distance, either up or traversing from side to side, and it can take place on large free-standing boulders or on any section of rock where a sequence of moves can be worked out. Many climbers see bouldering as a sport in its own right. Although some will take it as being a pleasant diversion from the real business of getting up routes, others will want to do nothing more than spend their climbing careers wearing only rock boots and a chalk bag, seeking out areas of ground over which they work out various moves. These sequences may not even top out, perhaps just being a short sequence to reach a suitable finishing hold, from where they downclimb or simply jump off.

Extreme effort and concentration is often needed in order to succeed

Bouldering will often be used as a training aid, where specific moves are practised in relative safety near to the ground before transferring these skills on to a roped climb. It is also used to build up stamina and finger strength, much in the same way that an indoor wall serves to keep a level of fitness going when the weather outside precludes climbing routes.

There are as many different varieties of bouldering moves and sequences as there are boulders. Problems of all types and grades can be worked out, and the most popular areas will have their own guidebooks and grading systems in place.

Slabs, roofs, crimps, jamming cracks and desperate finger pocket pulls will be but a few of the climbing styles that need to be mastered to complete a boulder problem successfully.

To make some problems harder, or to increase the height climbed, sitting starts are sometimes incorporated. These tend to increase the grade of a problem, as your bodyweight will be out further from the rock than if you were starting from a standing position. They are quite strenuous, the more so the taller you are, and they totally change the character of a problem.

Some boulder problems end so far above the ground that most people would consider them as being short routes. These are called highball problems, and this indicates that a fall from the upper section could be very serious indeed. To climb a highball efficiently means that you must be supremely confident of your strength and technique, and have your mind totally focused on the sequence needed for success. Having a good mat and a spotter or two also becomes very important.

EQUIPMENT

One of the attractions of bouldering for many climbers is the minimal amount of gear needed. A pair of rock boots will suffice to start with, although a chalk bag and, ultimately, a crash mat, will be advantageous to anyone taking it more seriously.

MATS

Many boulderers will invest in a mat soon after taking up the sport. Also known as a pad or crash mat, it will perform a number of functions. Firstly, it will even out the landing area and give some protection against injury on hard ground or adjacent rocks. Secondly, it will protect the boulderer's feet from becoming dirty with mud or other debris from the ground below the move or sequence. Thirdly, and very importantly, it will reduce the environmental impact on the ground beneath the boulder itself. The effect of many pairs of feet starting and finishing at the same point may cause irreversible erosion, and a mat will help to protect vulnerable terrain.

A mat is constructed by using a cover of a hardwearing, waterproof and non-slip material, usually either square or rectangular in shape. Into this will be inserted two or more layers of impact-absorbing foam. These will usually be of differing densities, with a light foam on the lower section to spread the load onto the ground, and a more solid foam on the uppermost side, to give a high degree of impact absorption.

The size of mats varies considerably, and it is worth thinking about the use to which they will be put. Some measure only half a metre (18in) square, and are used to cushion the impact of a feet-first landing. At the other end of the spectrum, large mats may be a couple of metres (two yards) square or more. These are useful should there be a need to field full body-length falls, such as may happen when negotiating a low-level traverse, or where the moves wander above the starting area so the landing point cannot be easily predicted.

Larger mats either hinge in the middle or roll up, being secured by a strapping system of tapes and buckles. They will also have a carrying system attached, often a couple of rucksack-style shoulder straps on the underside that can be removed to avoid them getting too soiled.

Crash mats are essential on tricky boulder moves

CHALK

Chalk is an important part of a boulderer's arsenal, and tends to be universally accepted as a suitable means of drying the fingers and providing a little extra grip on hard moves. However, some bouldering sites still frown on its use as it can cause severe and rapid polishing on some rock types, so check the local etiquette before use. More worryingly, studies have found that a high concentration of chalk in popular bouldering areas has had the effect of altering the pH balance of the surrounding ground, consequently affecting local plant growth.

Chalk, more correctly known as magnesium carbonate, comes as a powder, a block or in a ball. The powder comes in tubes from climbing gear suppliers or boxes from chemists. It tends to be finely graded, in particular the pharmaceutical version, and may not give the psychological reassurance of a grainier version, such as block chalk. This comes as a block a few centimetres square, which is then broken up by the climber and used as required. Although only loose powder formed into a shape, broken up block chalk gives a reassuring grainy feel to the fingertips and is the favourite of many climbers.

Chalk balls consist of loose chalk wrapped in a fine gauze material. Grasping the ball allows a small amount of chalk to be deposited on the fingertips. Some boulderers feel that this is not sufficient to cover the hands and allow a high degree of grip, but it is often the only type of chalk application allowed at many climbing walls and indoor facilities. Some chalks come in colours designed to match certain rock types, in order to minimize the visual impact of using it.

Chalk can provide the key to tricky moves

CHALK BAG

This is a small pouch, designed to be tied around your waist and used on the move. It will usually have a fleecy interior, which allows you to effectively dust your fingertips with the desired amount of chalk, and will have an attachment point for a belt or carrying strap. Some will have a small carrying slot for a brush, useful for cleaning holds. There will be a drawcord around the top to prevent the contents spilling out when transported, although some use a spring mechanism to do the same job.

There are some larger styles of chalk bag that are designed to stand freely on the ground. They hold a great deal of chalk and are used as a base camp supply. If you are attempting hard, low sequences of moves and keep falling off, with a conventional bag around your waist the chalk would keep being knocked out. The larger bag lets you dip in when on the ground without having to carry anything on the problem with you.

POF

This is a cloth rag containing a resinous substance that is used to make holds, in particular slopers and small crimps, easier to hang on to by increasing the grip. Made from tree sap and known as colophony, the resin in the pof is applied by slapping the cloth against the relevant holds, depositing a small amount of its contents in the process. It is very sticky to the touch, greatly increasing grip, and as such could be seen as cheating.

Its use is outlawed in many bouldering areas, as the resinous deposits can make the holds very smooth after a short period of application, dramatically reducing friction and making them useless to subsequent climbers. It is important to check local protocol before using a pof, and if in any doubt, avoid using it altogether.

TOWELS AND CARPET

These are useful additions to the basic kit, and are used to help keep your rock boots clean. A small rectangle of towelling can be carried over the chalk bag belt and be used to clean any dust or debris from your boot sole before climbing. A beer-towel is ideal, and easy to obtain (ask first!) from a handy local bar, otherwise any offcut of hand towel will do the trick.

A square of carpet, such as those used as samples by carpet showrooms, is useful as a more aggressive scrub, placed on the floor near the base of the boulder problem. Make sure that you take the carpet home with you though, and as much as possible use it on a flat piece of rock rather than on the ground, as it can cause erosion if you constantly rub your feet on it when it is placed on soft ground.

BRUSHES

Popular problems in some areas end up with a lot of chalk build-up, which makes the holds slippery. There is also always the chance of dust or other debris collecting on them. To rectify this carry an old toothbrush. More technical brushes are also available, and these often clip in to the end of extension handles, allowing high holds to be cleaned. Only use nylon-bristled brushes and never a wire one, as this can irreversibly scar and damage the rock.

Brushing a hold

SPOTTING

Spotting can be included under the 'Equipment' heading, as a good spotter is an essential piece of gear! Spotting is the means by which you provide some degree of security to a fellow boulderer whilst they work out a problem. If they slip off at any point on a problem and are not spotted, there is a chance that they could turn an ankle or stagger backwards out of control and trip up, causing themselves even greater injury. Efficient spotting means that, should they slip, you guide them down to a safe landing, ideally towards a mat, and help them to keep their body upright, thus reducing the stress on their knees and ankles.

There are many ways that spotting can be done, but the most efficient will be to take up a braced position behind them, with one leg behind another making an inverted V shape. Your arms should be outstretched and positioned at a point that will give the greatest support should the boulderer slip. This will most likely be around the small of the back, or one could be there and the other higher up by the shoulders. Should they fall, you are not catching them, as that would be almost impossible to do, but you are guiding them down to a safe landing area and stopping them from falling uncontrollably backwards.

It is important that you look out for your own safety when doing this, otherwise you could be injured by the climber landing on top of you. Watch out for your footing, and always maintain a position just back from the climber's possible landing point.

Efficient spotting is crucial on hard moves

A chalk bag is lightweight and easily carried

Training on an indoor climbing wall

CLIMBING WALLS

The vast majority of climbers will, at some stage of their careers, have visited a climbing wall. This may be for a quick fix when the weather outside precludes getting on to real rock, or as a regular training regime during the winter months. Indeed, there are some who choose only ever to climb indoors on artificial structures, never venturing outside at all. It must be said that climbing on an artificial wall definitely helps you to build up stamina and fitness, as well as allowing you to enjoy moving vertically in reasonable safety.

TYPES

There are many different types of climbing wall around, from the simplest, a few holds or a fingerboard bolted on to the roof beam of a garage or spare room, through to massive indoor structures offering climbs from slabs to huge roofs and everything in between.

Many serious climbers will make their own training facility at home, and these can be categorized under the heading of climbing wall. A fingerboard is the basic piece of kit, and this allows you to perform a number of manoeuvres, mainly with the intention of exercising the fingers and arm muscles. Although restricted in

A fingerboard mounted on a garage rafter

A basic brick-edge climbing wall

A purpose-made climbing facility

size, a well-designed fingerboard used imaginatively can provide a good workout, giving valuable exercise during spells of bad weather or when time precludes a trip to the crag. Most boards come supplied with a suggested training schedule, but it is very easy to make up your own. As with any facility, a proper warming up sequence is important to help prevent soft tissue injury and to increase the value of a training session.

Moving on to larger purpose-built structures, many schools and gymnasiums will have a wall incorporated at one end, and these are very often made by leaving out or adding bricks in order to create the holds. Concrete is sometimes also used to enhance them by giving ledge and overhang features. These walls are very basic, and climbers should take care not to injure their fingers on the sharp brick edges when pulling up. Often, these walls will have been improved by the addition of a number of bolt-on holds, giving variety and colour to what would otherwise be a fairly monotonous training area.

A common sight these days are purpose-built climbing centres, where a building, or a large portion of it, has been dedicated to the provision of a quality facility. Here you can boulder, top and bottom rope and lead, with routes set up in the various grade ranges, and at busy centres these are often reset every few days. Equipment is often provided, as is instruction for those that need it, and there may be a shop and cafeteria on site. The holds tend to be of the bolt-on variety, and this allows routes of different colour and grades to be set up and altered when needed.

Although most walls are indoors, some are designed to be used outside. In particular, competition walls that can be erected for an event and then stripped down will sometimes be placed in or near busy climbing towns, allowing large audiences to watch the competition unfold over a number of days.

An outdoor competition wall, designed for the world climbing championships

USING A WALL

Getting to use an artificial wall is usually very simple. Once any monies have been paid, possibly with a declaration of your ability to tie on and belay safely, you are pretty well free to do anything that you like, obviously within the confines of safety. Soloing high on main lead walls is usually not permitted. Many indoor walls insist on the use of chalk balls instead of loose chalk.

Some facilities provide ground anchors for you to use, and these could be permanent fixings into the floor, or heavy sand bags with a suitable attachment point. Whichever you end up using, make sure that you are belaying from them correctly and that there is no chance that, in the event of holding a fall or during a lower, you can be pulled forwards and trip over them.

Leading on walls is very similar to clipping bolts on a sport climbing route, and the skills for this are covered under the 'Sport Climbing' section. However, very often the extenders or quick-draws will be in place, requiring you to simply clip your rope in and continue on and up. Remember to clip the rope the correct way through the extender, so that it is feeding out of the front

and has no chance of rotating the karabiner, leaving itself open to a chance of the rope unclipping during a fall. Also bear in mind that, when clipping the second extender up the route, you may well have the chance of hitting the floor if you slip off before successfully doing so. This is because the amount of rope that you have pulled through may have introduced sufficient slack into the system to be a hazard, so always make sure that you are in the correct position to clip and have a good hold.

ICE WALLS

Some climbing centres have the facility to offer ice climbing. A complicated procedure to get right, indoor ice climbing is a very good substitute for being out of doors, and allows training to continue throughout the year and in all weathers. You will often be able to hire all of the technical gear at the centre if you need to, but if you are bringing your own remember that, apart from axe and crampons, a helmet is essential. Some form of eye protection is also a good idea.

Clipping extenders on a climbing wall

An indoor ice climbing wall

4: SUMMER
TRADITIONAL CLIMBING

This is the term given to climbing routes where the leader places all of their own protection in the form of running belays, and the subsequent climber or climbers strip it all out again. This demonstrates the difference between traditional or 'trad' climbing and sport climbing, where all of the protection is already provided in the form of expansion bolts and staples that are permanently fixed into the rock.

For many, traditional climbing is seen as the purest form of the sport, as the skill of the leader is used not only to overcome the physical problem of progressing up the rock, but also the important process of placing secure and effective running belays.

EQUIPMENT

Following on from the equipment entry in the 'Basic Skills' section, the gear that you choose to carry on trad routes tends to be based very much on personal preference, along with wealth and experience. For instance, if you are going to be climbing long slab routes on granite, having a large range of very big chocks and camming devices may not be appropriate. Conversely, if you are enjoying a lot of easy grade chimneys on dolerite, having a rack made up of micro-wires and tiny cams may also not be the best choice. Equipment choice all boils down to the route that you are going to do, and in an ideal world you will have the ability to chop and change your rack as required.

FULL RACK

It is hard to say what a full rack may consist of, as there are so many variables. However, a general-purpose rack, and one that will get you climbing safely on many traditionally protected routes may consist of the following. Firstly, two sets of wires in sizes from 1 to 10, arranged on two separate karabiners. Secondly, a number of camming devices, say sizes 1, 2 and 3 to start. Chocks are useful, so a range of four that take over where the 10 wire left off will be handy, and some slings, two at 120cm (8ft) and one at 240cm (16ft), each equipped with a screwgate karabiner. A set of extenders will also be needed, perhaps eight in number, some short and some long. Finally, a belay device, a couple of spare karabiners, prusik loops and a nut key will complete the kit. This list can be expanded upon, particularly in relation to camming devices, as you progress up through the grades.

Equipment racked on a bandolier

Equipment racked on harness gear loops

RACKING GEAR

How you carry this kit depends very much on personal preference. It is important to have a consistent arrangement that works for you, as this will make it much easier to choose the correct piece of gear when it is needed on the route. The first decision will be whether you are going to carry the gear on your harness, on a bandolier, or on a combination of the two.

Racking kit on a harness means that it is all to hand and fairly easy to locate when needed and will be a lot of people's choice, although a bandolier, worn over a shoulder and under the other arm, has a couple of advantages. If swapping leads, such as on multi-pitch climbs or on short routes, it makes it a lot quicker to pass the gear from one person to the other. Also, if climbing on a sea cliff and you are unlucky enough to take a ducking, it is possible to shrug off the bandolier, and thus the heavy weight, fairly quickly.

However, two main things are against using a bandolier. Firstly, the gear tends to crunch up together in the middle, making unclipping a centrally positioned piece of kit quite fiddly. Secondly, on steep or overhanging routes the bandolier tends to swing out behind you, altering your centre of gravity and making it harder to balance and hold on.

A compromise that some will make will be to have all of the placement kit on their harness and all the subsidiary kit, such as extenders, on a bandolier. Personal preference, though, will be the deciding factor, so it is worth taking some time to decide which method works for you.

If you choose to use the harness gear loops to carry the kit, as is my own preference for trad climbing, a system of racking needs to be worked out. My own method is to have, on my right-hand side, wires, small to large cams and then chocks, running from front to back. On my left-hand side I have the extenders, with any extra kit such as belay device and prusik loops, clipped well out of the way around the back.

Another thing that might help is to clip the gear on to your loops in an upward motion. This tends to make clipping a lot smoother, as the open gate is less likely to catch on loose clothing or other bits of kit, and the weight of the rest of the gear on the rack helps the karabiner to get into the right position easily.

You can carry the slings around your body, with the ends clipped into each other (see 'Basic Skills'). Don't do up the sleeves on the screwgates, as there is little point in doing so when carrying them and it just slows down getting them off from around you.

Chocks that have long rope loops or tape attached to them tend to catch on the rock sometimes, quite apart from clanking together with monotonous regularity. To get over this pull a short loop up from the head of the chock and clip it in to its carrying karabiner. This can now go back on to your gear loop and it won't catch. When needed for use, take it off your harness, let the loop at the head of the chock drop out of the karabiner and you are ready to go.

Clipping upwards on to a gear loop

Clipping a chock so that it doesn't swing around

STYLES OF ASCENT

There are different styles of climbing ascent, although the differences only really become important if you are claiming a new route or are saying that you have climbed a specific route in a certain style, but perhaps where a practice ascent or two has taken place beforehand. An on-sight ascent is the standard style of climbing for most people, where you turn up at the crag, choose a route and climb it from bottom to top. It is seen as being very pure, and those operating at the highest levels will aspire to on-sight the climb that is their latest target. If they subsequently fell it would not be seen as a clean on-sight ascent, as they would have knowledge of the moves below the fall point. Other styles, such as redpointing, where all of the moves are practised before a full ascent is made, are usually the preserve of climbers trying the very highest grades of route.

LEADING

There are many elements that go together to make a successful lead of a route. Not least amongst these are the mind games, where you have to get your head completely attuned to the idea of being on the sharp end of the rope. When you are starting out, this is one of the hardest things to achieve, and there will most likely be many doubts in your mind as to whether you can get to the top of the route or not. Experience is important here, and as you make your way through your climbing career you will become able to ignore negative messages from your brain and deal with any problems that may occur, such as lack of runner placements or the route being harder than you first predicted. There are a few things that you need to be aware of when leading that will go to help things run smoothly, and the most important of these are detailed below.

PULLING UP THE ROPE

Before clipping in to a runner, you will obviously have to pull up some slack rope. It would be worth making sure that your belayer is paying attention, as they should be doing all the time, to help make the clip swiftly and easily. A common problem is a belayer letting through a series of very short sections of rope at a time, in 30cm (12in) spurts, instead of letting you take through all the rope that you need in one smooth movement.

If you are electing to clip the runner while you are below it, simply reaching down to the rope and pulling the required amount of slack up will usually do the trick. However, sometimes you may have to pull the rope through a couple of times in order to get enough slack to make the clip, so exactly how you hold on to the first length of rope before pulling up another is worth thinking about.

Keep the karabiner steady with your middle finger and hold the rope between thumb and forefinger

The commonest method is to pull up a length and hold the top of the loop in your teeth, before reaching down to pull up some more. This is very effective, and you will only have to hold the rope in your mouth for a couple of seconds. Another method, as long as you are in reasonable balance and have a good hold, is to trap a bight of rope under the thumb of your supporting hand whilst reaching down for the next length. Obviously, take care if doing this, as you could potentially fall some distance if your supporting hand lost grip of the rock.

If, once you have pulled some rope through, you find that you need to move your position slightly to get a better purchase on the rock prior to clipping, don't be tempted to climb up a way with the rope still in your hand or between your teeth. Let it drop so that your belayer can take the slack in, make your adjustment and then pull the rope up again. By doing this you will be better protected than if you kept hold of the rope and subsequently slipped off, resulting in a long fall.

HOLDING A KARABINER TO CLIP IT

This may initially seem like a fairly basic procedure, but when you are some way up a route with your gear at arm's reach above you, the karabiner swaying in the wind, it suddenly becomes a bit more of a problem! The main thing is to be positioned as comfortably as possible, as you will be there for a little while, placing the protection and then either clipping an extender to it or just clipping the rope in to the gear's own karabiner.

The simplest method will be to use a finger clip style. Hold the rope between your thumb and forefinger and bring it up to the gate side of the karabiner. Now place your middle finger in to the karabiner at its lowest point to hold it steady, and press the rope on to the gate with your thumb. It will drop in easily, with the weight of the rope and gravity completing the job for you.

There are obviously other ways in which the rope can be introduced in to a karabiner, including one where the rope is across the palm of your hand and you squeeze it on

to the karabiner gate. However, you will probably find that the finger clip style will deal with most situations.

It is important that the karabiner is clipped with the rope running in the correct direction, as Z clipping and back-clipping are not desirable at all. These problems are discussed below.

Z CLIPPING

This is most likely to happen where the leader is on steep ground and probably feeling a bit nervous, and to clip the gear that they have just placed they get hold of the rope from below the previous piece and clip that section in by mistake. This means that the rope runs from the belayer, up to the top runner, through the lower one then back up to their harness. This is only possible if the gear placements are close together. It not only means that they are no better protected than they were before clipping in, but that there will be a huge amount of rope drag which will make it difficult to move upwards. Also, there is a chance that the lower piece of gear will be lifted up and out of its placement.

Your second will often be in a better position to see what is going on than you are, and hopefully they will let you know before you try to move up. The best remedy is not to unclip the higher runner but to undo the lower one so that the rope straightens, then clip it back on to the rope in the correct place.

Using your thumb, press the rope on to the gate

STEPPING THROUGH

This is fairly commonly seen, and is one of those actions whose consequences are not often thought through or understood until it happens. It occurs where you put your foot on to a hold off to the side of the line of the rope, but between the rope and the rock. If you subsequently fell off, the rope would run between your legs from behind you and when you went down past your last runner you would be flipped upside down, possibly causing back, neck or head injuries. Once again, this is easier for your second to spot.

BACK-CLIPPING

Avoiding back-clipping a karabiner on a piece of protection is very important, especially for sport climbing, under which section it is covered more in more depth. Back-clipping means that the rope from below runs up and through the front of the karabiner on the extender or whatever, and out from the back to your harness. As you move up, this will have the effect of rotating the karabiner, leading to a couple of possible consequences. Firstly, if the karabiner is attached directly to a placement that is not well seated, there is a chance that it will be rotated out of position. Secondly, and of more importance, is the fact that, in the event of a fall, the rope may not be clear of the gate and will therefore have a much

Stepping through

A back-clipped karabiner

increased chance of rubbing across it, with the possibility of it unclipping itself.

To avoid back-clipping a karabiner, first think about how the karabiner will hang from the protection. Now clip your rope so that it runs up from the back of the krab and exits from the front. This means that as you move up, the orientation of the karabiner will not be changed and the problem of the rope running across the gate will have been removed.

Note that the problem of back-clipping and subsequently the rope undoing itself from a karabiner in the event of a fall is far increased when bent gate karabiners are being used.

BACKING OFF

This is simply a type of enforced downclimb, where you have decided to come down from a route instead of continuing on and up. There are various reasons why you may choose to do this, such as the route being too hard, the weather changing for the worse, being off line, loose rock issues, and many more.

If the climbing was not too hard up to that point, the simplest remedy will be to just climb back down, retrieving your gear as you go. Watch out for your own safety of course, particularly if it has started raining or the rock is loose, but this will be the answer for most situations. However, if you are coming down from a high-point as the route is too hard or the gear is not

as good as you had hoped, you will very likely need to have a rope from above to give you security. If your top runner is a really good placement all is well and good, as your belayer can simply lower you to the ground, and you can strip out all the other gear as you go, perhaps leaving the second-to-top placement as a back-up. These two pieces can then be retrieved by abseil.

However, if your top runner is of questionable quality, lowering will not be a good idea. This is because, once you are hanging on the rope, it is not just your weight that the runner has to hold but also most of that of your belayer as well. In this situation, it will be far better, and safer, to downclimb, along with the extra security from above. If possible, place another piece of gear as soon as you can, and this will back-up the top runner.

SECONDING

Although seconding is sometimes seen as being a bit of a dead-end job, it is extremely important to get it right, and to become proficient at belaying a leader takes a lot of time and experience. Managing the rope, watching out for problems and potentially holding falls are but a few of the jobs that need to be mastered.

As you will be in one place for some time, get yourself as comfortable as possible. Sitting down is not an option unfortunately, as this will change the way that the load generated by a fall is transferred via the harness to your body. However, you can be relaxed and even leaning back slightly, although the confines of a ground anchor (see 'Basic Skills – Belaying'), if one is being used, will dictate your final position. Make sure that the rope is running in an orderly fashion up the line of the route, and that the spare rope is piled close to hand. Watch as the leader makes their way up the rock, and be ready for them to pull in some slack to clip a high runner. Belaying tends to be a lot of paying out and a bit of taking in, as runners are clipped and climbed past, and you need to give the leader your constant attention. For a leader to be trying to make a vital and delicate clip when their belayer has dozed off in the sun does not make for the best of relationships!

GEAR RETRIEVAL

Once you have started climbing, lifting the gear out will be your main job, apart from enjoying the climbing of course. Stop at a suitable point below the placement and make sure that you are well positioned so that you do not have to overreach, and

that if the gear comes out suddenly you will not be thrown off balance. Leave the gear clipped to the climbing rope while you retrieve it, as this stops it being dropped down the crag by accident.

All gear should be taken out the same way that it was put in by the leader. Thus, a camming device will have been placed with its stem pointing downwards and outwards a little, so this is the orientation that should be maintained when removing it. If you move the line of the stem, making it horizontal for instance, there is a chance that one of the cams could catch and jam in the crack, making subsequent retrieval very difficult and time-consuming.

RETRIEVING WIRES

The same goes for wires as for cams. It is wrong to hold on to the end of the wire and give it a smart jerk upwards, as this bends and possibly damages the wire at the point that it enters the alloy head. Instead, move your thumb and forefinger up as close to the head as possible, grip the wire and give it a wiggle. If this does not work, press your thumb against the wire as high as you can, to help it release. If this is still not working, it will be time to use the nut key.

Place the rounded heel at the end of the nut key on to the head of the nut, just at the point that the wire exits from it. Be careful that you don't damage the wire, as strands are easily stripped, rendering the unit useless. Now give it a good push with your hand, and this should dislodge the placement. If this still does not work, you will need to get two hands to it. Get your leader to take you in tight so that you can work safely, unless you are on a large ledge. Holding the key in the same position, give the end of it a bang with the heel of your hand. Finally, if even this is not working, you will need something more solid with which to get the wire out. This will often best be done by abseil once the route is complete, if this is possible. A stone or piece of rock will do the trick, but obviously make sure that you cannot drop it on to anyone's head, so keep people clear below you. Place the key back on the nut and give its end a smart tap with the stone. This will normally be enough to shift the wire from its placement and release it. If this still does not work, you may have no option but to abandon the gear.

RETRIEVING CAMMING DEVICES

Camming devices are notoriously difficult to remove from some placements, but the really important trick here is to not get them stuck in the first place! If they have been properly seated and are of the correct size for the crack, have been extended appropriately to avoid any rope movement, and you, as the second, have not altered their position at all, then they should come out without any problem. However, if something untoward has occurred then you may need to do something a bit more proactive.

If the cam has a cylindrical trigger bar that is hard to reach, the end of some nut keys have holes designed to fit over them. Alternatively, the hook section of a key may be enough to provide purchase on the pulling mechanism. If this is still not enough, you can use a couple of wires to help you. Pull the heads back a distance and clip both to a karabiner. The other ends of the wires, the ones that you would normally clip an extender into, are put over either end of the cam trigger bar. The karabiner now clips to an appropriate strong point on your harness. If you lean your weight out slightly on to the wires and hit the end of the stem, this is often sufficient to allow the cams to retract enough to pull out.

Small camming devices can have a short length of accessory cord fitted to them, just in case the trigger becomes deeply imbedded in the crack and difficult to reach. Pulling on the cord with a nut key, at the same time as pushing on the end of the central bar, will help the cams to

retract and the unit to be retrieved. Use a narrow diameter cord, as this will be less bulky, and make sure that the finished loop does not impede the workings of the cam in any way.

RETRIEVING SLINGS

Although getting a sling back from a spike runner is relatively straightforward, a threaded sling can present a bit of a problem. If the hole through which the sling is wrapped is large, then it should not be difficult to do. However, if it has been teased though a tight opening, there is a danger that it could become jammed in the constriction and be immovable. Use a delicate touch, as to tug it means that it will almost certainly become stuck, and make sure that the sling is flat and not folded over several times. The sewn section is often the bit that gets caught, so take particular care when unthreading this part and move it to the widest area of the gap, easing it through with your fingertips. You may find that a nut key is, once again, a very useful item, as the hook can be used to pull part of the sling through and the end can be used to push it through sections that your fingers cannot reach.

AT THE TOP OF THE CLIMB

Once you have completed the route, step away from the edge and let your belayer know when you are safe. You can then untie and help to get the rope coiled up, but don't be over-keen and take the belayer's anchor apart until you have checked that they have finished with it. It is not unheard of for a helpful second to dismantle an anchor, only for their belayer to then lean out over the edge to take a photograph or check for gear, with obvious consequences.

Take a moment to lay the gear that you have retrieved on a suitable rock, all unclipped so that it can be put back on to the rack in the correct order. All that now remains is to descend and do some more climbing.

A small camming device with retrieval cord pre-fixed

Sport climbing lets you concentrate on movement and not on placing protection

SPORT CLIMBING

Sport climbing relies on having protection already placed in the rock, usually by the first ascensionist, with the climber just clipping extenders in as required. Drilled bolts, held in place either by an expanding sleeve or by a special gluing process, are placed at frequent intervals up the line of the route, with each stance and/or the top of the climb being equipped with a lower-off point with two bolts linked with a chain, or similar set-up. Although most pure sport routes will be set up in this manner, it is worth remembering that this will not always be so, and some climbs, particularly those on long mountain routes, may also require the placing of conventional protection.

Many of the issues and techniques outlined below are also of value when climbing on an artificial climbing wall, in particular the issues related to leading and the correct manner for clipping protection.

A clip stick in use

EQUIPMENT

EXTENDERS

Extenders, also known as quick-draws or tie-offs, come in a variety of lengths and styles. Generally, as sport route protection tends to be kept straight, short extenders will be fine for most occasions. However, it is worth carrying one or two longer ones, as the bolts may sometimes be a little off to one side or the other, and need to be brought back into line.

One end of the extender is often supplied with a rubber retaining loop, which is designed to hold the rope-end karabiner rigid and correctly orientated whilst clipping the rope in. This helps when making quick clips, especially when allied with a bent gate karabiner that will let the rope drop in easily.

CLIP STICK

This is used to reach distant bolts. It is a telescopic pole with a device at one end that accepts a karabiner and extender. The rope is connected and the karabiner can then be lifted up to the bolt and clipped in. It can be used to protect the start of climbs, or may even be used extensively when climbers are working a route, making their way up to the top before lowering off and climbing from the bottom up. This is known as a redpoint style of ascent, where the climber has practised the moves and pre-placed the extenders, before going from bottom to top without falling off.

A multi-loop sling used as a cowstail, larksfooted to the harness

COWSTAIL

This is a sling or length of rope, used to make a connection between your harness and, most commonly, an anchor point as you arrange the rope in order to descend. It is very important that it is connected properly, as it will be holding your weight as you untie from the rope.

The simplest method will be to thread a 60cm (4ft) sling through your harness, locked off with a larksfoot, and clip a screwgate karabiner into the other end. This can be clipped into a gear loop, ready for use. An alternative is to use a length of climbing rope, with one end tied around the strong point of your harness and the other having a loop tied in it with a screwgate attached. A third method uses a sewn daisy-chain, with loops ready-made along its length, giving a variety of options for clipping length.

SPARE KARABINERS OR MAILLONS

It may be worth, on long routes, carrying a karabiner or two that can be abandoned if you have to retreat. Old screwgates are ideal for this, or alternatively a maillon can be carried for the same reason. If so, make sure that the sleeve opening is large enough to allow it to be clipped to the bolts on the route you are climbing, as some types of bolt, particularly the glue-in style, are made of thick metal and small maillons simply won't fit.

FROG

A variation on a standard extender, this has a grasping mechanism that is pushed vertically upwards on to a bolt hanger. Two arms then snap shut in a scissor-like action, fixing it into place.

An advantage of a frog is that you can be at arm's length below the bolt and still clip it, gaining a few centimetres over a conventional extender that has to be hooked in. However, it is considerably heavier and more expensive than a wiregate extender rig, so carrying one for really tricky clips will probably be your limit.

CONVENTIONAL PROTECTION

You may need to carry a small rack to deal with rigging runners on some climbs, particular longer, multi-pitch mountain routes. Any specific kit that is required will usually be mentioned in the guidebook, but even if a multi-pitch route is thought to be fully equipped, a lot of climbers will still take perhaps six or eight wires, and a sling and karabiner, just in case.

A frog

A variety of maillons

LEADING

Although sport climbing appears to be a safe activity, it is still climbing to height and as such has inherent risks. The nature of sport climbing is such that many leaders will push their grade and expect to fall off, knowing that a mechanism is in place to keep them safe. This is not always the case, so it is important that you treat the apparently clinical appearance of sport routes with respect.

There are a number of problems that can occur when leading a route, such as Z clipping, stepping through and so on, and these are covered in the traditional climbing section. There are a couple of points worth reinforcing here, and these are the height from which you clip the bolt, and the effect of back-clipping.

CLIPPING HEIGHT

This relates to the position that you are in when clipping the bolt. It becomes important because, if you are a distance below the placement and slip off whilst trying to place the rope into the extender, you have the potential for falling a long way. For instance, if the last bolt that you clipped is at or around waist height and the next one is a metre and a half (4ft 6in) above it, you will be pulling through around three metres (9ft) of slack rope. Should you then slip, the resulting fall will be a good six metres (19ft), a significant distance. If, however, you were at or very near waist level with the higher bolt and slip whilst preparing to clip, you would only drop three metres (9ft).

Very often, you may be below the bolt but positioned on a reasonable ledge with a good handhold, and this stance will let you make the clip without any problem. However, if you are in a position where the clip has to be made quickly due to the holds being difficult to use, or if you are not in balance, then a bit of

Clipping at waist height, thus minimizing the possible fall distance

forethought as to where you clip from would be a good idea. Basically, the closer that you are to the bolt the less distance you will potentially be dropping.

There are obviously other factors that need to be considered here. Even though the maths states that you will fall less distance when next to the bolt being clipped, your head may be telling you otherwise. Thus, being below and in the comfortable area around a 'safely' clipped bolt, even with a lot of rope needing to be pulled through, will in fact be better as you will be more relaxed. Nerves make climbers fall, so being relaxed makes a big difference.

Having an alert belayer is absolutely essential here (as they are, indeed, anywhere!). If you elect to clip from below and fumble the move, which then causes you to drop the rope, hopefully your belayer has the foresight to be ready to take in very quickly, thus reducing the distance any fall may be. This will then allow you to recompose yourself and go for the clip again.

A very common error is for the leader to hang on to the rope for too long when positioning themselves prior to clipping. They pull up a length of rope, find that they cannot reach the bolt easily, and hold on to the slack whilst repositioning themselves or moving up slightly. Obviously, the chance of slipping here is quite high, so if you find yourself in that situation, let the slack rope go so that your belayer can protect you properly, move to where you want to be and pull up the rope again.

Always be careful when clipping the second bolt on a route from some distance below (and this is relevant to artificial climbing walls as well as outdoor bolted routes). The slack that you pull up could easily be enough so that you hit the ground if you slip before making the clip. Gain a bit more height before pulling the rope through or, if the route is hard and the landing poor, consider the use of a clip stick.

Clipping from low down, which increases the possible fall distance

Concentrating on leading

BACK-CLIPPING

This is where the climbing rope is incorrectly clipped into the extender. This sounds like a fairly basic procedure, but it is undoubtedly the most frequent mistake made by both beginners and experienced climbers alike. Back-clipped karabiners can, in certain circumstances, cause the rope to undo itself from the whole extender should a fall occur. It may also happen that the extender is rotated by the movement of the rope in such a manner as to cause it to unclip itself from the bolt.

Because of this, it is extremely important that the line of the rope in relation to the direction that you are climbing, along with the orientation of the karabiner gate, is taken into consideration. Make sure that the rope runs up from your belayer and behind the karabiner, coming out from the front of it, and also ensure that the rope runs across the back bar, away from the gate. This may mean that you have to turn the karabiner around in the extender once it is clipped.

Most climbers on sport routes use extenders with a straight gate karabiner at one end and a bent gate at the other. The straight gate should be used for clipping into the bolt, and the bent gate must only be used for holding the rope. Although a bent gate is designed to make clipping the rope in much easier, important when having to move fast on technical terrain, it can, in some circumstances, also cause the rope to become unclipped as easily. This chance is far increased if the karabiner is back-clipped, as the rope has a chance of running across the gate in the event of a fall, and becoming unclipped.

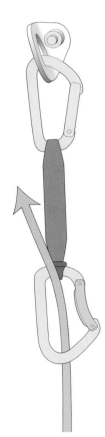

The rope correctly clipped through an extender

An extender back-clipped

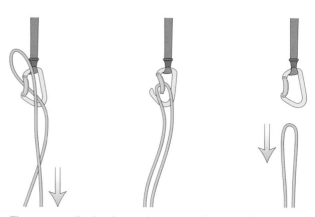

The rope unclipping from a bent gate, due to a fall after back-clipping

Another possibility with back-clipping is the chance of the rope moving the karabiner around the bolt so that it ends up in a position where it can unclip from the hanger. The diagram shows that the rope, having been back-clipped along the back bar, turns the extender so that it can come away from the bolt, either under its own weight or with that of a falling climber.

Back-clipped in the same manner, the next diagram shows the sequence that could occur if the run of the rope causes the extender to lift. In this situation, the karabiner connecting the extender to the bolt rotates. If the climber causes the rope to change the direction of its run, such as when pulling up slack quickly to clip a subsequent placement, the weight of the rope swinging across could cause the extender to undo itself from the bolt karabiner.

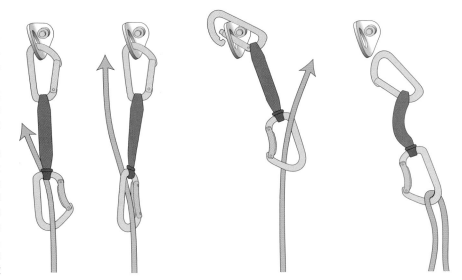

A sequence showing a karabiner unclipping from a bolt due to the rope being back-clipped

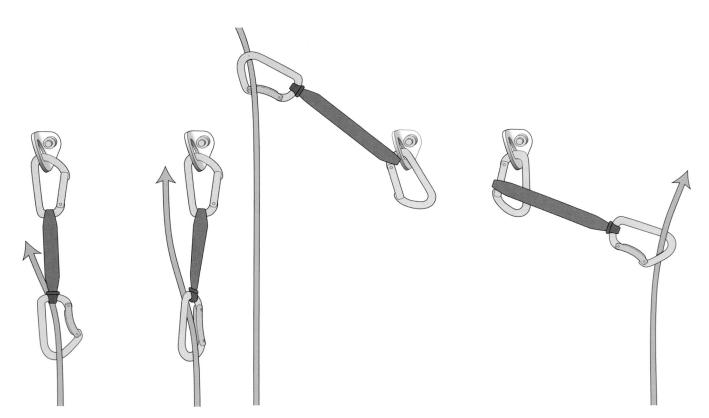

A sequence showing an extender unclipping from a karabiner due to the rope being back-clipped

DOUBLE-CLIPPING

This is where two extenders are clipped into the same bolt. Although not normal practice, it can pay dividends when making an awkward move over a bolt that has perhaps not been placed as well as it might. It is also used in situations where the leader needs every possible psychological advantage before making a move, and having the knowledge that the bolt below them has no chance of becoming unclipped may make all the difference.

Obviously it is only possible where the size of the bolt hanger will allow two karabiners to be clipped in and you position the extenders so that the karabiners on each open in different directions to each other. The rope should still be clipped through in the correct manner, running from back to front.

Another method, if you know that there will be an awkwardly placed bolt to clip, is to have an extender ready with two screwgate karabiners on. Doing both of the gates up after clipping will ensure that both the karabiners on the rope and the hanger stay in place.

A bolt double-clipped before a hard move over a bulge

Steep sport climbing on limestone

SOLVING BOLT PROBLEMS

As long as the solidity of the bolt is beyond question, and the rope is clipped through the extender in the correct manner, there are not a lot of problems that can occur. One thing that is worth being very careful of is to monitor which karabiner is being used to clip into the bolt. On extenders that have a straight and a bent gate karabiner, this will not be a problem, as obviously the straight gate will always be on the bolt. However, if you are using two straight gates it is worth marking which one will be used to clip into the bolt. This is because some hangers have sharp edges, and any loading on the karabiner can cause it to be come burred. If that karabiner is subsequently used on the rope end of an extender, the rope could easily become damaged, especially in a fall. Similarly, if the karabiner is used to clip into a wire, for example, on a traditionally protected route, it could also cause damage that may weaken the overall system.

A piece of tape or other marking method is therefore recommended, so that you can easily identify which karabiners are only to be used at the bolt end of an extender. Alternatively, extenders can be made up with a plain-coloured straight-gate karabiner on one end and a coloured one on the other, with the plain one always being used to clip into the bolt and the coloured one only ever used on the rope.

MISSING HANGERS

Some routes may have bolt stubs sticking out from the rock, but no hanger in place. These may have been removed to stop non-climbers from continuing up, through damage or simply due to vandalism. If you have wires with you, you can solve the problem by pushing the head of the wire down a short way to expose the loop at the top. Place this over the bolt stub and slide the head back up again. The wire can then be clipped in the normal manner with an extender.

Bear in mind that this is not ideal and should only be seen as a temporary remedy, and used as a last resort.

DAMAGED HANGERS

Most bolts that have damaged hangers should be avoided if at all possible. As a likely reason for the damage is rockfall, this could have also greatly weakened the inserted expansion section of the bolt, thus making the entire placement weak. However, if you are high on a route and have no choice but to make the clip, a wire would again make the placement usable.

If the hanger is only slightly bent, you could push the bottom eye of the wire down through it so that the head of the wire is sitting on the top. Clip an extender into the bottom of the wire and you can use it as normal, a bit like a thread.

If the hanger is nearly flattened, push the head of the wire down to expose a loop. Push this up through the hanger and clip a karabiner into it, to stop it from falling back out. The wire can now be clipped as normal.

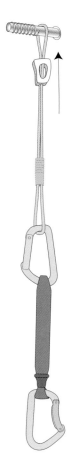

A wire over a bolt stub

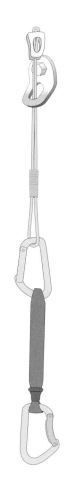

A hanger with a wire threaded down though it

A hanger with a wire pushed up through it

LOWERING OFF FROM SINGLE-PITCH ROUTES

Once you have reached the top of a sport route, you will commonly find that an anchor for lowering off has been drilled into place. Take care when arranging your rope for getting down, as this process is the cause of a number of accidents, either due to a mistake when clipping or tying into the system, or by loss of control by the belayer.

The style of lower-off point varies considerably from venue to venue and even route to route, but there are three types in common usage. Firstly, some will have a single-point lower-off, consisting of a one bolt placement, typically equipped either with a snap-link or a spiral pigstail. Then there are those constructed with two bolts linked by a length of chain, the bottom of which has a welded ring or snap-link through which the rope can be placed. Thirdly, two independent bolts can be found, either ring-bolts that have a smooth inside radius or hangers with tightly closed maillons attached. Note that for all of the techniques whereby you need to spend time at a lower-off, it is important to have a cowstail pre-clipped to your harness ready to use.

CLIP-IN LOWER-OFFS

Arranging to lower from the type that uses a snap-link or spiral pigstail should not present any problems. You arrive at the top, place your rope through whatever device is in situ and are then lowered off by your belayer. Some single-point lower-offs will have a bolt placed next to them. You can use this to clip an extender into, so that you are protected by your belayer whilst you arrange the rope. Alternatively, you can clip your cowstail in so that you can use both hands on the anchor if necessary.

SINGLE-POINT LOWER-OFFS

The type of rig that has two bolts linked by a chain, with a welded ring attached at the bottom, needs a bit more thought and time to use correctly. There are a couple of ways of dealing with this, and we will start by looking at the most common one first.

Once you have arrived at the top of the route, clip yourself into the chain or suitable bolt, using your cowstail and use it to hold your weight. This can be clipped directly into the ring, but may also be placed away from it, perhaps into one of the links of the chain nearby, or directly into one of the bolts. Now pull up a bight of rope and pass it through the ring, and tie a figure of eight knot in it. This is then clipped into the abseil loop on your harness with a screwgate karabiner.

You can now untie the rope knot on your harness. Doing this gives you a length of spare rope, so pull it back through the ring and tuck it into a suitable point on the harness to stop it hanging down by your feet, otherwise you may trip over it during the descent.

You now need to pull yourself in close to the lower-off point as your belayer takes in any slack rope and holds you tight. Lean back out again and put all of your weight on the rope with your belayer holding you to check that everything is connected properly. If there was a problem with your tie-in, you are still connected to the chain with your cowstail. After a final check of the system, remove the cowstail and you can then be lowered to the ground.

If you are concerned that the rope will only just be long enough to reach the ground, you may wish to tie back into it in order to save the long tail. This process is only slightly different to the one above.

Once you have arrived at the top of the

A snap-link lower-off

A tail-shaped lower-off

A two-bolt and chain rig, equipped with a thread-through ring

1. Having clipped in a cowstail, the climber passes a bight of rope through the ring

2. Climber ties a figure of eight in the rope

3. This is clipped into their abseil loop with a screwgate

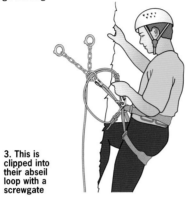

4. Climber unties from the end of the rope, pulls it through, removes the cowstail and is lowered off

The process of arranging a lower-off using the figure of eight method

1. Rope clipped into extender to prevent loss

2. Climber unties the rope

3. Climber threads the rope through the ring and reties

4. Climber removes the extender and cowstail and is lowered off

The process of lowering off using the retie system

1. Cowstail clipped into one bolt and rope clipped on to extender to prevent loss

2. Climber unties from climbing rope

3. Rope threaded through bolts and tied back to harness

4. Cowstail and extender holding rope removed and climber descends

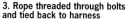

The process of lowering off from two unconnected bolts

route, clip yourself in to the chain using your cowstail as before. Pull up a bight of rope from about a metre (39in) down and tie a knot such as a figure of eight or overhand knot on the bight in it. Clip this loop on to the lower-off chain using a spare extender or other karabiner, as this prevents the rope from being dropped during the next part of the process.

You can now completely untie from the end of the rope and thread it through the ring, retying on to the end once you have done so. An acceptable alternative to this would be to tie a figure of eight on the bight in the end of the rope and clip it into your abseil loop with a screwgate karabiner.

You can now take off the first knot that you tied, the one to keep the rope in place, and remove the extender or karabiner. The final section is just as before, where you pull yourself in to the chain whilst your belayer takes the rope in, and then you put your weight on the rope to check all is OK. Once you are happy, take off your cowstail and be lowered.

You may well come across routes that have two bolts with captive rings (or large-diameter headed glue-in bolts) at the top but no linking chain. In this situation the process will be, in the first instance, to make yourself safe by clipping your cowstail into one of them. Then clip an

extender or spare karabiner into your cowstail karabiner. Tie a figure of eight or overhand knot on the bight on the climbing rope about a metre (39in) from you and clip it into the karabiner to prevent the rope from being dropped. Now untie from the climbing rope, thread the end through both of the rings and tie back on. An alternative is to tie a figure of eight on the bight on the end of the rope and clip this to your abseil loop with a screwgate karabiner.

You can now take the spare extender off your cowstail and untie the knot. Pull yourself up to the bolts and have your belayer take you in tight on the rope, and sit back under tension to check the system. Once you are happy that everything is in order, unclip your cowstail and go down.

ON THE WAY DOWN

As you are being lowered, and assuming that you have led the route, you will have to retrieve all of the extenders that you placed on the way up. It may be that your partner wishes to lead the route with the extenders in place, quite a common occurrence, but if not they need to be stripped out.

If the route is overhanging to any extent, or perhaps goes over a roof or bulge, you may find it tricky reaching the lower extenders as you are swinging out from the rock. If you clip an extender between your

harness and the climbing rope running up the route, this will keep you closer to the rock during the lower and make reaching each bolt easier. It also means that you can reach the climbing rope at all times, in order to pull yourself in closer if needed.

Take care when you remove the bottom extender, as the rope will very likely be at a tight angle at that point, coming down from above and out to your belayer, and could flick out and hurt. It would be best if your belayer moves close in to the base of the route, which will let you remove the bottom extender easily.

On very steep routes, where the lowest bolt is quite close to the ground, you need to be careful that you don't swing out once you have unclipped it and hit something, such as the ground or a nearby boulder, because of the arc of the swing, possibly exacerbated by the rope stretch. There are a number of things that you could do to solve this problem, and the simplest will be to leave it in place, be lowered to the ground and then climb up to unclip it from below, without tension on the rope, perhaps being spotted by your companion. Alternatively, you could leave one or two extenders in place above it, go down to the bottom one and remove it, and then climb back up to retrieve the others. This means that any swing will be from a higher position, consequently with much less chance of connecting with anything as you swing out. On the steepest routes, it may be worth lowering off and reclimbing the route on a top rope, unclipping on your way up, and lowering off again from the top.

Bottom roping is a very common way of climbing a sport route, especially when there are a few of you, or perhaps you have someone with you who doesn't climb quite as hard as yourself and they want the security of a rope from above. If you are stripping out the extenders in order to bottom rope a steep route, think about the chance of any subsequent climbers swinging out from the route and hitting another section of rock or perhaps a tree. If this is a possibility, one or two extenders can be left in place to keep the rope running close to the rock. Once the climber has finished on the route, you can get them to swing in whilst being lowered and either remove the extenders if that is the end of the session, or reclip them if someone else is going to have a go.

Any time that you are lowering (and this does not just apply to sport climbing, it is relevant anywhere, even in winter), it is essential that the dead end of the rope is secured so that there is no chance that it can slip through the belay device and pull right out. This is quite a common cause of accidents, as the belayer is watching the climber they are lowering and is unaware that the end of the rope is about to slip through their fingers. This happens, for example, if the route is longer than half the length of the rope, and the team have not noticed the fact.

If a rope mat is being used, make sure that the dead end of the rope is tied securely to one of the tabs, as this will never pull through the device. Alternatively, tying a knot close to the end of the rope, about a metre (39in), will also do the job, and act as a warning to the belayer. Or the belayer themself could be tied in to the other end of the rope, and this will certainly be the most secure and foolproof method.

LOWERING OFF FROM AN INTERMEDIATE BOLT

This is something that should not happen very often, indeed ever. Although it would be quite common for a leader to be lowered off from a bolt part way up the route, only for their partner to take over and complete the pitch, to lower off and strip the route without reaching the top means that something has gone wrong. Usually, it will be because the leader has found the climb harder than they thought, and their belayer does not want to have a go. Alternatively, it may be because time has run out, or the way ahead is unclear. Whatever the reason, coming down from an intermediate bolt will often mean abandoning gear.

If you are on a route and realize that you have to descend, you can simply lower off from an extender. However, this would obviously mean leaving the gear behind, something that not many climbers are prepared to do, so thinking ahead will help solve the problem. Instead of using an extender in the bolt, use the spare karabiner or maillon that you have been carrying for just such a situation. Clip it into the bolt and put the rope into it, making sure that any gate or sleeve is done up tight. Once you have reached the ground, it should be a simple matter to pull the rope through, leaving just one piece of kit behind instead of a complete extender.

It may be tempting, if the bolt is just above a ledge where you can stand in balance for example, to untie from the rope and thread it directly through the hole in the bolt. If this were a large ring-bolt that may work, but having the rope running through a hanger with a narrow radius or sharp sides should not be contemplated. Apart from the possibility of dropping the rope when untying, being lowered with the rope running over sharp metal will not do it any good at all, and the soft fibres could easily be severely damaged or even cut through under body weight.

Many of these problems can be solved simply if you were able to climb down the route. Just reverse the way that you came up, unclipping each extender from above head height once you have passed it, with your belayer swiftly taking in the slack. If the ground immediately around you is too difficult for this to work, an alternative will be to lower off, untie and pull the rope through. Now tie back on and lead the route, clipping the extenders. When you get below the last one, reach up and unclip it from the bolt, as you are now protected from below. The rest of the route can now be reversed.

A maillon on a bolt being used to lower from

Never run the rope directly through a thin metal hanger

Your cowstail is clipped into the bolt underneath the extender

Remove the extender and put a maillon or spare karabiner in its place

If this is not possible, and it is essential that you descend, leaving an extender may be your safest bet. It would be far better to do this than to risk your life to save a bit of money. However, there is a process that you can use if the eye of the bolt is large enough for two karabiners to be clipped in, and you want to change the extender for a maillon. Although the simplest answer will be in the situation where you can stand in balance and reach the bolt without any problem, simply clipping the maillon in over the extender and then removing it, we will assume that the ground is steep and holding on for any time is not an option.

Clip your cowstail into the bolt, underneath the extender, and rest on it. If you put it on top, the extender will be very difficult to subsequently remove. Now unclip the extender and rope from the bolt, and clip in the maillon or spare karabiner. If possible, this will be best positioned underneath the cowstail karabiner. Make sure, whilst you are doing either this, or any other section of the procedure, that you are maintaining a downwards loading on the bolt placement and not outwards, as this will pull it in its weakest direction. Now clip the climbing rope into the maillon, and pull yourself up towards the bolt so that your belayer can take the rope in. This allows you to unclip the cowstail and be lowered to the ground.

Some bolts are quite large with their eye having a smooth, wide inner surface. As long as the eye has a radius of at least eight millimetres (1/3in),the rope can be threaded directly through it. However, if there is any question whatsoever about

the bolt's properties, a separate karabiner should always be used.

To thread the rope through, start by clipping yourself to the bolt with the cowstail, and let it take your weight. Once again, try to get the cowstail karabiner under the extender that is already there. Unclip the extender from the bolt and take the rope out of it. Replace the extender on to your cowstail at an appropriate point, most likely into the karabiner, tie a figure of eight or overhand knot on the bight into the rope and clip this to the extender. This ensures that the rope is not dropped during the next part of the procedure. Untie from the rope and thread the end through the bolt, and either retie into your harness or connect yourself to the rope with a figure of eight on the bight and a screwgate karabiner to your abseil loop. The securing knot and the extender can now be removed. Pull yourself in towards the bolt, maintaining a downwards loading on it, have your belayer take the rope in tight, and remove the cowstail after checking all is well. You can now be lowered to the ground or stance.

You should remember that, with all of the above techniques, your safety relies totally on the security of the bolt. If there is any question as to its stability, even if there is the smallest question in your mind, backing it up with a wire or similar piece of protection should be considered. Although this extra kit will probably end up being abandoned in the long run, it is far better to do this than risk bolt failure and its consequences.

After clipping in with your cowstail, secure the climbing rope with an extender

Take the climbing rope off your harness, thread it through the bolt and retie

Remove the extender and any extra knots, unclip the cowstail and descend

LOWERING FROM STANCES ON A MULTI-PITCH ROUTE

This form of lowering does not happen very often, but may occur if you are climbing with someone less experienced than yourself. Descent from a multi-pitch route will usually be via abseil, down the line of ascent. However, if the person that you are with is unable to abseil for some reason, or it would simply be quicker or more effective to lower them, then this course of action might be decided upon. Bear in mind that a lower can use a full rope length, whereas an abseil can only take place over half that distance. Worth remembering! Most intermediate stances, however, will be equipped with abseil and belay stations, commonly two bolts linked with a chain, thus dictating the distances between points that you travel. Using two ropes will vastly increase the distance, as well as the speed, that you can descend, perhaps two pitches at a time.

Either a direct or semi-direct lower can be rigged (see 'Lowering' section). It would be very unusual for a semi-direct system to be put into place, because the provision of the anchor will make a direct lower far quicker to set up, as well as being a lot more comfortable for the operator.

To set up a direct lower, either a belay device or an Italian hitch could be used to control the descent. However, as there is a chance that you will have been using a suitable active self-locking belay device when belaying your partner, this would also be a good piece of kit to use for the lower, with the obvious proviso that only one rope is going to be used.

It should be reiterated that self-locking belay devices are not designed to be used hands-off, so take care when using them that you are not tempted to let go of the dead rope, even if the device appears to lock off perfectly when needed.

When clipping the device to the anchor, make sure that you are able to reach and operate it effectively. You may need to use a sling to bring it down into an appropriate position for use. Also consider the manner in which the device works. Most of these types rely on part of the body moving or camming in order to grip the rope. Thus, it is essential that they are not placed in a way that stops them from working properly, such as tight up against the rock. If they cannot move as designed, there is a chance that the rope will simply slip straight through, making it impossible to hold the weight of the other person.

Although it is most likely that once the lower is finished you now abseil to join your companion, you could in fact be lowered down yourself if it was felt that would save time.

Once the first person down has reached the next stance, they make themselves secure. You now clip the rope into the anchor, to make sure that it is not dropped down the crag and lost, and disassemble the lowering rig. Now thread the rope through the ring on the anchor chain and either tie in or clip it to you with a figure of eight and a screwgate karabiner on to your abseil loop. Your partner below now takes in all the rope between the two of you, so that you are tight on the rope coming through the chain. After checking the system, and each other, your partner can lower you down to join them. Once you are safe, and having used a cowstail into the anchor for security if you are still on

a ledge, you can untie from the rope and pull it down.

It is obviously essential that the rope can at no time be dropped down the crag and lost. Having one end or the other always secured will prevent this from happening. Equally important is having the end of the rope on the dead side of the lowering device secured or knotted in some way, so that it is impossible to let it run all the way through the device and be lost, possibly along with your partner. Tying a knot or two near the end will be the simplest solution, or clipping it to a suitable part of the anchor will also do the trick.

It cannot be overemphasized how important it is that the strength of the anchor is beyond question. You should not hesitate to back it up if there is any doubt, or even avoid using it altogether and look for an alternative.

Lowering off using an active self-locking device

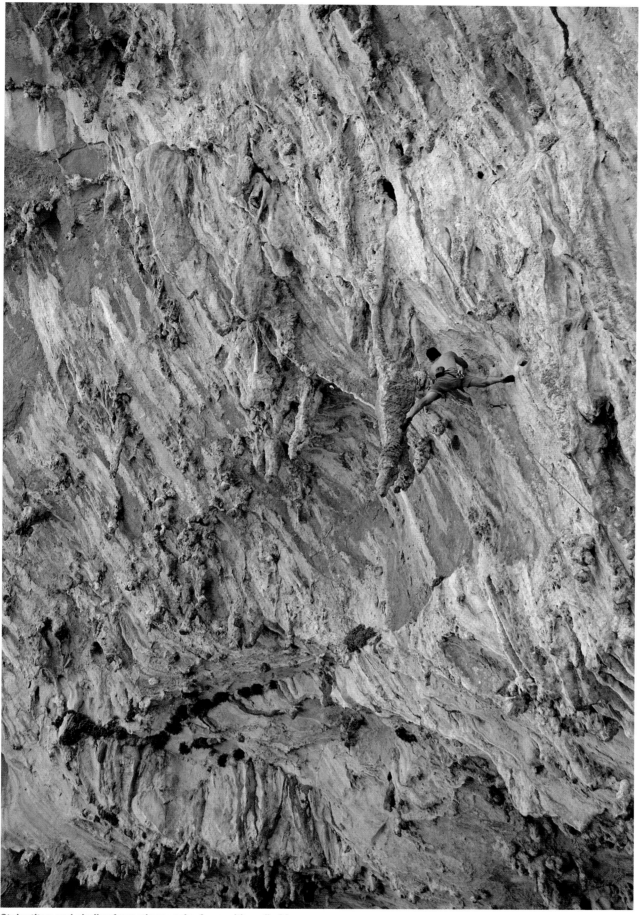

Stalactites and similar formations make for exciting climbing

Via Ferrata gloves

VIA FERRATA

Taken from the Italian for 'iron road', these series of ladders, bridges and other elements fixed to cliff faces provide an entertaining way up, around and down sections of cliff. Originally used by the military in the Dolomites during World War I for troop movement, the number of people now enjoying the delights of Via Ferrata trips grows from year to year. Akin to scrambling but in a far more clinical atmosphere, where all of the safety equipment is (normally!) in place for the entire tour, it is well suited to families and those who are just starting to experiment with moving on craggy terrain. There are also many people who just enjoy Via Ferratas for their own sake, rarely venturing on to any other forms of crag or mountain environments.

Although it may seem at the outset that everything has been done to negate any risk inherent in the activity, this could not be further from the truth, and even the simplest circuits will hold many hazards. You will be connected to a lanyard at all times, which is in turn connected to various cables and strong-points around the route, but a fall of some distance, especially when clipped to a cable, is a very constant danger.

Having said that, Via Ferratas are fun, with the lower grades of circuit offering plenty of excitement and interest for anyone wishing to give it a go, and the top grades being long, committing and usually requiring determination, fitness and a severely calm head for heights!

EQUIPMENT

The specialist equipment, as it is exactly that, can usually be hired from the Via Ferrata ticket office at your chosen circuit. Apart from this, a helmet is important, as is footwear that offers good grip on metal surfaces, as you will probably be climbing on ladder rungs a great deal. A harness is essential, and a couple of slings and screwgate karabiners should be carried. If the circuit is likely to take a couple of hours or more, a small rucksack with the normal additions of a snack and something to drink, along with sunglasses and sunblock would be a good idea.

LANYARD

These are specialist bits of kit, so don't be tempted to make one up yourself unless you know exactly what you are doing. It is essential that a form of shock-absorbency is incorporated into the design, and this is done either with a fail-safe stitching system that rips under a certain load, thus absorbing energy, or by a section of the lanyard running through a series of metal loops, causing braking through friction in the event of a fall. Just using a sling or two, with karabiners attached, gives no shock-absorbing properties and should never be contemplated.

The lanyard will have two long tails and one shorter central loop. Each of these three points will need a quick-release, large-opening karabiner attached to it, and these will often be supplied fitted when the lanyard is purchased. It is best to use large steel karabiners, as those made of alloy will wear through when rubbing on wire cables.

ROPE

It is worth carrying a short length of rope on most circuits, as this increases the security of your party members, thus everyone's enjoyment. A length of 30m of a thin (9.2 to 10mm) full weight rope would be fine, and it can be used for a variety or tasks, not least providing reassurance on steep sections of ladder, in addition to the lanyard.

GLOVES

As you will be working with metal-runged ladders or crag staples a lot, a pair of gloves, fingerless being fine, would be of benefit. Apart from protecting your hands from any sharp edges and the effort of holding on to narrow rungs, there is a chance that the metal will be cold, particularly in shaded areas, and you will find it hard to grip after a while.

Some gloves are made specifically for this use, and they will be a snug fit, often with a Velcro adjustable back, hardwearing and with a non-slip palm.

TANDEM PULLEY

Some circuits include a zip line, often as a finale. A pulley with two wheels is not only smoother and safer than one with a single wheel, but will give a lot more stability during the ride. It is important that the pulley you choose is designed to be used with wire cables, and that it has a good attachment point for a karabiner at its central point.

MAILLON

This is useful when you are going to be riding a zip line. Alongside the main wire that the pulley runs on will be a second one as a safety line. If you clipped your usual lanyard karabiner on to here, it could get badly damaged and grooved by the friction of running along the steel cable at high speed, as the alloy of the karabiner is very soft. A steel maillon will not only be a lot more resilient to wear and tear for this job, it will also be a lot cheaper to replace.

A tandem pulley and a maillon

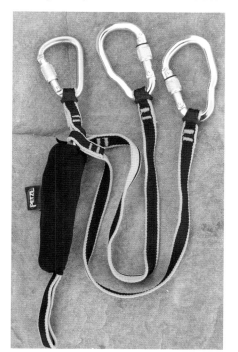
A Via Ferrata lanyard

SAFETY ON THE CIRCUIT

Although it may feel that you are in a clinical environment, you need to keep your wits about you when going round the circuit, and knowing how to deal effectively with all possible hazards is essential.

CLIPPING INTO SAFETY CABLES

Nearly all sections of a Via Ferrata circuit, be it a ladder, bridge or cargo net, will have a steel safety cable running alongside them, into which you clip your lanyard karabiners for security. These will be anchored to the cliff at various points along their length, commonly around 2–5m (6–15ft) intervals. It is important that you are always clipped in to this cable where one is supplied, with at least one of your lanyard tails at any time.

Starting at the bottom of a ladder sequence, for instance, you would have both of your tails clipped in to the cable. Let's say it is running on the left-hand side. Start your way up the ladder, letting the tails tow along beside you. One thing that you could do here is to have your left arm under the tails, so that they run over your forearm which in turn keeps them high, as doing this helps to avoid them dragging and catching too much on obstacles. As you approach a cable anchor, stop a short distance below it, unclip your upper tail from the cable and put it back on above the anchor. Thus, if you slip, you will only fall a short distance. Now unclip the second tail, clipping it back on next to the first.

Only by doing the unclipping and clipping in this way will you be sure of always having at least one connection point to the cable, in case you slip during the swap-over process.

USING PIGSTAILS

Many cable anchor points, particularly along the line of ladders, will be fitted with curly pigstail rope connectors. These are provided so that you can use a rope for any members of your group who may need a little extra confidence, or in areas where the cable protection isn't quite as good as it might be. Moving together skills can be utilized here (with the connection to your harness being the same as that for scrambler's coils, covered in the 'Alpine Climbing' section), but you must understand that, if you are in the lead and your partner falls off, you will very likely be pulled backwards as well. Thus, a different method of using the rope needs to be found, and the one that follows is an option and quite simple to remember.

Both you and your companion tie on to the rope, with them being left in a safe position, or at a point where they are well

Climbing ladders, using a lanyard for security

secured by being clipped to a part of the safety cable or a handy rung. You make your way up the section of ground, looking after your own security with the lanyard as normal, but this time clipping the rope through the pigstails provided. On short sections of moderate ground that go straight up this may not be necessary, as the rope will run in a straight line to your partner. However, if the route is overhanging or wanders around the rock face a bit, as will often be the case, the pigstails help keep the rope in line for the benefit of your partner, so that they will always be supported by it and not be pulled off line.

Once you have gone past the tricky bit, you can then belay them up. This is quickest done with a direct belay on an Italian hitch, on to a karabiner and sling around an appropriate part of the metalwork, perhaps a solid cable attachment point or ladder step. Once they have joined you, you can either repeat the process if necessary or pack the rope away and continue as normal.

If you are using the rope to negotiate difficult sections, you may want your second to belay you as well. In this case,

they can do so using an Italian hitch off their harness, unless of course a belay device is available. You can use the pigstails as before, but might also want to create extra security by placing a sling around a ladder rung every so often as an extra runner. Once you are past that particular section you can belay as before and bring your second up, who will strip out any gear that you have placed.

The rope running through a pigstail

A steep ladder section

In descent, the rope can be used as a safety line, being paid out as needed from an anchor, normally on a direct belay, with the person being safeguarded running it through the pigtails as they descend to ensure that they are being protected from the correct direction all the time. If you also need to be protected as you descend, you can run the rope through the top ladder rung, for instance, and your partner can pay the rope out to you as you go down. Once you are safe, you simply untie and pull the rope through.

LADDERS

These are a major feature of most Via Ferrata circuits, and will either be continuous ladders or a series of U-shaped metal rungs drilled into the cliff, sometimes called stemples. These ladders provide access up and down sections, and will also have been placed on very steep and overhanging terrain, ground where only cargo nets could otherwise provide passage.

Those placed on steep ground can be quite tiring, so make the most of any rest opportunities that may present themselves. The karabiner on the short loop on your lanyard will be useful here, as you can clip this directly into a ladder rung and use it as a resting point if you need a breather.

Take care in wet or icy conditions, as the ladder rungs can be quite slippery. Also, make sure that your hands aren't getting too cold, as it will be difficult to hold on for long if they do. This is where the purpose-designed non-slip gloves come in.

BRIDGES

These come in a variety of styles and constructions, but can be roughly categorized as those with a solid platform underfoot and those simply consisting of wire. The first type looks to be the most solid, and they certainly allow for good foot placements. However, due to their weight and the distances that they span, they tend to oscillate, both up and down and side to side. Take it slowly at first so that you get your balance right. Keeping your feet to the centre line will stop the bridge from wobbling sideways quite so much. Once you have got your confidence up you can walk as normal; a springing gait is helpful in compensating for the movement of the bridge. If there are other people on the bridge and you are a bit nervous, it may be worth waiting for them to cross so that you are not being affected by their foot pattern.

Bridges will have a safety cable running alongside, normally at a slightly higher level, and you should always clip into this for extra security.

Wire bridges come in a variety of styles, the commonest being either the two- or three-strand crossing. Curiously, most people find the two-strand crossing the easiest to deal with, as your feet are on the lower wire, your hands on the upper one, and you can get yourself into a position that feels quite stable, usually leaning back slightly. Three-strand bridges, where you will be in a Y shape when holding on, can feel a little less secure as your body weight can move around quite a lot.

A shuffling motion with your feet sideways to the cable will normally be most comfortable, although crossing them over would be fine. You can either swap your hands as you go along or shuffle these as well. Be particularly careful, though, that there are no loose strands of wire sticking out from the cable, and for this reason the use of gloves is highly recommended.

There will be a safety cable, usually in addition to the bridge wires. This should be used, and don't be tempted to clip your lanyard on to one of the bridge wires unless there is absolutely no other option. Apart from having the karabiners knocking into your hands all the time, it would be easy to catch a finger or glove if you slipped, and end up suspended from these and not the lanyard.

As with the more solid bridges, it may be best to wait until anyone else ahead of you has finished their traverse before stepping on to it, for their sake if not your own!

Crossing a wooden bridge

CARGO NETS

These provide an alternative method of climbing up bulging and overhanging areas of rock. The difference between these and rungs is that with ladders you will be hanging out on your arms from the cliff, with a net you are usually on the inside looking out, using your legs a lot more.

Climbing up them is generally simple, as you have many options as to what to hold on to for both hands and feet. There will also be a safety cable, which once again should always be clipped for safety.

ZIP LINES

These are an exhilarating section of any circuit, and they are often left until right at the very end. Basically, they will consist of two lengths of cable, one of which is for the pulley and the second being for

Crossing a wire bridge

Preparing to ride a zip line

your safety lanyard. Often there will be an option for you to bypass this section, as not everyone will want to take part.

A pulley is connected to the main cable and clipped to your harness with a screwgate karabiner. This karabiner will often be the one on the short tail on your lanyard, as this gives you important clearance between your body and the cable. Alternatively, you can use a sling from your harness and adjust it to the correct length: long enough for you to be hanging away from the cable but short enough that you can reach the cable to help yourself up at the end of the line if necessary.

Onto the second cable you put your maillon, and do it up. Clip a tail from your lanyard into this, with the other tail clipped out of harm's way at the back of your harness. It is not recommended that

you just clip the lanyard's alloy karabiner directly on to the safety wire, as the karabiner will be damaged as the cable slides through it.

Make sure that if you have long hair it is tucked well out of the way under your helmet. It is absolutely essential that you do not touch the cable as you go along the line, as you will be travelling at quite some speed and could severely damage your hands, with either the wire or the pulley, so ensure that you are happy with the position that you will be hanging in before you set off. Holding on with both hands to the short tail, underneath the karabiner that connects you to the pulley, will be fine. Get yourself into a starting position, with your weight just coming on to the cable and your feet pointing forwards in the direction of travel. Once you are ready and have done a final

check, commit your weight to the cable and off you go!

The speed will seem incredible, as will the noise from the pulley, but soon it will be time to think about landing. If you have used a steel maillon on the safety rope, pulling down on your lanyard will slow you down a little. Don't do this if you are not using a maillon, as the alloy karabiner on your lanyard will be damaged. Lift your feet up to reduce the bump at the end, although many circuits will have padding as a safety measure. Once you have stopped moving, get yourself to the end of the cable if you aren't there already. Use the spare tail of the lanyard (the one that you clipped to the back of your harness) to clip into the safety cable on the rock to keep you secure whilst you dismantle the pulley and maillon. You can now continue as normal.

5: WINTER

AVALANCHES

These are an accepted part of mountaineering wherever snowy conditions may prevail. They are, in many cases, avoidable through judicious observation of weather and snow conditions, on-site tests and reference to any avalanche forecasts available for the area that you are visiting. However, it can be difficult to tell exactly what the snow conditions are like, both at your site and higher up the mountain, particularly in remote areas, so a few pointers may be of use to help deal with the problem.

TYPES OF AVALANCHE

There are many types of snow avalanche, quite apart from ice or rock avalanches that are a little rarer but still do occur. Loose snow avalanches slough off the surface of the snowpack, slab avalanches are caused by the lack of cohesion of a buried layer and a large section of snow sliding downhill. Avalanches can be full depth, where all the snow down to ground level slides, or partial depth, where an intermediate layer provides the fracture and sliding surface. They can be channelled, such as in a gully, or open, as on a wide slope. They may also stay low and flow along the ground, or become airborne as powder avalanches.

Many factors contribute to cause avalanche activity. Wind can blow the snow crystals across the ground, pulverizing them into irregular shapes that, when deposited out of the wind on lee slopes, can sit in an unconsolidated manner for a considerable time, until cohesion takes place either through their own metamorphism or a change in air temperature. This is the classic formation of a slab avalanche hazard, one of the most powerful and

The debris from a hard slab avalanche

most deadly. Constant cold temperatures can also keep unpulverized crystals in an unchanged state for quite some time, and these can sometimes release under loading to give large powder avalanches, very destructive during their descent and preceded by extremely high winds. An increase in temperature can cause the snowpack to become moist and heavy, also triggering a slide. It can also lubricate layers within the snowpack, or the ground itself, causing large full-depth avalanches.

Cornices, the large overhangs of snow that are created by the wind, may often collapse, triggering snow slides underneath them. Factors that can cause them to fall are rising air temperature or rainfall, which increases their weight, and addition to their mass by falling or windblown snow. Avoiding ground beneath cornices for 24 to 48 hours after any of the above would be a very sensible precaution.

EQUIPMENT

There is some kit that it would be sensible to carry when travelling in snowy terrain. Apart from being useful when studying the snowpack and making avalanche predictions, it can also be used for building emergency shelters and a host of other jobs.

SHOVEL

A lightweight shovel with a telescopic detachable handle is an essential piece of kit, and does not weigh much. At least one of these should be carried in each party, and preferably more.

AVALANCHE PROBE

This is a long lightweight metal pole, used for probing snow and avalanche debris for a victim. They pack away very small, sometimes fitting into the handle of a shovel, and can be quickly assembled.

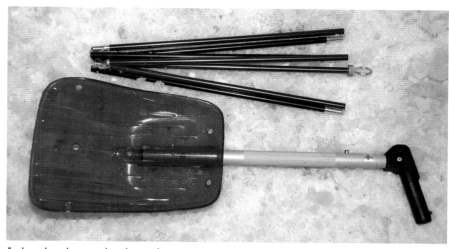

A shovel and an avalanche probe

A large cornice, drooping under its own weight

TRANSCEIVER

These are not very frequently carried by mountaineers, and are more the preserve of off-piste and backcountry skiers. There is no reason for this, and transceivers have proved to be very effective at locating buried victims. They take some training to become proficient with, and the efficient locating of a buried person requires good organization and leadership. All group members should carry one, and they must be turned on to be of any use. There should be a number of shovels and avalanche probes in the party as well. The correct use of transceivers means that a buried person can often be found far quicker than with conventional observation and probing techniques.

TESTING THE SNOW PACK

There are a number of tests that can be done to assess the state of the snow. None of these should be taken in isolation, but used to help build up a picture of what the snow conditions in that immediate area are likely to be. All should be carried out in a safe area, at the same height, altitude and aspect of the slope to be crossed or climbed. When you have moved on any distance the conditions will have changed, so it is important to build up a picture by performing a number of similar tests as your day unfolds.

THE SQUEEZE TEST

Making a ball of snow in your hand allows you to make a quick assessment of the temperature of the outer surface of the snowpack, useful when deciding what state the underlying snow may be in. If

the snow falls apart when you open your hand up, this shows that the temperature on the surface is below freezing. If you can easily make a snowball, the temperature is probably just above freezing. If you squeeze and can make water come out, then the temperature is relatively high.

Snow below freezing may be unconsolidated, leading to a powder avalanche risk if there is sufficient build-up. Conversely, wet snow will create a problem as the moisture could percolate through the snowpack, run downhill on a harder, buried layer or the surface of the ground, and cause a wet slab avalanche.

SNOW PIT ANALYSIS

Dig a pit into the ground and make the back wall vertical. The depth of the pit will largely depend on whether a shovel is available, but try to cut down to a hard layer that has been made solid by a melt/freeze process. Inspect the back wall for signs of different layers, and assess the change in hardness between them. Using a scale of 1 to 5 is useful, where 1 is a fist, 2 is gloved fingers, 3 is a single finger, 4 is an axe spike and 5 is an axe pick. What you are looking for here is a difference of more than 2 between adjacent layers. For instance, if a very soft layer that your fist penetrates, giving a 1, is sitting on a hard layer that only accepts your axe pick, 5, you have a large difference and the chance that the layers may not be strongly bonded together.

Also look out for layers that appear inconsistent with the others. In particular, layers of ice crystals or round pellets, loose grains of ice or air gaps all show a high degree of instability and will give an almost total lack of cohesion between adjacent layers.

Each layer could also benefit from the squeeze test, mentioned above. This will determine if there is any significant moisture in the snowpack, once again causing possible instability

THE WALKING SHEAR TEST

If you have decided that there may be some instability within the snow, you can check a section for cohesion by performing this test. It is made far easier if a shovel or two are to hand, as a reasonable amount of snow will have to be excavated. It should be sited in a safe position where you will not be threatened by the snow above, and on a slope of around 30 degrees.

Dig out the sides and lower face of a block measuring a metre by a metre, with its depth going down to just below a solid melt/freeze layer, taking care to not disturb it whilst doing so. Now very carefully cut through the upslope edge, completely isolating the block on all four sides. It is now subjected to a series of tests, running from 1 through to 7. 1 is where the block fails, which means that it slides on a layer below surface level. 2 is when it fails as you approach the block from above, and debris that you dislodge causes it to slide. 3 is when it fails as you stand up carefully, heel to toe, along the back edge. 4 is failure as you do a quick down-sink using your knees. 5 is where it goes after a small jump, 6 is failure after a few jumps, 7 is no failure at all.

If the block slides at anything from 1 to 4 then you need to be very cautious how you proceed, as there are unstable, non-cohesive layers within the snow pack. Even if it does not fail at the test site, this does not mean that the slope will be safe a little farther on or higher up. Check the state of the shear layer as well. If it is smooth then that further confirms that the layers are not cohesive, if it is jagged and uneven then cohesion is taking place.

The block being excavated

This block slid out once isolated on the up-slope side

It also split into three sections, showing smooth shear planes throughout

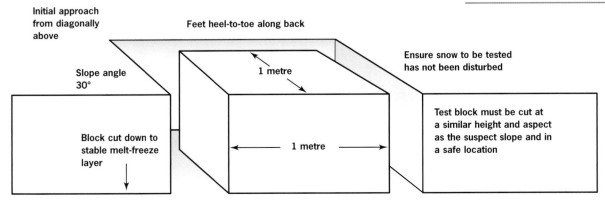

Initial approach from diagonally above

Feet heel-to-toe along back

Slope angle 30°

1 metre

Ensure snow to be tested has not been disturbed

Block cut down to stable melt-freeze layer

1 metre

Test block must be cut at a similar height and aspect as the suspect slope and in a safe location

The walking shear test

THE HASTY PIT

This is a small version of the walking shear test, with the advantage that it can be constructed easily with just an axe and the test carried out very quickly, hence the name. It does, however, only tell you what is happening in the layers near to the surface, and you may miss instabilities deeper down.

Isolate a block 30–40cm (12–16in) in the same manner as for the larger test, cutting away the sides and downslope face. This should be done down to just below the layer that has given you cause for concern, perhaps a hard or soft layer detected when you pushed your axe shaft into the snow. Now carefully isolate the block on the upslope side by using your axe pick, taking care not to disturb it, and widen this slot so that you can place your hands in it. With your fingers outstretched, put both of your hands down the back of the block and slowly pull, don't lever, downslope. You are finding out how much effort it takes to make the block move. If it slides off as you isolate it, that indicates severe instability between the adjacent layers. If it slides when you touch it with your hands, or with a slight downslope pressure, that too shows that a sliding hazard exists. Even if it fails with a harder pull, or seems to disintegrate, indicating cohesion between the layers, this again does not guarantee that the rest of the snowpack will be consolidated.

As you will probably be performing a number of these tests throughout your journey, make sure that the size of the block is constant each time, otherwise you will be getting a different feel for the snow at each stop, leading to a variation in conclusions.

Pulling down-slope to test a hasty pit

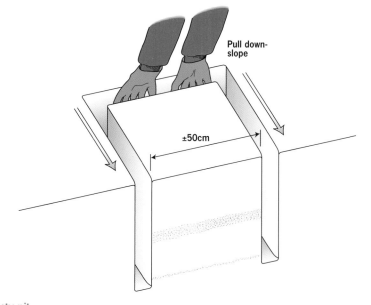

The hasty pit

THE INTERNATIONAL AVALANCHE GRADING SYSTEM

This is a system used in a number of countries across the world where avalanche prediction and monitoring takes place, and the results are posted up on notice boards and the Internet on a daily basis for walkers, climbers and skiers to refer to. The predictions should always be used in conjunction with your personal observations of the snow, as well as weather patterns, but they do provide a good source of important information, useful when planning a journey or climb.

DEGREE OF HAZARD	SNOWPACK STABILITY	AVALANCHE PROBABILITY
1 (LOW)	The snowpack is generally well bonded and stable.	Triggering is possible only with high additional loads on a few very steep extreme slopes. Only a few small natural avalanches (sloughs) possible.
2 (MODERATE)	The snowpack is moderately well bonded on some steep slopes, otherwise generally well bonded.	Triggering is possible with high additional loads, particularly on the steep slopes indicated in the bulletin. Large natural avalanches not likely.
3 (CONSIDERABLE)	The snowpack is moderately to weakly bonded on many steep slopes.	Triggering is possible, sometimes even with low additional loads. The bulletin may indicate many slopes that are particularly affected. In certain conditions, medium and occasionally large sized natural avalanches may occur.
4 (HIGH)	The snowpack is weakly bonded in most places.	Triggering is probable even with low additional loads on many steep slopes with an incline of more than 30 degrees. In some conditions, frequent medium or large sized natural avalanches are likely.
5 (VERY HIGH)	The snowpack is generally weakly bonded and largely unstable.	Numerous large natural avalanches are likely, even on moderately steep terrain.

BEING AWARE

Statistically 30–45 degree slopes are those with the higher incidence of avalanches, although they obviously occur well beyond both ends of the scale, so taking care on any type of incline is important. Also look out when crossing convex slopes, as these hold the snow under tension and will be a likely point for the snowpack to fail. Open snowfields and gully lines will be more prone to slides than buttresses and ridges, with the latter being a safer option in suspect conditions.

When travelling across snowy ground, look for evidence of avalanche activity. Snow deposition, where the wind is transporting snow, is also a warning sign, and don't forget that it doesn't have to be snowing for there to be an increase in avalanche hazard during the day, as the action of the wind can cause this. Anything over 2cm (1in) per hour is seen as being a high build-up and a potential risk. An increase in temperature should mean that you stay away from potential problem areas, such as under cornices, and snowballs or 'sun wheels' rolling past you down the slope are an indicator of the snow surface warming.

Any booming underfoot should be seen as a warning that you are walking on a slab layer, with a squeaking sound, either underfoot or under your walking poles, confirming this. If you have irregular blocks breaking away underfoot, that shows a high slab hazard and you should take extreme care in that area.

Irregular blocks breaking away underfoot indicates a slab hazard

PREPARATION FOR CROSSING A SUSPECT SLOPE

The first and most important consideration is, 'Do you have to?' It may be far safer to backtrack and choose a different route, rather than risking crossing a dangerous snowfield. Remember that going directly up or downhill may be safer than traversing, so try to build this into your plan.

If you have no option but to continue, make sure that each person knows what they need to do and where the route goes. You can make the most of islands of safety (large boulders or scoured sections of ground) as intermediate points, and identify a place where you are all going to reunite. Make sure that all transceivers are turned on to 'transmit' mode.

Do up your clothing, including sleeves and collars, put your hood up and wrap something over your nose and mouth, such as a scarf or neck warmer. Take off walking pole and ice axe wrist loops. Rucksack hip belts can be undone and shoulder straps loosened. Although they hold all of your emergency kit, rucksacks can be anchors in moving snow, and cause victims to become buried, sometimes upside down, before they can be shrugged off.

WHAT TO DO IF YOU GET CAUGHT

If you are unlucky enough to get caught by an avalanche, you need to do all that you can to avoid burial. If you can, run to one side or the other of the slide, as the nearer the edge you get the more slowly it will be moving. Get your axe into the snow as an anchor as high above you as possible to delay being pulled downhill. Shout to attract attention, and do all that you can to stay on top of the debris as you start to move, with rolling to one side perhaps being enough to get you near the edge. Self-arresting may also help to delay your departure down the slope (see p. 150).

If you are taken downhill, get rid of walking poles and rucksack. As the avalanche slows down make a huge effort to clear a space in front of your face and take a deep breath to give your chest room to expand. Also try to get to the surface, or at least stick a hand or foot out, so that you will be easier to find by your companions. It sounds easy to say don't panic, as this seems to be the natural thing to do, but try as much as possible to remain calm, as panicking uses up a lot of the oxygen that you will need to remain conscious.

The crown wall, where the fracture line of a partial depth slab avalanche can be seen

WHAT TO DO IF A COMPANION IS CAUGHT

If your companion is taken away by the snow, make a note of the point at which you last saw them. Don't attempt a rescue if there is any chance of further avalanches in the same area, but if you are sure that you will be safe, make a quick search of the area where you last saw them, working your way downslope looking for any signs. This could be a hand or foot thrust out of the snow, blood, clothing or other debris. It is worth listening for any sounds, although snow is a poor conductor even if someone is shouting a short distance away.

Probe the most likely areas quickly, and then make the search more systematic, marking the areas already searched with kit or obvious piles of snow. It would now be the time to send a person down for help, if someone is available. Up to this point you have needed everyone to search, as the survival probability for the buried person is about 90 per cent for the first 15 minutes, decreasing to about 10 per cent after two hours. Those remaining should continue searching, as you are the victim's only real chance of survival, and they may well be alive for quite some time after the initial incident, perhaps with their head near an air pocket or simply at the surface somewhere you have not yet searched.

When found, a live victim will need their airway cleared and a space around the chest to be excavated to allow them to breathe easily. They can then be dug out and any appropriate first aid administered. Rewarming through shared body heat, extra clothing and use of a group survival shelter will help. If necessary, evacuation by the emergency services, if any exist in the area, should be called upon.

Even when on ice, watch out for pockets of unstable snow

SNOW SHELTERS

There is a difference between snow holes and snow shelters. A snow hole is a base that has been constructed for a planned stay of one or more nights, and suitable equipment, such as shovels, sleeping bags, stoves and so forth, have been carried for the purpose. They can range in size from the most basic, which will sleep two people, up to those sleeping twelve or more. A snow shelter will be constructed in an emergency, in order to shelter from the effect of the elements, and may be little more than a glorified scoop in the ground. To spend more than a couple of hours in a snow shelter means that things must really have gone bad.

A SNOW HOLE

This will be best constructed in a steep bank of snow, as this means that you will have to dig in for less distance before being able to dig upwards to form the living area. However, the slopes that make good sites are also those that will be holding a large weight of snow, thus they may be avalanche-prone. More than one person has been carried off by an avalanche while looking for a suitable place to stay, so be aware of your surroundings, the nature of the terrain and the state of the snowpack, testing for avalanche danger if necessary. In some situations, particularly when on expedition to the higher mountains, a suitable snow hole site could be found in the gap of a bergschrund or even a suitable crevasse, although it may be time-consuming to enlarge.

Digging in snow is very damp work, and it is worth wearing a full set of waterproofs with only light clothing underneath to save perspiring too much. Your gloves will get sodden, so having an old pair to use for the digging process is a good idea, saving a decent pair for when the work stops.

The use of shovels is important, otherwise the task will take a very long time indeed. You may also want to have tested the area with an avalanche probe, to make sure that the snow is of sufficient depth and that rocks won't be struck after a short time. In hard snow conditions, a snow saw will help you to cut through any difficult layers, and to construct blocks to help seal up the entrance.

There are a variety of ways of digging a snow hole, and here we will look at one that assumes that two of you will be digging at the same time. You will be starting with two doorways, so mark out the shape on the slope in front of you, approximately shoulder width and 120cm (48in) high. These will initially be your entrance passageways, although one will be blocked off at a later stage. Tunnel directly inwards and slightly up, throwing the debris away behind you. How far in you go before starting to enlarge the hole depends on the angle of the slope into which you are digging and the quality of the snow.

Once you have dug in for an appropriate distance, the hole can then be enlarged by digging upwards and sideways, to create an area that is big enough for you and your companions to lie down, and at least sit up, if not stand up, in. The floor of the sleeping area needs to be higher than the access tunnel, as this will serve to keep warm air trapped in the living space, allowing cold air to roll out of the door. It also allows for easy removal of the snow whilst digging, and this can be made easier by letting the debris fall on to a plastic bivi bag beneath where you are working. This can then be dragged out and emptied at regular intervals.

At some point, your section will join up with the one being dug by your partner, and this increase in space will allow for even more efficient digging and debris removal. Towards the end of the digging process, debris can be packed into one of the access tunnels, sealing it off completely. This will now make for a handy storage area.

The living area, once finished, can be dome-shaped. Make sure that you provide plenty of headroom and don't end up with anything too cramped. Ensure that the floor has a smooth and level surface, otherwise you will be sliding about during the night. The ceiling and the walls should be smoothed over with a gloved hand or the back of the shovel. This helps to reduce the drips as the temperature within the hole rises during cooking and when affected by body heat.

As a final touch, you may want to roof over some of the entrance tunnel, particularly if the slope that you have dug into is at an angle, or the wind is transporting a lot of snow. Doing this will help to prevent any ingress of wind-blown snow, and it can be accomplished by cutting blocks that may then be used as handy building material. You might also wish to reduce the size of the entrance, in order to keep as much wind out as possible.

Being organized means that you will end up having a comfy stay, so spend a bit of time getting things just right. A couple of long shelves for storing kit can be made by digging into the walls. Don't leave items such as spare clothing loose on the shelf, as they will attract moisture from the atmosphere. Gear placed into plastic bags or boxes will stay dry.

Keep the stove in the centre of the hole and quite near the door. This is useful in case of any spillage, and also allows the poisonous vapours created by the cooking process to sink down the entrance tunnel to the outside and not be trapped in the hole itself. Cooking will be quite a long process, so make sure that all of the necessary food items and utensils are to hand. Most likely, you will be operating from inside your sleeping bag, which will be inside a waterproof breathable bivi bag to keep warm, so get yourself comfortable from the outset. Have a pile of snow chunks ready to melt in the pot. Only put in a little at a time and wait for it to melt before adding more. The base of the stove may

well get hot during the cooking process, so don't have it on any sleeping mat or touching any kit. If possible, place it on a flat piece of stone. Alternatively, you may have a light piece of plywood or similar carried for the purpose. This will prevent the stove from melting itself into the floor of the snow hole and causing the pot to tilt over. Take care with boiling liquids for this very reason.

Light can be provided with a candle, and a shelf or two with candles on them will light up the living area very effectively. Scoop out the back of the shelf to make a snow reflector, and a good deal of light will bounce off its surface.

It is important that the entrance to the snow hole does not drift over. If this is a possibility, perhaps due to high winds during the night, it may be necessary to get up frequently to dig out the front of the hole to ensure that adequate ventilation is maintained. If this is cut off, cooking becomes extremely hazardous as poisonous fumes are given off, and it should not be undertaken if there is no fresh air available.

If you need to go outside during the night, ensure that you can relocate the snow hole. This is surprisingly difficult to do, even in good visibilty, let alone when the mist is down or spindrift blowing about. On a clear night, the glow of a candle from inside the hole can be seen from some distance and act as a marker, but in poor weather a climbing rope may have to be tied around anyone venturing outside, so that they can find their way back. If you have to go out during the night, ensure that you have plenty of clothing with you in case finding the hole again takes some time.

A snow hole site needs to be left spotlessly clean. Matches, candle stubs and plastic bags are classic bits of debris often left behind, and there is no excuse for it, so a search about before leaving the site will help to sort this out. Human waste is not only unsightly but also a pollutant, so consider carrying it out with you. Do the business into a strong plastic bag, place this into a tough screw-top plastic container, and carry it out for disposal at a suitable site back at civilisation.

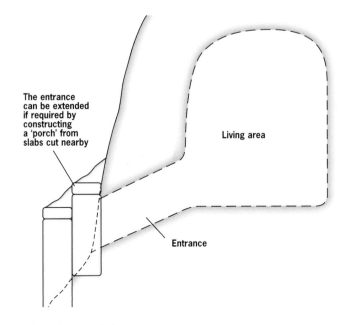

The entrance can be extended if required by constructing a 'porch' from slabs cut nearby

Living area

Entrance

A cross-section of a snow hole

EMERGENCY SHELTERS

An emergency shelter is exactly that, designed to be used only when dire straits dictate that safety from the elements has to be sought, perhaps when your partner is injured or extremes of weather make movement impossible. Prior to making the decision to dig in, every effort should be made to get down off the hill or into some other area of safety, such as a local hut or other habitation.

Digging an emergency shelter is very tiring work, using up a lot of effort and calories. Often it will have to be constructed with the minimum of equipment, and most likely you will end up spending time in it with only the clothes that you are wearing, as it would be unlikely that you would have a sleeping bag with you on a single-day mountain trip. Anything that can be done to make the digging and construction easier should be seized on, and gear to hand such as ice axe, deadman, a plate or lunch box can be put to use for digging into the snow. A lightweight shovel will greatly simplify the digging process, and it is recommended that at least one is carried between group members during winter trips.

There are many types of emergency shelter that can be constructed. Large boulders will often have drifts of snow behind them, and these can be scooped out to create a shelter. Below the tree line, the lower branches of fir trees in particular, will often support snow but leave a sheltered area underneath by the lower section of the trunk. This can also be dug into and end up being quite spacious.

However, in a mountain environment digging into the snow may be the only realistic option. We will look at three methods here, each relevant for different situations.

SITTING SHELTER

The sitting shelter is the most thermally efficient of the three, and may be the most comfortable to spend any time in. It requires a steep bank of snow to be dug into, and these will often be found on stream banks or re-entrant features (see 'Navigation' section). The idea is to end up in a sitting position, with minimal contact with the snow. This position, with the entrance low down, allows warm air to be retained around the head and torso.

Digging straight into the snow and then tunnelling upwards is one way of building the shelter, but this means that you are lying on the snow all of the time and will get very wet, not a good idea if you are to spend the night in the same clothes. However, in soft snow conditions it may be the only choice. A much better option requires you to do a little more work, but it keeps you off the snow throughout, making it a more pleasant experience.

A wedge-shaped slot of around shoulder-width is cut into the snow bank, high enough to ensure that your head ends up below surface level. You will need a seat to sit on, and this can be made at the back of the slot from debris as you near the end of digging. Once the slot is dug, it will need to be roofed over in order to keep snow out and warmth in. One way of doing this is by weighing down a bivi bag or group shelter, using snow blocks around their edges, perhaps supported across the slot by walking poles. In hard or slabby snow conditions, it is much better to cut a series of snow blocks, slightly longer than the width of the slot, which can be placed over the shelter to provide a roof. These can be placed one above the other until the slot is covered, leaving only a small entry gap at the bottom. Cut them from a section of ground above the shelter, as this will make them easy to slide down into place.

The seat should be insulated with anything to hand, such as a rucksack back insert, and your feet can go into the sack itself once you are in place. Marking the top of the bivi would be a good idea, best done with walking poles or an ice axe.

Snow is a very good insulator, but you need a few centimetres (2–4in) of air gap around you. Don't be tempted to make the bivi too big, otherwise the heat-retention of the system will not be as efficient as it otherwise might be.

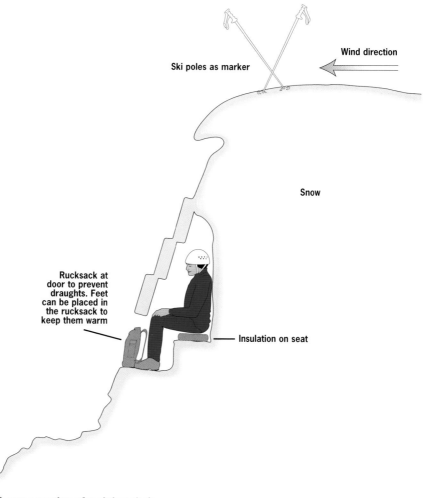

A cross-section of a sitting shelter

(figure labels: Ski poles as marker; Wind direction; Snow; Rucksack at door to prevent draughts. Feet can be placed in the rucksack to keep them warm; Insulation on seat)

A SHOVEL-UP

On flat terrain, or where a suitably steep slope for a sitting bivi cannot be found, two other methods are possible. The first is called a shovel-up or mouse-hole bivi, and is very suitable if shovels or other methods of moving snow are available.

Place everyone's rucksacks on the ground and, if possible, cover them with a bivi bag or shelter. Now heap as much snow as you can on top of them to create a large molehill. Gently firm the snow down with shovels and hands every now and then as you go. You can now dig a small entrance on the side out of the wind and remove the bivi bag and rucksacks. The inside can be cut out to shape to give more headroom (be careful not to dig up too far!), and then smooth the roof over to prevent it dripping.

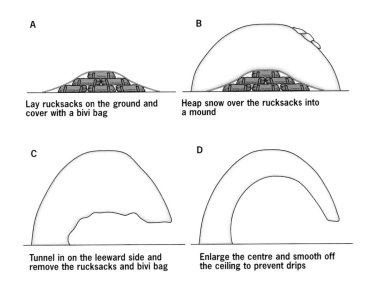

A Lay rucksacks on the ground and cover with a bivi bag

B Heap snow over the rucksacks into a mound

C Tunnel in on the leeward side and remove the rucksacks and bivi bag

D Enlarge the centre and smooth off the ceiling to prevent drips

The stages of building a shovel-up

THE SNOW GRAVE

Another method, suitable for use on the flat in solid ground such as wind slab, is the delightfully named snow grave. This name stems from the position that you take when using it, laying on the ground under the surface of the snow.

Using the pick of your axe, cut out an outline on the ground. This should be around shoulder-width and a metre or so (39in) long. Divide this into slabs widthways and lift them out. Now scoop out the snow underneath, hollowing out an undercut section for your feet. If possible, try to leave a lip around the hole for the slabs to rest on when they are replaced. If this is not possible, other longer slabs from a position away from the hole will have to be cut. Once the hollowing out has been completed, place a couple of slabs back in place, climb inside and lower the others down on top.

Make sure that you use any spare gear to help minimize your body contact with the snow which, as you are lying flat, will be considerable.

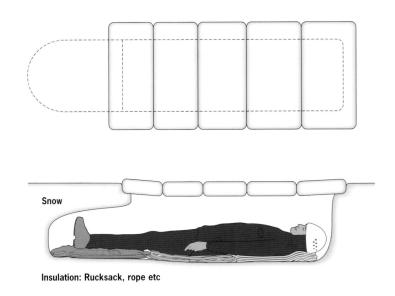

Snow

Insulation: Rucksack, rope etc

Top and side view of a snow grave

Winter mountains, the type of terrain where efficient step kicking becomes important

STEP KICKING

This is the fundamental way of moving on snow and demonstrates that, along with an ice axe, your boots are one of the most important pieces of winter kit that you will ever use. Your feet are your only contact with the ground and they should be comfortable, well supported, kept warm and provided with a solid base with which to walk without slipping.

For serious winter walking and mountaineering, boots should have very stiff soles and have little or no give. Boots whose sole can easily be bent more than ten degrees at the toe section are too bendy for serious use in winter. A deep tread, with good square edges all round, is also important, as worn boots become a real hazard to the wearer. Those with cut-away or stepped heels should be rejected, as they are not suitable for use under proper winter conditions.

Be firm when placing your feet on hard snow. Lightly placing your feet and relying on balance for progress, tiptoeing along as though on an icy pavement is not the technique to be used on a mountain, and a well-directed series of kicked steps is what is required, both when ascending and descending.

SLICE STEPS

The most frequently used of all steps is called a slice step. This relies on the cutting action of the edge of the sole to create a platform, hence the need to ensure that your boot soles are in good order. To progress up a slope, swing your foot forwards from the knee in a slicing action, so that the rounded section of the upslope part of your boot sole carves out a ledge. At times just one swing will be enough, but in harder conditions three or four may be necessary to make a suitable ledge. This needs to be long and wide enough to safely support your boot, but will probably not be the length or width of the entire sole, just a percentage of it. Keeping the outer edge of the boot slightly higher than the inner will help to stop it from sliding off the step. Repeat the process with the other boot a little higher to progress. If you are on terrain where you are taking more than six or seven kicks to create a good step, it is time to think about wearing crampons.

Once you have kicked a few slice steps in one direction, use your ice axe for support and turn yourself around, then kick steps up in the other direction. By doing this you should be able to effectively zigzag up the slope.

To descend, kick a slice step with the downslope foot, then move the higher one into the step just vacated. The ice axe can be used above you for support.

Boot position for a slice step

PIGEONHOLE STEPS

On steeper terrain pigeonhole steps are excellent for progressing up, down or even across the slope. These are made by swinging your leg from the knee down and kicking in with the toe of your boot. Once you have made a step, keep your heel a little higher than your toe, which helps to prevent the step from crumbling.

Pigeonhole steps

HEEL-PLUNGE STEPS

Heel-plunge steps are very effective for use in descent, but take care that the snow is not so hard that your heel will not be able to dig in. Face downhill and lock off your hip, knee and ankle, lifting the toe of your boots up slightly. Drop your body weight straight down through your leg on to your heel, which will then punch a small ledge into the snow. Do not be tempted to swing your leg back into the slope, as this is less effective. Done correctly, the movement needed is more akin to a hop than a step. Bending your knee slightly helps to reduce jarring in harder snow.

Heel-plunge steps

Cutting a step with an axe

STEP CUTTING

Although the art of step cutting has suffered in favour of crampons, it is actually one of the most essential tools in a mountaineer's armoury. It is a method of crossing short sections of snow-covered terrain, where stopping to put crampons on may be unnecessary and time-consuming.

Use a wrist loop on your ice axe to avoid it slipping from your grasp whilst being swung. Another important consideration is that when being used for cutting steps, the axe head will not be in the correct orientation for the adze to sit into the shoulder and allow a self-arrest (axe and self-arrest are covered below) to be performed. Watch out for this and be prepared to turn the axe around should you slip.

Cutting steps, like any excavation in the snow, such as bucket seats or anchors, is much easier if a sequence is thought through. In the diagram, section A is cut first, then B, C and D. If you start cutting at D and proceed forwards to A, there will be a good deal of resistance from pulling up against the snow, a lot of effort will be needed and it will become tiring very quickly.

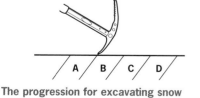

The progression for excavating snow

SLASH STEPS

The commonest style of step is known as a slash step, and these can be used in ascent, descent or when traversing. A good way to practise is to start by cutting in descent, as this allows you to get to grips with what the step should look like and to get used to the swing of the axe. Start to swing the axe with your hand holding the bottom of the shaft and the adze pointing behind you. Wearing a wrist loop here is important, as it helps with grip and ensures that the axe is not lost. Using this pendulum motion, start to bend your knees and lower your shoulder until the adze is just scraping the ground about 15cm (6in) directly down-slope from your boot. Use as many cuts as necessary to form a step, making sure that it is at 90 degrees to the slope.

This step should be angled very slightly into the slope to stop your foot from sliding off it and longer than your boot sole to give a level platform. Once this step is completed, stand up, put your right foot into it, move your left foot down to the step just used by your right, and repeat the process. If you are managing to cut each step with just one swing of the axe then that's fine, but security is the prime consideration here, and if you need five

swings, take five swings. Once you have got used to the pendulum motion, add a wrist flick at the bottom of the swing, as this will put a little more force into the axe head and make it cut a little easier.

Slash steps are very effective when cut for going uphill, usually zigzagging, changing direction after every ten or twelve steps. Face across the slope with the upper foot no more than 15cm (6in) higher up than the other, and in advance of it so that the toe of one is in line with the heel of the other. Lean your upper body forward, hold your axe in the uphill hand and, swinging from the shoulder as before, cut a step on the up-slope side. The downhill foot is then moved up and into this step, crossing over the other one, and the process repeated. Don't try to reach too far when cutting, as this causes the step to be cut at an angle across the slope, instead of horizontally. When you need to change direction, cut yourself a larger step and place the axe into the snow above it for support. Stand into the step with both feet, turn yourself around and change hands with the axe, drop your downhill leg to the last step cut in the previous line, and continue on and up.

Cutting slash step going downhill

Stepping through on slash steps, going uphill

PIGEONHOLE STEPS

On steep ground, pigeonhole steps can be cut to form a ladder, and they can be used for both hands and feet. In soft snow, use the adze to create a series of holds, each being wide enough to accept the width of your boot with a flat base. Work two or three holds in advance, as you will find these easier to cut. If you are going to use them for your hands as well as your feet, a small lip can be created on the front edge to make them easier to hold on to. If the snow is hard or it is icy, you will need to cut a teepee shape first with the axe pick, then chop out the centre with the adze.

LETTERBOX STEPS

Letterbox steps are cut with the outside hand, the one away from the slope, and they make for a very secure way of getting up reasonably steep sections of ground. Lean on the snow for balance with your up-slope hand, holding the axe in the other. The shaft should be at 90 degrees to the snow surface and just in front of your body when making contact. Cut a slot in the snow with four or five swings, but the axe should not follow through, simply cutting into the slope. Work a couple of steps ahead of yourself, cutting them approximately 30cm (12in) above and about half a step's length in advance of the previous one. Kicking your boot into them, you will appreciate their worth, and the finished steps should look like a series of letterboxes, providing excellent support for both hands and feet.

TRAVERSING STEPS

Going directly across the slope is possible, with the steps ending up looking like slash steps. However, they are cut in a slightly different manner. Start with one foot about 10cm (4in) above and heel to toe in advance of your other foot. The axe can be held in your strongest hand. Start by cutting the lower step, and the first cut with the adze should be in line with the toe of the uphill boot, the cutting progression mentioned above being followed. It will take five or six swings to achieve a good step, and obviously it's not possible to follow through, as your leg is in the way! Make sure that it is longer than the sole of your boot, and that you have not left any lumps on the surface that would cause your foot to pivot off. Drag the debris from the step with the adze to leave it tidy once it has been completed. Now repeat the process for the upper foot, starting the first cut in line with the toe end of the step that has just been prepared, avoiding the temptation to reach too far ahead. You can now move your feet, first the downhill one and then the other, and cut the next two steps.

RESTING STEPS

Cutting or kicking steps up a slope is tiring work on the legs, and a rest might be called for. You may also want to cut a resting ledge when walking with crampons, as your calf muscles will probably get tired after a long stretch of uphill ground. To quickly manufacture a good resting step, hold the axe shaft in both hands and chop away at the ground in front of you, using an appropriate number of blows from the adze. The object of the exercise is to create a large step, big enough to make you feel secure when standing on it, at least the width and length of both of your boots.

Pigeon-hole steps on steep ground

Letterbox steps being cut

CRAMPON TECHNIQUE

Walking with crampons is a fundamental skill and pivotal for safe and successful movement in the hills and mountains. To have a slovenly technique is a sure way to trip over at some stage, perhaps with dire consequences. You need to spend a good deal of time practising your technique in a controlled situation before progressing on to steeper and more technical terrain. Wearing a helmet would be a good precaution if learning, as would using gloves. However, you may decide to put your ice axe to one side for the initial steps, as this can cause you to alter your balance and not be as smooth when walking. Obviously, the axe is essential at any other time, and you will probably introduce it into your session as soon as you are feeling more confident, or when moving up a slope where a slip could cause you to slide any distance.

FLAT-FOOTING

Walking on a gently sloping section of ground is a basic movement, and should be practised first. Known as flat-footing, maximum security will be found with all of the downwards-facing points being in contact with the snow or ice, and you should concentrate on getting this right from the outset. Try to make the walking movement as natural as possible, so lift each foot and place it in front of and slightly to the side of the other. Be constantly aware of the need to maintain a gap between the points of your crampon and your other foot, as it is all too easy to have your feet close together and snag a point. You will have to flex your ankles as the ground gets a bit steeper, and you will probably need to turn your feet across the slope a bit in order to get all of the points in. Lift your feet high so that you can cross them over each other and maintain a safe clearance between points and boot. Zigzagging up the slope will be the best way to progress, changing direction after a few steps. Always make sure that your feet are not getting too close together as your confidence grows.

Descent on moderate ground can also be done by flat-footing. Face directly down the hill and flex your ankles, bending your knees as required in order to get all of the downward-facing points in contact with the snow at the same time. Note that this is different to the heel-plunge steps that we use when kicking steps without crampons, and if you lead with your heel on hard ice you have a real chance of skating off down the hill. Keeping all of the points in contact will be far more secure.

AMERICAN TECHNIQUE

On slightly steeper slopes, we can introduce a variation in the way that we walk. Known as the American technique, it is a very logical method of ascent. One foot is placed into the snow using the front-points, the other is placed in the flat-foot position. This foot may need to be turned out to the side at an angle of up to 45 degrees, depending upon the gradient of the slope, but it is important that all downward points are in contact. Using this technique, you can go straight up the slope if need be, or at any angle. Pure front-pointing is quite tiring on the calf muscles, so when the leg that is front-pointing starts to get weary, simply swap over so that the flat-foot side is now front-pointing, and the front-pointing foot is now placed flat. This method is only really suitable for going up, and is very difficult to use in descent.

Using the American technique

Flat-footing with crampons

Flat-footing in descent

FRONT-POINTING

When the ground becomes very steep, front-pointing will be required. This uses the front two, four or six points of each crampon in turn, depending on the hardness of the snow or ice. The crampon is placed on to the snow or ice with the sole of the boot horizontal, and it is important that you keep it so once the points have been placed. If you drop your heel, the front-points will be levered out of the placement by the next set of points. If you raise the heel, the points could be dislodged because of the toe of the boot pushing against the surface, causing them to be levered out. Make the most of any irregularities on the surface of the snow or ice, such as ripples and old axe or crampon placements, to give the crampon more purchase and the leg muscles a rest, as this technique is quite tiring. On long sections of steep ground, you may find it useful to cut a resting step at intervals, in order to give your legs a breather. This is true of any crampon technique, as a few moments on a flat ledge will do a great deal to help your leg muscles to recover.

Front-pointing is eminently suitable for climbing down, and once again the boot soles should be kept horizontal when placed.

Balling up

Using front-points on steep ground

TRAVERSING

Traversing a slope needs to be practised, and this can be done by either flat-footing or front-pointing. If the ground is fairly easy-angled, face across the slope and flex your ankles so that you are flat-footing. Take care to maintain a good gap between your feet, remembering that the up-slope foot only has a small gap to pass through, so keep it high. If you need to traverse steep ground it may be necessary to crab-crawl. Face in to the slope using your front-points, and bring one foot to the other. Don't cross your legs, as this will greatly increase the chance of you catching a crampon point.

When you do use the axe, be careful that it does not tempt you to lean too far forwards out of balance. Maintain an upright posture wherever possible and move naturally. If placing it above an ice bulge, make sure that you keep your soles horizontal and don't lean too far forward, otherwise your crampons will come out.

BALLING UP

One hazard that is difficult to remedy satisfactorily is balling up. This occurs when the snow is moist, such as when there is a slight thaw in progress. It then builds up between the points of your crampons into a stilt that stops any of the points from touching the snow, consequently leading to loss of traction and possibly a slip. Many crampons are supplied with anti-balling plates which go some way to prevent the snow sticking in the first place. If there is still a problem, a sharp tap on the side of your boot with the axe should be enough to dislodge the balling. In very poor conditions, this tapping will have to be done at every step.

OTHER CONSIDERATIONS

If you need to rest or stop for any reason, don't be tempted to just sit on the snow. You will immediately shoot off down the slope, possibly going head over heels and out of control. If you need to stop, cut yourself a good sized ledge to sit in, or better still make your way across to a suitable boulder and sit on that.

Once you have negotiated your slope, make sure that you are well away from the edge before removing your crampons. It is very easy to take them off too early, with the consequence that you slip back down to where you started.

Holding the axe correctly is very important, as this will be the key to getting all of the subsequent techniques correct. When carrying it, hold it with the adze facing forwards. This means that it is in the right position for bringing up into the self-arrest stance, covered a little later on. Your thumb and forefinger should be around the adze, middle finger in line with the shaft and the other two around the pick. Hold the axe loosely but securely, as to grip it too tightly will make subsequent techniques tricky to perform.

SELF-ARREST

Also known as ice axe braking, self-arrest is a fundamental skill and one that should be learned at the outset by anyone who is setting off into the mountains where there is snow present. Any slip or trip in this terrain could result in you sliding at an increasing rate down the slope, potentially with fatal consequences, and having the knowledge of how to stop by using an ice axe is paramount.

Holding the ice axe in the correct manner, so that it can be used for self-arrest effectively

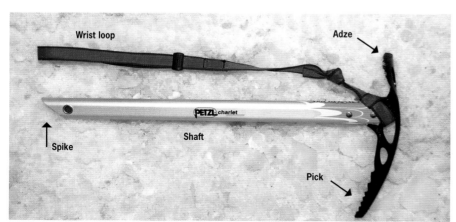

Wrist loop Adze

Spike

Shaft

Pick

The parts of an ice axe

THE SELF-BELAY

It is very important that any slip does not become a slide. If it does, this makes it very difficult to arrest, with an increased chance of losing control during acceleration. Your first line of defence is known as a self-belay, and is an essential skill to learn.

When walking on any slope, it is important that the axe is always carried on the uphill side of your body. This is so that it can be effectively placed for support, and also allows the self-belay to be used if needed. The axe spike is placed firmly into the snow each time it is moved forwards, and the shaft kept vertical. Should your feet slip, your downslope hand is quickly placed on to the axe shaft at the point where it meets the snow surface. It is important that the hand is kept as low as possible as this reduces any leverage. The hand holding the head of the axe can be pushed uphill slightly to counter any chance of the axe shaft pulling out. With your feet having slipped away from under you, you will now end up in a lying position suspended by the axe, hopefully with it holding you in place. Kicking a hole in the snow with your feet will help you to get upright again.

If you are walking on easy-angled terrain, where the shaft of the axe will not be in

The correct position once a self-belay has been carried out

contact with the snow at each step, a self-belay can still be carried out. Should your feet slip, bring the downhill hand up and grip the axe shaft a short distance above the spike. As you go down, ram the axe vertically into the snow, so that you end up in the standard self-belay position.

Should your attempt at self-belay fail for some reason and the shaft pull out through the snow, you should get yourself into a suitable position to perform a self-arrest.

SELF-ARREST

If you start sliding on the snow, you need to have practised a method of stopping yourself. There are a variety of positions from which an arrest can be effected, and these will include on your front with head up-slope, a sitting position, head first face down and head first face up. There are, of course, many ways to fall, but those mentioned above are the best to know, with any variation being solvable through a bit of forethought and cunning rehearsal.

When setting out to practise self-arrest, the area that you are going to use must be carefully selected. It should be a concave slope that allows a safe run-out in the event of you making a mistake when trying to stop, be free from boulders, and be steep enough to allow a slide to be made but not so steep as to be terrifying. An ideal surface for practising on will be a couple of centimetres of fresh snow on a base of older hard snow.

Helmets should be worn at all times. Crampons should never ever be worn

The correct hand position to effect a self-belay

when practising slides of any type. Should a crampon point catch in the snow, severe trauma to the ankle or leg can occur.

To avoid slipping around too much when getting organized, some of the starting positions of the techniques will be best gained by digging a pit in the snow. Consider subsequent users of the slope, and fill in any holes at the end of the session. Waterproofs should be worn, as should gloves, as your hands will be in frequent moving contact with the snow. When you become a little slicker at each technique, try performing them with a rucksack on, as this will obviously make a difference to how each method feels.

For the sake of the following descriptions, we will assume that the axe is being held in your left hand, although it is essential to be equally proficient at arrest skills with both hands. Remember the importance of the self-belay, where the axe will alternate between the left and right hand, as it will always be on your upslope side.

The correct position for walking with an ice axe, ready for self-belay

THE BASIC POSITION

The basic position, that of face down and head uphill, is important, as it is the position into which all of the other variations will end up. Getting this right is key to effective arrest, and time should be taken to get it right.

Practise getting the axe into the correct position across your body whilst still standing. Bringing it up from the walking position, allow your hand to rotate on the axe head so that your hand ends up pulling down on the axe head. The adze should now slot into the recess under your collarbone, with the shaft of the axe running across your chest to the opposite side hip. Your right hand must cover the spike, which ensures that it does not dig into the snow, or indeed into you! Both elbows need to be tucked in to the side of your body, and make sure that you look away from the head of the axe. This is important, as it not only prevents injury to your face if the axe catches on a section of hard ice or a rock, but it also directs the weight correctly on to the shoulder over the axe.

Now lie face down on the snow in a flat area. Raise your feet into the air to ensure that crampon points (which you are not wearing during practice of course), cannot dig into the snow and flick you over backwards, or cause other injuries. Your knees must be apart, around one and a half times shoulder width.   This is

The body position on the snow

to ensure stability when sliding, as you will probably not be going in a straight line. Your backside and stomach must be raised slightly, and chest and shoulders lowered. This allows a good deal of body weight to be transferred on to the axe head, very important when sliding on hard snow at speed.

Once you are happy with the basic position, move yourself a little way up the slope and try it with some movement. Slide a short distance and then place the axe pick into the snow, firmly but without jabbing it in, maintaining the correct posture until you stop. Slowly increase the speed and distance that you slide as your confidence builds. It is very helpful to have a companion around at this stage, as they will be able to correct you on anything that

is not quite right, such as your feet getting near the ground when stopping.

The axe being held across the body, as if seen from underneath

THE SITTING ARREST

When you are happy that you can arrest efficiently in this basic position, it is time to introduce a variation. Should you slip whilst walking downhill facing out, a slide in a sitting position will occur. For this, the axe is held in the usual manner, across the body and into the shoulder. You will need to turn over so that you are face down on the slope, and to achieve this it is essential that you roll on to your chest by turning your body towards the head of the axe. For instance, if the axe head is held in the left hand, you would roll over to the left-hand side, completely over on to your front and into the basic braking position. It is important that the axe stays as part of your body. Don't be tempted to dig the axe into the snow and then jump on it, as it will be snatched out of your hands if you are travelling at any speed. Remember to keep your head clear of the adze as the axe goes into the snow, as the pick touches the snow surface before your body has finished rotating. Also, bend your knees slightly as you rotate, as this has the effect of keeping your feet away from the snow, important when wearing crampons in a real situation.

ARRESTING HEAD FIRST FACE DOWN

It is possible that you could trip over your crampons on the way down a mountain, and thus end up sliding head first face down. The starting position to practise this is far easier to get into if a slot is cut across the slope for your boots to hook in to, and this will allow you to get in to the ready position without immediately sliding away. Lie face down on the slope with your head downhill, feet hooked into the slot. Your axe is held exactly the same way as for all the other techniques, one hand on the head, the other on the spike. If the axe head is in your left hand, the pick is placed into the snow as far out to the left as possible, in line with your shoulders. Look across at the axe, and not down the slope, as this will help the start of the turn. How you place the pick into the snow is important, as if it is jabbed in it could be snatched out of your hands, but if it is not placed firmly enough then the rotation needed for the arrest to happen will not be performed efficiently.

Take your feet out from the slot and allow yourself to slide down the slope. Once you are sliding a little, place the axe into the snow out to the side and your feet will swing round to the right. Keep the knees very slightly bent once this manoeuvre starts, as it helps to keep your feet clear of the surface. When you are halfway round, approximately across the slope, lift your axe out. The momentum created should keep you rotating, and as you do so arch your back, place the axe into the shoulder and brake as normal. It is very important that you remove the axe from the snow and divide this technique into two parts, the rotation and the arrest. If you leave the axe in the snow until you have fully rotated the right way up, it will be impossible to apply the correct amount of body weight to it. It would also be impossible to pull your body weight upslope on to the axe whilst sliding down.

Make sure that you do place the axe well out to the side in line with your shoulders. It is very tempting to place it in front of your body but that means that not only will the rotation be inefficient, but that you may run over the sharp adze with painful consequences.

The starting position for a face down head first arrest

ARRESTING HEAD FIRST UPSIDE DOWN

Should you really manage to fall down in a complicated manner, you may end up head first face up, sliding on your back! To practise this, first make your slot from the previous slide into more of a seat, as this will hold you whilst you get into the correct position. Now sit on it and run your feet round so that they are upslope and you are lying on your back. Pull the hood of your jacket up and over your helmet before starting, as it may get damaged or just slow you down.

The axe is held as normal, one hand on the head, the other covering the spike. Assuming that you are still holding the axe in your left hand, it is placed out in the snow on the left-hand side in line with your hips, with your left arm straight and the pick about 50cm (20in) out, and your right hand somewhere near your left hip. Let yourself slide and place the pick in the snow as before, not too fast, not too slow. Doing this creates a pivot, and your legs will swing round to the right. As they swing round, you must rotate what will now be your downslope hip, in this case the right one, upslope, in other words

you are performing a sit-up towards the head of the axe. Keep your feet together and have your knees slightly bent, as this helps to keep your boots clear of the snow surface.

What you are doing here is pivoting your body through 180 degrees, with your head ending upslope and you being on your front. As your body rotates, take the axe out of the snow, and arrest in the normal manner. Once again, it is important that you remove the axe between manoeuvres and the whole process is separated into two parts, the pivot and the arrest.

A common and quite understandable mistake is for you to end up rotating the wrong way when pivoting, thus performing a log roll down the slope. This is extremely dangerous, as not only will you soon pick up speed but you will also be rolling over the business end of the axe.

THE AXELESS ARREST

It is also possible to self-arrest without an ice axe, although this should not be used as a first line of defence! However, it is possible that you lose your axe during a fall or it is snatched out of your hand when

you place it in the snow, and an axeless arrest may have the effect of slowing you down or even stopping you.

To practice this, lie on the snow, head upslope and face down, with your arms out to the sides. Now lift your feet and start slipping down the slope. As you slide, place your feet back on the snow with just the inside edges of the soles in contact with it, and push your body weight up with your hands. These should be placed at just over shoulder width apart, ending up with your arms straight. The finishing position looks similar to that of a press-up, but your arms and legs will be spaced a little wider.

When doing this arrest, make sure that you use the edges of the boots, not the toes, as to do the latter could cause you to injure your Achilles tendon. Also, it is obviously not a suitable technique for use with crampons, although in real life you will do anything to try to slow yourself down or stop.

The final position for the axeless self-arrest

The body position when starting to rotate whilst sliding head first downhill

USING AN ICE AXE ON STEEP GROUND

There are a variety of ways in which a single ice axe or pair of tools can be used for self-arrest, and the following techniques are the most common. Firstly, if just using a single axe, it can be held diagonally across but away from your body in an extended arrest position. This allows you to dig it in to the slope and use it for support, ready to arrest with it if need be.

The extended arrest position

Daggering with two axes

It can also have the shaft plunged into soft snow, as this will give more purchase than simply using the pick, which may pull through. If using two axes, both shafts can be pushed deep into the snow and the axe head pulled on, a good technique for getting over small cornices.

Daggering is an efficient way of climbing moderately steep slopes. Place your hand on top of the axe with the pick forward, and push it into the snow at chest height. Now push down on it as you move your feet up. Using two axes makes this technique useful for quickly gaining height, as a good rhythm can be set up. The only drawback is that the axe is not in a good position for self-arresting, so don't use it if a long fall is a possibility.

Swinging the axe over your head is the technique of choice for most on steep ground. Holding the end of the shaft, swing through a full curve to make the pick bite in. With a reverse curve technical axe, a flick of the wrist at the end of the swing will make it bite in efficiently. Don't be tempted to over-drive the pick, as this

will make retrieving it very difficult, so moderate the size of the swing according to the snow and ice conditions. Keeping the axe shaft parallel with the snow will also improve the placement, and stop your fingers from getting bruised. On thin ice, or where there are many old axe marks, simply hooking the tip of the pick over the irregularities will be enough to provide purchase.

On hard fragile ice, hook the picks into existing holes or irregularities in the surface

Arranging a buried axe anchor

ANCHORS

Selecting an effective anchor under winter conditions can be quite tricky. As you are dealing with a medium – snow – that changes its state even from hour to hour, your judgment about the stability of an anchor at the start of a route may be completely different a few hours later at the end of the climb. However, well-constructed anchors in good quality ground can be very strong, and they can be used for a variety of applications, such as belaying, abseiling and as lowering points.

BURIED AXE

This is a fundamental anchor and has many uses. It can be placed behind a bucket seat to give a system with the ability to hold a leader fall, or can be used on its own as a direct belay in good snow conditions, useful for bringing a second up or lowering a climber down. The strength of the system is in the snowpack downslope of the placement, thus care should be taken to disturb this as little as possible.

A cut is made across the slope using the pick of the axe. This should be at 90 degrees to the direction of loading, and a little longer than the length of the axe shaft. A second cut is made parallel to it, about 15 centimetres (6in) higher.

The adze is then used to remove the snow between the two cuts, taking care not to disturb the downhill internal face. The depth of this slot depends upon current snow conditions, but as a rough guide a slot of around 20cm (8in) deep will be fine in very hard snow, and around 40cm (16in) in soft snow.

The axe shaft will end up resting against the downslope edge, so it should be made as flat as possible, in order that the entire length of the shaft will be touching the snow.

A vertical slot now needs to be made. This will be for the connecting sling and rope to fit into, so it can be initially cut out with the axe pick. To widen it, the shaft of the axe can be used, dragged through the snow to create a channel. Do not use the adze, as this will make a slot that is too wide and may weaken the overall placement. This slot should run for approximately one and a half metres (60in) below the level of the snow, before emerging at the belay point. This would be a bucket seat if you are belaying a lead climber, or a small ledge if using a direct belay system.

A clove hitch is tied in the sling, which is then placed onto the axe shaft at around halfway along its surface area. It is worth wrapping one side of the sling around the back of the axe, as this inverts the clove hitch and ensures that it grips the shaft tightly when loaded.

The axe, with the pick pointing downwards, is placed into the main slot, with the sling running down the vertical one. Ensure that there is no debris in any of the slots, in particular the one holding the sling, as any loading could cause the sling to pull incorrectly on the axe and lift it out of position. The sling should be tugged sharply a couple of times in the direction of loading, to ensure that everything is seated correctly. A karabiner is now attached, with any subsequent rope system, such as a direct belay, being clipped in to it.

When digging this style of anchor on sloping ground, look after your own security. It would be a good idea to clip yourself to the anchor as soon as possible, or have a spare axe or hammer to hand in case you should slip before the job is completed.

If the snow conditions are soft, it would be worth pushing snow from upslope of the slot down onto it and packing it in place as added security.

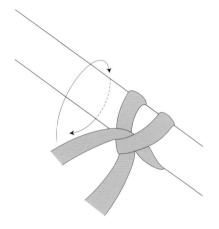

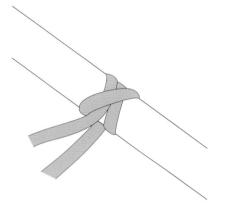

Inverting a clove hitch

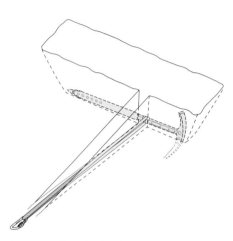

Cross-section of a buried axe anchor

REINFORCED AXE

This is a method of improving the buried axe anchor, for use in softer snow conditions.

Once the initial axe placement has been made, a second ice tool is placed at an angle just back from vertical, at the top of the vertical sling slot. It should be just touching the horizontal axe but not moving it. The spike of this axe is placed between the two sides of the sling, and is pushed down as far as possible, at most until its head reaches the level of the shaft of the horizontal axe. A tug on the sling will help to ensure that everything is sitting snugly.

A variation is known as the 'T' axe belay. This is where a sling is clove-hitched around the top of the vertical axe, which is pushed down behind the horizontal one so that the sling rests on top of it. It can be used where there are a number of hard snow layers close together within the snow pack, but as quite a judgment call has to be made about when it is appropriate to use, a standard reinforced buried axe anchor, as detailed right, will normally be found to be superior.

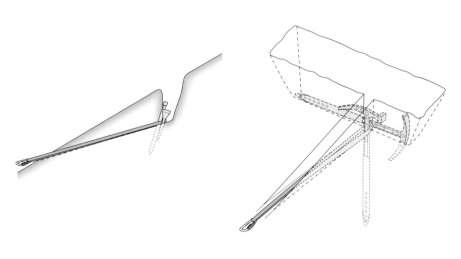

The reinforced buried axe anchor

DEADMAN

Looking like a flat plate about 20cm (8in) square with a wire attached, a deadman anchor is very useful in place of a buried axe. The main advantage is that the climber will still have their axe to hand, essential for looking after their own personal security. It can be used for a variety of tasks, such as anchoring a belayer, as a direct belay attachment or as a securing plate for the end of a fixed rope.

A deadman is of most use in a climbing situation where the ascent will be predominantly on steep snow, where the burial of the axe and thus the danger to the climber whilst they construct the anchor is not a good idea. However, they can be notoriously difficult to carry and place correctly, and for this reason are often overlooked in favour of a buried axe system.

Getting the placement of the deadman correct is critical to its security, as it requires a 40 degree angle between it and the snow on the upslope side. If it is placed too steeply into the snow there is a chance that it could pull out when loaded, if canted too far back it could bury itself deeper into the snowpack and have reduced holding power.

Placing a deadman on steep snow is a tricky process, and even though it will give a solid anchor once finished, if there is any danger to you whilst arranging things then a different anchor, perhaps rock, should be found if at all possible.

It needs to be placed in an area where the snow layers are consistent. If a very soft or very hard layer runs across the face of the plate, there is a chance that it will be tilted to the wrong angle when loaded and therefore fail. As with any snow anchor, care should be taken that the downslope snow area is left undisturbed as much as possible, as it is here that the strength of the system lies.

The ice axe is placed into the snow at 90 degrees to the slope. This angle can be checked by using the sides of the deadman as a square. The deadman should now be placed across the slope, at 90 degrees to the direction of loading, with its pointed base close to the shaft of the axe, but not resting up against it.

The angle between the ice axe and the slope is now bisected by the deadman to give 45 degrees, and the top is then tilted back a few degrees further in order to reduce the angle to 40. The deadman is pushed into the snow a short way so that it stands on its own.

The slot into which the deadman will sit can now be cut with the axe. Using the deadman as a guide, cut a deep line into the snow with the pick of the axe at exactly the same angle, just off to one side. It is important that this slot is cut carefully, as it will become the face down which the deadman is driven and, as such, be the guide for the correct angle of placement. The snow on the upslope side of this slot is now removed for a few centimetres width and depth, taking great care not to disturb or alter the lower face of the snow.

The wire from the deadman will need to sit in a slot of its own, running vertically down the slope to the appropriate belay position at 90 degrees to the horizontal slot. The pick is used to cut a narrow slot running vertically downslope for approximately two metres (78in). The deadman is now placed into the horizontal slot and held in place whilst being hammered in from above, ensuring that it follows the front guide-face all the way.

Once the wire attachment point is below the level of the surface of the snow, pulling the wire taut whilst hammering will keep the plate at the correct angle as it is driven in. The depth to which it is buried will depend upon the condition of the snow, but in good conditions, where the snow is firm, the top of the deadman needs to be no further than 5–10cm (2–4in) below the surface.

Any snow or ice that has been inadvertently knocked into the vertical wire slot must be cleaned out, otherwise when the deadman is loaded the pull may be from a sufficiently wrong angle to dislodge it.

With the wire running in the vertical slot, the shaft of the axe or hammer is placed through the end loop of the wire and is used to give it a tug. This will help to both seat the deadman into place and help the wire pull straight through its slot. Once the whole system is set up, a screwgate karabiner is attached to the loop at the end of the wire and whatever system is being used can be run from there.

After use, a plate in hard or very cold snow will have to be dug out. In softer conditions, a tug uphill will often be enough to unseat it. Care must be taken that the wire is not damaged whilst the device is being dug out, as it could render the deadman useless for the future.

Carrying a deadman can prove awkward, so it will be best to wrap the wire around the plate a number of times and then use a screwgate karabiner to secure the end of the wire through one of the lightening holes. This karabiner can then be used to clip the plate onto a suitable part of the rack. As the plate is an awkward shape, the best position in which to carry it may well be clipped into a subsidiary gear loop on the rucksack, tucked well out of the way.

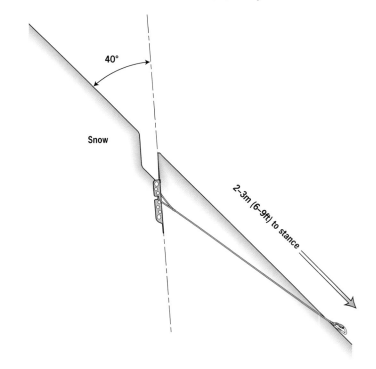

40°

Snow

2–3m (6–9ft) to stance

Correct placement of a deadman

BUCKET SEAT

This a very effective method of belaying on snow slopes, in particular when allied with a buried axe or deadman anchor. Its simplicity makes it an effective tool that is often all that is needed to safeguard a climber moving up towards you or when protecting a climber during descent. However, a bucket seat on its own is not suitable for protecting a leader, as the forces exerted on the belayer when holding a leader fall of any distance may well be sufficient to lift them clear of the seat with disastrous consequences. Should the seat be used to protect a lead climber, then it must be linked to a second anchor, such as the buried axe or deadman.

The seat works by any load pulling the belayer down onto the front edge, with most of the load being taken by their thighs. For this reason, the construction of the front section of the seat is the most crucial part of the anchor.

The finished shape is going to be roughly a semi-circle about a metre (39in) across, and this can be described in the snow with an ice axe pick, holding on to the end of the shaft and rotating around your elbow. The straight section should be at the front, at 90 degrees to the line of possible loading. Having cut round this shape with the pick, the snow inside can be chopped out, using a combination of adze and gloved hand. The front of the bucket seat should not be disturbed, as this is where the strength of the system will lie. This front side is cut down perpendicular to the surface, with the depth being determined by the length of the belayer's thighs, which should be supported for their entire length.

A ledge cut downslope of the bucket seat, and slightly off to one side, will make a placement for the rope to sit on. Otherwise, if setting up the system on a slope, the rope can end up hanging down the pitch and getting in the way of the ascending climber, or even snagging on a protrusion.

STOMPER BELAY

The stomper belay is a very versatile method of safeguarding a climber who is either ascending or descending the terrain below you. This type of belay method is not designed to take a shock-loading, such as may be created by holding the weight of a falling leader, and if such a loading occurs the system could quite possibly fail, with the axe being pulled out of the ground.

Quick and simple to set up, it can be used in many situations, such as safeguarding someone investigating a potential cornice obstacle when searching for a descent route, bringing up a second on moderate ground, or it can be used for lowering one or even two people at a time.

The most important factor to be considered when deciding to use this method is your own safety when operating the system. There is no direct attachment for you to the stomper, so this method should only be used on terrain where you are happy that there is no chance of you either stepping off the stance accidentally or being blown off your feet by the wind and falling downhill. Having some knowledge of the snowpack is important, as should the system be set up across layers of widely varying hardness there may be a tendency for the axe to lever out when under load.

The belay can be set up on either flat or sloping ground. In either situation, the snowpack needs to be firm enough to support a sideways pull on the axe, but not so icy that it cannot be pushed or stamped in right to the head. On terrain that is sloping, a ledge is either cut or stamped into the snow, inclined slightly back into the slope. Ending up wedge-shaped, this ledge should be just wide enough for you to stand on with your feet together. To help stability, make the ledge deep enough so that the snow on the upslope side supports the backs of the calves. Standing on the ledge and kicking back with the heels will help to shape the back wall to fit your leg-shape.

Standing in position on the ledge will have made an imprint of your soles. The ice axe will be pushed in spike-first at the point where your heels stop, just at the instep. Prepare a hole by pushing the axe straight in to the snow at an angle of 90 degrees for about three-quarters of its length and then remove it.

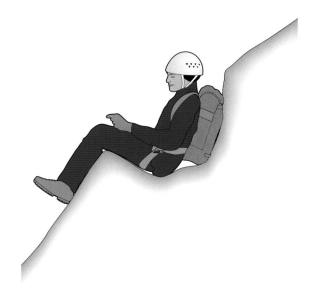

Cross-section of a bucket seat

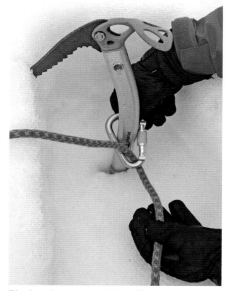

Placing the rope and karabiner on to the axe shaft for a stomper belay

An HMS karabiner is best suited to this belay system, and the rope running to the person to be safeguarded is clipped to it. The rope should be at the narrow end of the karabiner and coming out from the bottom of it. Place the karabiner around the shaft of the axe and slide it up to just below the head.

The axe can now be pushed into the hole, making sure that the axe head is running across the slope and the rope is on the downslope side. Push it right down so that the head is flush with the surface of the snow. It may need to be stamped into place if the snow is hard. Ensure that the rope can run through the karabiner smoothly and that there is no way that it can snag. The system relies on your bodyweight to make it work safely, so you now stand on the head of the axe with your heels against the back wall. Do not take your weight off the axe head when the system is in use, as this would severely reduce the strength of it.

To manage the rope, a right-handed belayer runs it up through the left hand, which is held down alongside the left leg, behind the back of the left shoulder, down over the front of the right shoulder and gripped by the right hand. There is no need to take a twist around this arm, as for a conventional waist belay, as there will be a lot of friction already created in the system. Reverse this process for a left-handed operation. The rope is then in a position to be used as a shoulder belay. Make sure that the rope does run up behind your back first. If it comes in front of your body and over your shoulder, a lot of the system's strength will be lost as you could easily be pulled down into a crunched position.

When the system is being used, it is important that there is never any slack rope between yourself and the person being safeguarded. If there were to be slack rope in the system, the shock-loading created by a slip could be enough to cause the axe to pull out through the snowpack. For this reason, a person being lowered should also always be below the level of the axe head before putting any weight on to the system, otherwise it could pull out if loaded in an upwards and outwards direction. For the same reason, if a climber is being belayed up a slope, they should stop just below the axe head level, unless it is set up on flat ground at the top of a route and they are on safe terrain. If dealing with less experienced climbers and the system has been set up on sloping terrain, it would be a good idea to prepare a ledge or bucket seat below the level of the belay for them to stand or sit in.

If you are wearing a harness, it is possible to belay by using a conventional belay device. In this situation, the rope would simply run up through the karabiner and into the device, with no wrap being taken around the body. As long as the harness is well fitting, this would be easy to do, but in some situations, such as in cold conditions or at altitude where extra clothing may be worn, the harness may feel as though it is being pulled down over the hips, and in this case a shoulder belay may be the best and more secure option.

On sloping ground, a ledge for the rope to sit just downslope and to the side of the belay ledge would be worth constructing, to help keep the rope management tasks simple and avoid tangles or snagging. Also, remember the precaution of securing the end that is not connected to the climber. If this is not tied into in some way, or at the very least has a large knot tied in it, there is a chance in a lower situation, if control is lost, that the end of the rope could disappear through your hand.

BOOT/AXE BELAY

A complementary skill to the stomper belay, this is a quick and efficient method of safeguarding the descent of a climber on snow-covered ground. It can also be used to efficiently lower one or even two people over moderate terrain should a speedy descent be necessary.

It simply requires an ice axe and snow of a reasonable density underfoot to set up. A huge advantage of this method is that your body position is low to the ground and thus quite stable in high winds. However, the disadvantage with the boot/axe belay is that it is purely designed for descent. If the person being lowered needed to make their way up the slope again, you would have to take a hand off the axe in order to take in the rope, which in turn would compromise the strength of the system.

Like the stomper belay, the boot/axe belay is not designed to take a shock-load, and for that reason there must never be slack between yourself and person being lowered, nor should it be used in a situation where the person being protected is upslope of the belayer, with the possible consequence of the system being shock-loaded in the event of them slipping.

The system can be rigged on level or moderately sloping ground. If the ground is not flat, a ledge should be cut that can accommodate your boot, sloping slightly back into the hillside. If crampons are being worn, the ledge can be flat but, if not, it is a good idea to create a 3–5cm (1–2in) lip on the outside edge of the ledge against which the outside of your boot can be braced.

The stomper belay set-up

For a right-handed person the right foot will be on the ledge with another smaller ledge having been kicked or cut about a metre (39in) downslope to accommodate the left foot. For left-handed operation, the right foot would end up downslope. Your boot, if no crampons are being worn, is placed against the downslope lip. With crampons, it is placed firmly in the centre of the ledge. The axe is now positioned with the shaft leaning slightly uphill from vertical, aligned just behind your shinbone, with the pick of the axe facing behind you. It is pushed into the snow, with a corkscrewing action sometimes useful in harder ground. The head should not go below the top of your boot, and once in position it should be snug against it.

The rope, having been prepared on a ledge cut into the snow behind you, runs through your legs, in front of the ankle of the right foot (assuming a right-handed belayer), loops around the head of the axe from under the pick and exiting under the adze, and then down to the person to be lowered. A stance is taken that allows you to lean with your right hand holding on to the head of the axe, with the left hand gripping the rope, positioned down next to the snow surface and just behind the right ankle. Holding the rope in this position moves the axe down tight on to the boot, which is in turn forced upslope on to the

axe. This opposition allows the system to stay in place and support the weight of the person being lowered. The stance that you take up is crucial, as once the system is loaded you cannot afford to let go of either the rope or the head of the axe, as to do this would mean that the weight of the climber would pull the system apart.

To introduce slack into the system so that the climber can be lowered, your left hand is brought forwards slowly so as to decrease the friction around your ankle, and the rope can be paid out in a shuffling motion. Bringing the hand back behind the ankle again will increase the friction, thus slowing or stopping the descent.

As always, consideration needs to be given to what is at the other end of the rope, and if the belayer is not tied on, a large knot should be tied at the end of the rope, as well as a smaller one about a metre or so from the end. This will at least give warning of the rope running out and avoid a disaster. Also, the rope must only be loaded when it is running parallel to the surface of the snow. If it is pulled upwards, the rope could travel up the shaft of the ice axe and cause leverage that may cause the system to fail.

The boot/axe belay

SNOW BOLLARD

This is a handy anchor to know and has a number of applications, with the advantage over other anchors that no equipment is left behind if it is to be used for abseiling. It can take a little while to construct, depending upon the solidity of the snow, but once finished provides a versatile and solid point of attachment for a variety of belay methods.

Its size depends mainly on the quality of the snow, and the width of it can range from 50cm (20in) in very hard snow to two or even three metres (80–120in) in less ideal conditions. The rope, once placed around it, needs to be resting against a single homogeneous layer of snow, so an inspection during the cutting process will help to identify where the layers change. Care should be taken not to disturb the snow either within the area where the bollard is to be cut or the ground immediately downslope of it.

The bollard will end up being a horseshoe shape, and this can be drawn in the snow with the pick of the axe. This should be symmetrical and have the lower section, where the rope is to exit, tapering towards the direction in which it will be loaded.

The basic shape can now be cut around, using the pick of the axe. Once the outline has been cut through, the adze can be used to chop out a narrow slot all round it. The depth of this will vary according to the underlying snow layers, but will most likely be in the region of 15cm (6in) deep.

The main loading area will be the top section of the bollard, so this should be mushroomed slightly with the adze to create a slight overhang, under which the rope can securely sit.

The bollard may be used for a variety of purposes, and lends itself to them all very well. It can be used in conjunction with a bucket seat, as a direct belay or an attachment point for fixed ropes. However, if being used as such it would be a good idea for the last person down to test-pull the abseil rope before abseiling to ensure that the rope has not frozen to the back surface of the bollard, making subsequent retrieval impossible.

Although the method described is for use on a snow slope, it is quite possible to fashion a bollard from near-ready material such as the gap between a rock face and the snow pack, particularly in gullies. Resembling a spike anchor, in good conditions this can result in a very strong attachment point.

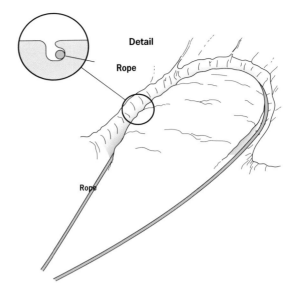

Detail

Rope

Rope

A snow bollard

A snow bollard being used for an abseil

RETRIEVING AN ICE AXE ANCHOR

Although categorized by some as being in the 'rope tricks' department, it is possible to abseil from a vertical axe anchor and then retrieve it, leaving no gear behind at all.

If you decide to do this it probably means that all other possibilities for an abseil anchor have been considered and then dismissed as being either impractical or unsafe. For instance, the use of a snow bollard would normally be considered well before that of a retrievable axe abseil, but the snow into which it needs to be dug may be of insufficient width, perhaps being in a narrow gully.

The axe is pushed vertically into the snow so as to make a hole no wider than the shaft. Take note of the state of the underlying layers as you do this, as if they are very soft a different location should be found. Attach a second tool, such as a hammer, to the axe, using a sling; this can easily be tied or larksfooted through a suitable hole in the head of both tools.

The bottom of the axe needs to have a length of sling or rope such as an unpicked prusik loop attached to it, measuring around a metre (39in) long. Once this is in place, the axe is pushed back into the vertical hole already prepared. Make sure that the cord or sling is not damaged or dislodged during this process. The head of the axe can, for the moment, be left protruding a few centimetres (couple of inches) from the surface of the snow.

The second ice tool is placed horizontally tight up against the axe at 90 degrees to the line the abseil rope will take, with its pick flat on the snow. This will allow the rope or sling connected to the bottom of the axe to be pulled without it cutting into the snow and possibly jamming.

The rope to be used for the abseil is placed around the head of the vertical axe, with the centre mark at the back. An overhand knot on the bight is tied on the rope close to the axe head, and a karabiner used to connect it to the sling or cord from the bottom of the axe. The head of the axe is now pushed down to the surface of the snow, ensuring that it doesn't go so far in as to snag the rope, which would prevent it from being pulled smoothly around the shaft.

The abseil rope and the sling connected to the bottom of the axe are run over the top of the horizontal tool, and the abseil rope can then be lowered or thrown down the slope. Make sure that the connecting knot plus any knot joining two ropes together if they are being used are both on the same side of the axe.

Once the abseil has been completed, retrieval is accomplished by a strong and constant pull on the relevant side of the abseil rope. This pull should continue until the tools have been recovered, as to stop part way through may result in them jamming in the snow on the ground above. Great care should be taken when the rope is pulled for retrieval, as two sharp ice tools will be accelerating towards the bottom of the rope. Everyone not involved should be kept out of the way, and the person doing the pulling should keep careful watch so that they can avoid the tools as they fly down.

If two ropes are being used and are of different colours, it will be easy to remember which one to pull. If it is the same rope, however, it would be a good idea to clip a free-running karabiner on to the relevant side, and this will provide a reminder once the next stance has been reached.

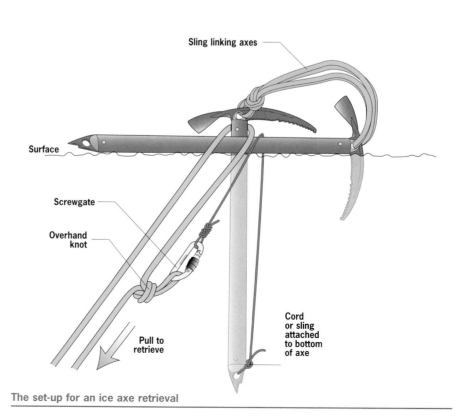

The set-up for an ice axe retrieval

GULLY CLIMBING

The ascent of a gully will often be the first introduction to snow climbing for many mountaineers. By their very nature, gullies tend to take lines provided by natural breaks and seams in the cliffs, and these can often be at a reasonably easy angle. As such, many gullies are in the lower grades of climbing difficulty, and provide an excellent way for novices to start to learn about snow-craft, winter ropework and climbing skills.

Having said this, there are a great deal of gully routes that take improbable lines up terrifying sections of rock, offering all sorts of challenges such as huge chockstones, hanging ice and blank rock steps. They are also a channel for debris, as snow, ice or rocks dislodged from above will be funnelled down the line of the route, making life for anyone lower down the gully very unpleasant, to say the least.

EQUIPMENT

No particular specialized equipment is needed for climbing gullies, at least at the lower end of the grade scales, with the main exception being the addition of a second ice tool, such as a hammer, to complement the axe already used for general mountaineering. It is very handy to have a matched pair of tools, in other words an axe and hammer that are similar in length, style and weight. This allows you to climb smoothly and efficiently, knowing how each tool will feel when placed.

The heads of the tools can have either a normal or a reverse curve to them, depending upon your current and future aspirations. A normally curved pick will be fine for easy to mid-grade routes, but if you are progressing towards harder climbs a reverse curve will be found to be beneficial. This will help to ease the retrieval of the pick after each placement, making ascent a lot easier and saving precious time and energy, as taking a classic curve pick out of hard snow or steep ice can be tricky when it is swung in too hard.

The same goes for crampons as for axes. Most general purpose crampons will be adequate for lower graded climbs, as long as they have front-points, but should you decide to attempt harder routes, a good pair of technical 12-point crampons, robustly designed and made with steep climbing in mind, will be needed. These will obviously need to be fitted to suitably stiff-soled boots, often utilizing a step-in binding system rather than straps for convenience. As far as the boots themselves are concerned, they need to have a good quality sole block and it should not be possible to bend them by hand. If you can, they are too soft for serious winter use.

Either a single or double rope system can be used, with the former simpler to handle and the latter better from a protection point of view for steeper, more technical routes. Protection during the climb will most often be provided by rock anchors, as these give good security when well placed. However, a deadman and a couple of ice screws may also be carried.

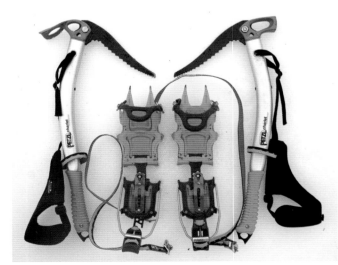

A good set of matched reverse-curve technical tools, with a slight curve to the shaft, along with a pair of 12-point step-in crampons

A deadman provides a very useful belay anchor on snow slopes, with the advantage that your ice axe is not buried, such as when using the axe to back up a bucket seat belay. If you really have to, the deadman can also be used to protect a section of ground where no other anchors are available, sited in the snow and clipped as a running belay.

Ice screws are handy if there is likely to be any ice encountered, and this will be particularly likely where melt-water has been running over the top of exposed slabs or down the front of jammed boulders.

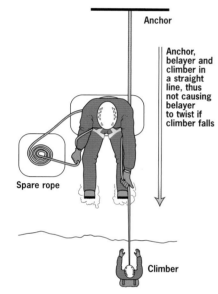

Correct position of belayer

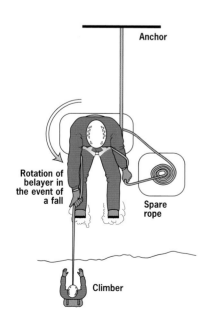

Incorrect position of belayer

BELAYING

All of the belaying techniques described in the 'Basics' section are relevant for use in gullies. However, if a snow or ice anchor is being used, it is important to use an indirect or waist belay if any shock-loading, such as when holding a leader fall, could be experienced. There is a very important consideration here, in the manner that you are tied on to your harness and then to the anchor. Imagine sitting in a bucket seat with a buried axe anchor, with the rope from the anchor coming to you under your left-hand side, but the live rope to the climber coming out from your right-hand side. If a long fall were held, there would be a severe twisting motion applied to you as the rope pulls itself into a straight line between the anchor, your harness and the climber. This could result in you being pulled from your stance, losing control of the rope, and also sustaining severe back injury as you are violently twisted round. It is essential that the rope coming to you from the climber is on the same side of your body as the rope coming in from the anchor.

Another important consideration is the direction that the route above will be taking. If your second climbs up to you, retrieves the gear and then leads on through to the next pitch, the direction that they take is critical to the safety of both of you, and you must plan ahead to keep things in order.

Let's say that you are belaying in the centre of a gully, facing out and using a waist belay. If the climber comes up to your left-hand side (as in the diagram), takes the spare gear from you and leads on, should they move across the gully behind you and then fall off, they will have unwrapped themselves from your waist belay and you

would not be able to hold them. Conversely, if they approached you from below and to your right and then traversed across above you, this would have the effect of wrapping the rope around you. A fall in this situation would mean that you could easily be injured by the rope running around your upper body or neck, it being pulled tight with their body weight.

It is very important, therefore, to plan ahead and decide not only which side of the gully will be appropriate for the belaying as regards the direction of the next pitch, but also which hand to use to hold the dead rope. This will need to be worked out in advance of constructing the anchor, in particular which side of the bucket seat the anchor rope should be running in to.

Another consideration will be the safety of the belayer. Gullies being debris chutes, it would be foolhardy for a belayer to be standing directly below the main section of a pitch, unless absolutely unavoidable. Taking a stance to one side, ideally with a convex section of rock just above to serve as protection and hopefully deflect any falling snow or ice, would be the best thing to do. Helmets are absolutely essential, as is alertness from all party members. The leader should be aware that if they dislodge any debris they must shout 'Below' to warn others that there is a risk of being hit.

If conditions are such that a good deal of snow, ice or rocks are dislodged during the early stages of a climb, it would be best to abandon the attempt for the safety of everyone involved. Climbing snowy gullies in warm weather can also be very dangerous, as rocks in particular, levered from the main cliff by the action of ice during a freeze, will be channelled towards anyone climbing below.

Having climbed up to the belayer's left-hand side, the climber traverses across above them, unwrapping the belay

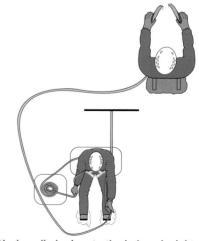

Having climbed up to the belayer's right-hand side and traversed above, the belayer is now tangled in the rope in the event of the climber falling

DEALING WITH CORNICES

A cornice is a large cap of snow that builds out over steep slopes, particularly gullies, creating a steep, if not severely overhanging, finish to a climb. These need to be negotiated in some manner, and there are various ways to deal with them. Firstly, if the snow is very soft or the air temperature is rising, the simplest advice is to avoid them altogether. Cornices can become very unstable in these conditions and, as they will weigh a considerable amount, being underneath one when it snaps off is very dangerous. A secondary problem of cornice collapse is that it could, in slab avalanche conditions, trigger the fragile snow pack below it, causing a large area of the slope to slide. Find out about the conditions and make an informed decision before climbing hundreds of metres to find your way blocked by a very unstable and scary umbrella of snow. However, cornices can be stable and provide a challenging end to your climb, so having some method for overcoming them is a good idea.

Firstly, as they are made of snow with little or no chance of any running belays to be found, it is a good idea to have a belay stance just a short way below them, but off to one side. This will stop you from falling much distance should you fail to get over on the first try, as there won't be much rope run out. Secondly, the sides of the cornice may provide an easier escape ramp than following the direct line up the gully would, so it would be worth investigating this possibility, deviating towards the side that appears to look the most likely route.

Failing this, you will have to go straight up. If the cornice is very small, perhaps little more than chest-high steepening or slight overhang, then you may be able to go straight over. Make sure of good foot placements, and it may be necessary to push the entire shaft of the axe into the snow to get enough purchase to progress. As you get up to the lip, reach over the top and push your axes well into the snow, away from the edge. These can be used to help work your feet up, moving the axes further back from the edge if need be. As you move your body over the final moves, take care not to lift your heels too high, otherwise the snow will be pushed in an

Surmounting a small cornice

outwards direction by your crampon points, causing them to become dislodged. Also avoid the temptation to use your knees as you top out, and step up in balance well away from any potential fracture line.

If the cornice is overhanging a little, it will be necessary to cut some of the snow away to keep your body in balance as you move up. You should be able to excavate a U-shaped slot in the snow without too much trouble, using the adze of your axe, and then climb up as described above.

If the cornice is very large, then there

Climbing through a U gap in a cornice late at night

Tunnelling through a cornice

are a couple of options, The first will be to go down. This may seem like admitting defeat, but the time it takes to get past a very large cornice is considerable and descending, especially if night is drawing in or bad weather is on its way, is a good option. However, you may wish to continue and that will mean tunnelling through. Before doing this, be absolutely certain that by digging a hole through the snow you are not compromising its strength, and there is no chance of it snapping off whilst you are burrowing inside.

Tunnelling a cornice is a very time-consuming process, not without its dangers and with, for most people, quite a high fear factor. To be inside many tonnes of overhanging snow, chopping away at

its very foundation, focuses the mind very effectively! Although tunnelling will usually just be carried out with the adze of the axe, a shovel may be available and in soft snow this will dramatically reduce the time it takes to get the job done.

You need to be able to climb through at an angle that lets you climb safely, but not at such a low angle as to have to cut through many metres of snow unnecessarily. A slope just back from vertical will be fine, and will allow you to climb in balance.

Dig away at the snow above you, letting the debris fall back down the gully and not knock you off your feet. Obviously, watch out in case there are other people below. The tunnel needs to be large enough to allow you to move with reasonable ease,

and also be a size that will allow your rucksack through on your back. In very hard conditions, where digging may take some time, you may elect to remove your rucksack to save having to excavate so much snow, hauling it up on the rope later. Pull your hood up as you progress, otherwise debris from higher inside the tunnel will find its way into your clothing and soak you over time. Squirm your way up and through, using your ice tools to pull you up, and avoid the temptation to lean your back on the snow as this could cause that section of the cornice to collapse. At the top, drive your tools into the ground as far away from the hole as possible and pull yourself upright.

Leading on steep water ice

ICE CLIMBING

Pure ice climbing is an acquired taste for many. Some find the ascent of a frozen pillar of water very worrying, with it being tenuously attached to the underlying rock in some places and totally free-standing in others. Others say that the climbing is repetitive and boring, with hand and foot holds wherever you want them and little skill being needed in order to complete the route. I have some understanding with the first sentiments, as just remembering that a cubic metre of frozen water will weigh a tonne is enough to make any sane man or woman question their reasons for crawling up an icicle! However, for those who say that ice climbing is never a challenge, I hold little sympathy. There are so many factors that need to be right to allow for a successful ascent of ice, certainly at the mid to higher grades, that anyone stout enough to attempt a route will certainly have long ago made their decision about whether the discipline of ice climbing is lacklustre or not.

EQUIPMENT

Ice climbing requires some equipment that may be seen as being specialized, such as ice hooks, Abalakov and V thread tools and protective visors. However, some of the rack will often be made up with rock gear, as rock runners will be infinitely more reliable than ice screws, particularly when associated with thin ice or narrow pillars.

AXES

Axes designed for pure ice will tend to have a pronounced curve to the shaft, which helps to keep your knuckles away from impact with the ice whilst ascending. It also serves to transfer your weight in a very efficient manner to the tip of the pick, allowing it to stay in place on even the most tenuous of hooks or edges. Indeed, modern ice tools are so efficient that the main problem is with over-driving them into the ice, which makes them difficult to extract, rather than worrying about them not providing enough purchase.

One main consideration will be the choice between leashed and leashless tools. Some do both jobs admirably, with the leash being removable in an instant, but if choosing a full leashless system, climbers will very often opt for a pair of tools with an efficient handle design, usually canted at quite an angle from the shaft. This type of tool is very popular for dry tooling (see below).

It is important that the pick is sharp and easily able to penetrate the ice with minimum effort from you. It is equally important that the top edge of the pick is kept sharp, as this eases retrieval as you move up, and saves you from having to expend valuable energy in removing the tool.

Carrying a file is a good idea if away for an extended trip, in order to keep the pick as sharp as possible. Spare blades are also sound insurance, as it is possible to snap one in use, in particular if there is a section of rock linking up ice pillars that requires any sort of aggressive technique to cross.

CRAMPONS

The choice of these will often come down to personal preference. For instance, I prefer two vertical front-points for general icefall climbing, but will revert to a single front-point, also called a mono-point, for hard technical routes and certainly if there is any linking rock to be crossed.

The second set of points should be quite aggressively set forwards, in order to provide a platform for the foot to rest on when the front set are fully engaged in softer ice, or if the heel is dropped slightly for resting. Other points can be of any configuration, as they will not normally be used for the main part of the climbing session. However, they need to be of a good standard, as you may end up using the flat of your foot for bridging moves, and to have poor quality or rounded ancillary points could cause you to slip off.

Most climbers will choose a binding system that allows for quick placing and removal of the crampons on the boots. This will most often be done with a wire toe-bale and lever-style heel mechanism. Although there is no real problem with using strap-on crampons, many ice climbers feel that the movement caused by the straps giving as their weight is applied to the front-points is sufficient to cause them to have to alter their footwork technique, not something that they wish to do. As step-in bindings keep the crampon rigidly fixed to the sole of the boot, this is the choice of anyone frequently climbing ice.

As with axes, it is important to keep the points fine and sharp, so having a file handy is a good precaution. Sharpening will usually need doing more often than with the axes, as the crampons may have to be used for part of the walk-in and will unavoidably come into contact with rock, causing them to dull a little.

Heel spurs can be useful in some situations, particulary with heel-hook moves and wrap-around moves on thin pillars. However, they take some getting used to and are generally not necessary on the majority of ice routes, particularly those non-technical in nature. Their use is also frowned upon on many routes as well as in competitions.

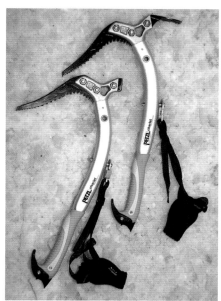

A matched pair of technical ice tools

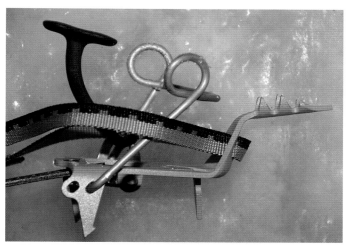

Heel spurs on technical ice crampons

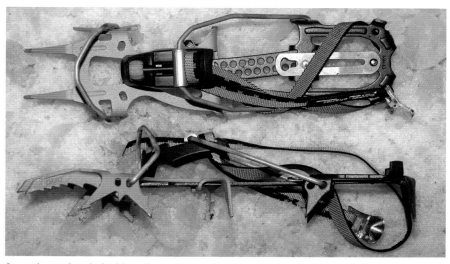

A good set of technical ice climbing crampons with twin vertical front points

ICE SCREWS

There are many types of ice screw available, and for climbing pure ice you will want to have the best that exist. They come in a variety of lengths and diameters, each with its own hanger configuration. As the screws will usually be placed with one hand, whilst the other holds you on to the ice, it is important to choose a type that not only cuts easily into the ice but also has a method by which it can be wound in swiftly and efficiently. Most modern screws come with a device, often attached to the hanger, which allows them to be quickly wound in with one hand. This may be a lever in a fixed position, one that is hinged up during placement, or part of the hanger itself. Whichever type you choose, it would be a good idea to practise swift and efficient placements low down, or even at ground level, before the need arises to place them on a route.

It is important that the screws are protected from damage, not just the cutting teeth but also the thread around the outside. Make sure that you do not bash them against any other gear or ice tool, and consider using a screw-tube, which allows the device to be carried safely and readily extracted when needed.

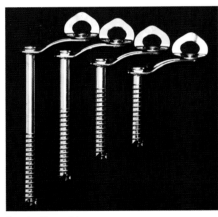

A selection of ice screws

Ice screw carrying tubes

ICE HOOKS

These are shaped like the pick of an ice axe, with a 90 degree bend and a hole at the bottom, usually with a sewn tape loop in place. They are not often used as conventional ice protection, but do have their place in some situations. For instance, they can be tapped into existing axe tip placements and used for direct aid or resting. They can also be hammered into narrow iced up cracks, albeit usually irretrievably. They are not a stand-in for ice screws, and shock-loading a hook placement could cause it to shear out and fail. Take great care, therefore, if choosing to use them, and always go for the better option of using ice screws for the majority of jobs.

The difficulty of carrying ice hooks is another reason why they will not be seen on every climber's rack, as they are very sharp and therefore tend to snag on gear and clothing at every opportunity.

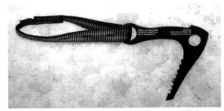

Ice hooks, with the tape ready sewn in place

ABALAKOV HOOKS AND ROPE

The Abalakov, also known as an 'ice' or 'V' thread, is a very useful way to arrange an anchor, often for abseiling from, leaving minimum gear behind. The actual rigging of an Abalakov is covered below, but a useful piece of kit to have is an Abalakov hook. This tool is designed to pull the threaded rope or tape through the hole made in the ice, a job that is otherwise very difficult to do.

You can purchase a ready-made thread hook, or make one up yourself from a length of coat hanger wire or similar. It needs to be less than the diameter of and just a bit longer than your longest ice screw.

LARGE CAPACITY ACCESSORY KARABINERS

These are very useful bits of kit, as they give you somewhere to stow an axe when placing an ice screw or when at belays. They consist of a large karabiner with a snap opening, often shaped to fit securely around the side of your harness. Two of these are useful, one either side of you, and they can also be used to carry a number of ice screws for quick selection and use.

HELMET VISOR AND GOGGLES

An addition to standard kit may be a visor for the climbing helmet or a pair of goggles. Ice, in particular that which has frozen very quickly and is brittle, or that with little air content, tends to break off in chips. This can be very off-putting for the leader at the very least, and can be extremely dangerous, as being hit in the face by a large chunk of ice could cause severe eye injury. Any attentive second, positioned at the bottom of an ice pitch, will also welcome the extra security.

A Perspex visor attached to the climbing helmet is one answer, with a number of manufacturers offering this option. A simpler alternative will be to wear light or clear-lensed ski goggles.

A helmet with a Perspex visor attached. This can be raised or lowered as required

A thread hook. This one has a protective rubber cover over the spike and a spanner built into the handle, useful for tightening axe-head nuts

USING ICE PROTECTION

NATURAL THREADS

A threaded anchor, or one that can be used as a running belay whilst a pitch is being led, is the term given to the use of natural ice for protection, such as when a sling is placed around a large icicle. The strength of the thread will only ever be as strong as the ice and its associated bond to the understructure, and great caution should be exercised before attaching any system to an anchor such as this. Icicles, in particular, may be structurally unsound, and the section that joins on to the lower surface may have meagre adhesion. Indeed, it may not be touching at all, and simply have a layer of snow masking the gap. This can also be true of the top edge of an icicle, for instance where it has dropped off from its original position and refrozen into place. Digging down a little should give you an answer, although if the use of the thread is critical, care should be taken to ensure that it is not disturbed any more than is necessary. If in any doubt, a different solution should be found.

The quality of the ice making up the thread can be hard to judge, although ice that has spent some time building up will be more stable than brittle ice that has formed as the result of a rapid freeze. Information can be gained whilst climbing, as the shattering of ice under axe and crampons will give warning of fragile conditions.

In extreme cases it may be possible to climb through a hole in the ice, thus threading both the leader and trailing rope at the same time. This sometimes happens with mixed routes, when leaving the rock and stepping on to the ice. Ensure that the rope is not going to become snagged by a downwards-facing icicle, or damaged by any sharp edges.

Natural drainage lines give good sport when frozen

ICE BOLLARD

The ice bollard is an effective but somewhat time-consuming method of arranging an anchor. It will most often be used for a lower or abseil descent, but it could also be utilized for belaying a climber up. The time that the anchor takes to construct is one of its disadvantages, and it can be quite tiring as well. Thus, it would only be in exceptional circumstances that a leader would choose to use one. However, in descent there may be a problem with having sufficient gear available to carry out multiple abseils, and the bollard, in this situation, requires no gear to be left behind.

It is, as the name suggests, a bollard (or mushroom shape) similar in design to the snow bollard, albeit on a smaller scale, and is chipped out of the available ice with an ice axe. It will only ever be as strong as the ice from which it is made and so a suitable location needs to be found that not only offers ice of good quality, for instance that does not shatter when struck, but that is also of a sufficient depth for the bollard to have holding power when constructed. Locating a slightly pronounced boss of ice would be advantageous, as it will make the creation of the bollard a little easier, but examination should be made to ensure that the bulging is not due to an ice fracture or some other undesirable feature.

An ice bollard will generally be around 30-40cm (12-16in) in diameter, with a depth of around 10cm (4in). This will vary, given different ice conditions, but the width will never normally be much less than 30cm (12in), as there would otherwise be too high a chance of any fractures within the ice pack meeting and causing the bollard to fail.

To start making it, select a suitable area of ice and scratch out an outline of the area to be cut with the axe pick. This should be horseshoe-shaped, and the lower ends must not meet, otherwise its strength would be severely reduced. The pick of the axe is now used to carefully cut around the shape, chipping along the line drawn. Take care to not cut or damage the inner bollard section. Once the basic outline has been cut, use a combination of axe pick and adze to enlarge it until the desired shape and depth is obtained. It should be mushroomed along the top edge, forming a lip under which the rope or a sling can sit securely with no chance of rolling off. If used for an abseil anchor, the rope can be placed directly around it, as the subsequent retrieval should be quite straightforward. If it is to be used for a lower or belay, a sling could be placed around it and a stance taken up a suitable distance below.

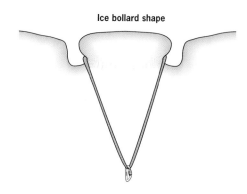

Ice bollard shape

An ice bollard from underneath, showing the mushroom shape

ICE SCREW PLACEMENTS

Ice screws used to be very awkward to place, requiring a cranking motion with the hammer or axe pick through the eye of the screw to get it to wind all of the way in, after it had been gently tapped whilst being rotated. This procedure took two hands, not something that is desirable, or even possible, when on steep ice.

Modern screws are very different, and money is well spent on choosing a good design with a large bore, prominent thread, easy wind-in mechanism and well profiled cutting teeth, four being the optimum.

The placement of an ice screw will only ever be as good as the ice into which it is made. If any dinner-plating appears (the shattering of surface ice, often breaking away in large plates), as the screw is wound in, it should be removed, the rotten ice removed with the axe, the surface cut down to an area flat enough to allow the hanger of the screw to rotate and the placement continued.

The screw needs to be held between hip and chest level, and placed at 90 degrees to the surface of the ice. Overreaching, particularly above the climber, although tempting, will not result in an efficient or even safe placement.

Efficiently placing an ice screw on the lead

Placements into good quality ice using modern screws should be a relatively simple process. The cutting teeth are rotated back and forwards for about half a turn three or four times in order to roughen the surface and so aid the teeth initially biting. Then the screw is wound in until it is fully home, ensuring that the hanger is on the downslope side in the direction of loading and that any folding handle mechanism is placed back in its correct position to avoid it snagging on the rope or extender.

The screw is designed to extrude a solid column of ice from its core as it is wound in, which helps to prevent the ice from being overstressed or shattering. Be careful if this core exhibits signs of melting or significant air pockets or gaps. If so the screw should be removed and another area tried.

It is important that the core of ice that remains inside the screw is removed once it has been extracted from its placement. This can be done by either gently warming the tube a little by placing it in a pocket for a short while, or by using a tool such as a V-thread hook and prodding it out. The screw will be unusable if this core is not removed and it freezes into place. Although gently tapping on the head of the screw may help to ease the core out, care should be taken not to hit the thread as this may damage it irretrievably and render the screw useless for future use.

Ice screws need a bit of maintenance after use, and should be properly dried out, rather than left in a rucksack. An application of a silicone-based lubricant is well worth doing, especially if they are not to be used for some period of time, as it will not only prevent corrosion but also help the screw to preserve its ice core clearing capability for the future. Regular checks should be made to ensure that they are kept sharp, and that the cutting teeth do not become burred or blunt. When sharpening is needed, it should only be carried out using a small hand file and not any form of mechanical grinder. Filing should be carried out so that the fine geometry of the screw's cutting edges is maintained, as any change in shape of the cutting teeth will dramatically alter its performance. Alternatively, you could send the screw away for professional re-sharpening on a specialist machine.

When being used as a belay anchor, ice screws should always be used in pairs, as the effect of shock-loading a single screw can easily be enough for the placement to fail. To avoid the chance of any dinner-plating causing problems, with the shattered area around one screw running into the ice around the other, the screws should be placed a metre (39in) apart diagonally. They should then be either brought to one point, using an equalized sling, or tied into using the rope, adjusted so that each screw takes exactly half the load.

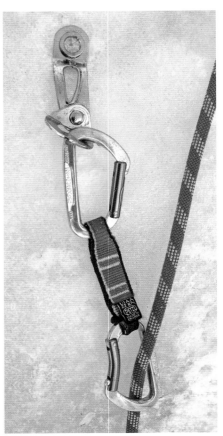

An ice screw with a rotating hanger eye

If the screw has not been fully wound home before it bottoms out, in other words it touches the underlying rock and cannot be seated any further, it needs to be tied off in order to reduce leverage. This can be done by clove hitching a sling over the shaft of the screw, pushed up flush with the ice. Alternatively, and if the problem is expected, an extender can be placed on the shaft with the top karabiner having been removed. The screw can now be wound in to its final position and the lower karabiner, which is still attached, clipped as normal. Some types of screw have a facility for moving the eye down the shaft in case they do bottom out, and it may be worth seeking these out if you are going to make a habit of climbing on thin ice.

If the screws are being used for some period of time, perhaps when rigging ropes on an icefall or when practising crevasse rescue, there is a chance that they could have their strength compromised by the heat of the sun. Solar absorption may occur that will slightly warm the screw and weaken the placement. To help to avoid this problem, once the screw has been placed into the ice, a few centimetres (couple of inches) of snow or ice can be packed over the top, helping to shield it from the heat of the sun.

ICE HOOKS

The placement of ice hooks needs to be carefully considered, as their holding power in the event of a shock-loading can be quite low. This is not the fault of the hook itself, more due to the nature of the ice into which it has been placed. They are often used to hook into existing holes made by axe picks on steep ground and used as resting points or temporary runners until a better ice screw placement can be made. Hammering them into pure ice may cause the surrounding area to shatter, making the placement less secure. They are useful, however, where ice and turf meet at awkward points, such as in thin corner cracks. Here they can be driven in and they hold well. The only problem is then getting them out again!

ABALAKOV, OR V THREAD ANCHORS

This is potentially a very strong and versatile method of anchoring on ice, and it has a big advantage in that, in a retreat situation, it leaves no expensive equipment behind. It can be used in ascent as well, should the situation dictate, and such a case may be where only one ice screw is left for the belayer to use and a second anchor needs to be found.

The depth of the holes that are drilled determines the overall strength of the anchor, and it will only be as good as the ice into which it is constructed. After some practice it should only take a little time to put together. Two or more threads can be constructed and linked so as to share the load, if it is felt desirable. If doing so, each set of holes needs to be not less than 50cm (20in) apart.

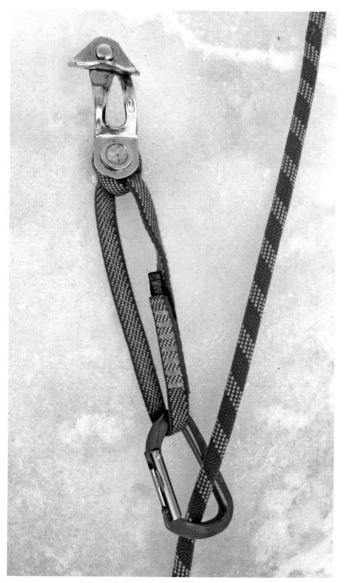

Using an extender to reduce the leverage on an ice screw

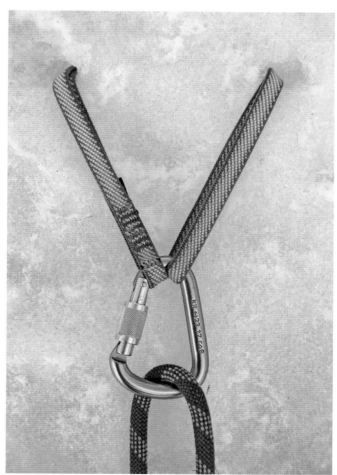

A threaded sling, with the ends clipped together with a karabiner

A long ice screw with a tilting hanger is ideal for making a thread, and it will be useful to have a thread-hook to hand. The rope or cord to be threaded could be some that is carried as spare in the rucksack and cut to length as required, or in an emergency it could be something like a prusik loop that has been unpicked. A thin sling could also be used, with the ends being simply clipped together with a screwgate karabiner.

First, select an area of homogeneous ice, which displays no evidence of the potential to crack or shatter. If the ice is very hard, tap a small starter-hole with the ice axe, place the screw at an outside angle of 45–60 degrees to the ice and wind it fully in. Two holes will have to be cut in the ice, and these must meet at an internal angle of between 60 and 90 degrees. Withdraw the screw and wind it in from the opposite angle, so that the teeth end up cutting into the end of the first hole. This second placement must not be started closer than 10cm (4in) from the first. Both of these holes also need to be arranged at 90 degrees vertically to the slope. On many qualities of ice, it is possible to discern the outline of the screw as it goes in, making the task of assessing the screwing angle a bit easier.

Remove the screw and thread the cord or sling through the tunnel system, and either knot it or clip it together to give an attachment point. Make sure that the apex of the cord/sling, the point at which the load is applied, is at an angle of no more than 90 degrees.

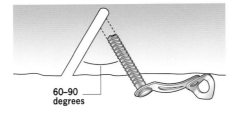

The angles for drilling an ice thread

If a second thread is going to be used to back up the first, it should be placed away at a 45-degree angle from the original one, and with the nearest holes no closer than 50cm (20in) from each other. If a third is to be used, the same criteria apply.

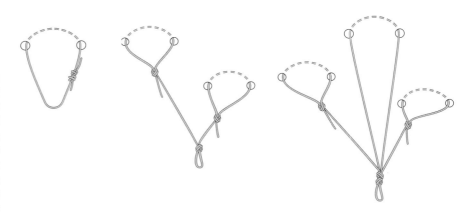

Linking adjacent ice threads

ICE SCREW RETRIEVAL

In some extreme circumstances it may be decided to abseil using a single ice screw. Although other methods of organizing an abseil anchor will be more appropriate and safer, such as an Abalakov thread, snow bollard or rock anchors, retrieval of a screw may be essential if gear is at a premium and everything must be done to keep equipment losses to a minimum. However, the pros and cons of committing weight to a single screw should be thoroughly considered, and if there is any chance of anchor failure a more secure method should be sought. This technique is one that is firmly in the 'rope tricks' category, but may prove useful to know, not least to impress your friends!

The screw is wound into a suitably strong section of ice, with the amount of complete turns that it took to place it being remembered. The hanger should end up a short distance above the top of the ice, perhaps a centimetre (half an inch) or so, as the rope used for the abseil will fit between it and the surface. The hanger should also end up pointing upslope, at 180 degrees to the direction of the abseil.

A length of cord or an untied prusik loop is fastened on to the eye of the screw with a secure knot, such as half a double fisherman's. This cord is then wrapped

around the top of the screw in the opposite direction to the teeth. In other words, as the screw was placed in a clockwise direction, the cord will be wound round it anti-clockwise. The number of wraps should be a couple more than the turns that secured the screw in the first place.

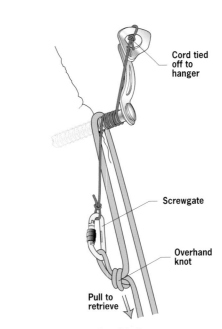

Cord tied off to hanger

Screwgate

Overhand knot

Pull to retrieve

The set-up for a retrievable ice screw system

The abseil rope is positioned over the screw, with its centre at the top. It is important that it does not exert any leverage, and it should sit snugly between the screw's hanger and the ice with no gap between either. A small overhand knot on the bight is tied on to one side of the abseil rope, close to the ice screw, and the end of the cord is clipped into this with a screwgate karabiner.

Once the abseil is completed, retrieval of the ice screw is accomplished by a firm and constant pull on the overhand knot side of the abseil rope. Doing this will cause the screw to unwind and it will eventually come out of the ice and fall down the slope attached to the rope. Care should be taken when the ropes are pulled for retrieval, as the ice screw will be accelerating towards the bottom of the rope. Everyone not involved should be kept out of the way, and the person doing the pulling should keep careful watch so that they can avoid any contact with the screw as it falls to the ground.

If two ropes are being used and are of different colours, it will be easy to remember which one to pull. If it is the same rope, however, it would be a good idea to clip a free-running karabiner on to the relevant side, and this will provide a reminder once the end of the abseil has been reached.

Once again, I should emphasize that this is a last-in-the-line technique, and should only be used if all other far more sensible methods have been excluded.

REDUCING THE LOAD ON AN ICE SCREW

The loading on any ice screw should be kept to the minimum. It will only be as strong as the ice into which it is placed and, although this will often be very strong, reducing the chance of a screw coming out under load is a wise precaution.

The simplest way to do this is to use a shock-absorbing, or screamer sling at key placements. This sling resembles an extender, except it is made up of a number of folds of tape sewn together. The amount and type of stitching is very carefully calculated, as it is designed to tear at a given loading. This allows the load to be partially taken by the sling itself, reducing the shock effect on the screw placement. Once fully torn open, the extender resembles a normal large sling, so there is no chance of the rope ever becoming detached.

The use of a shock-absorbing sling is a good idea on multi-pitch climbs. When leaving the stance of a multi-pitch route, protection should be placed as soon as possible, most often by placing it from the stance itself, in order to reduce the fall factor (see Appendix II) and subsequent shock-loading on the belay system. Using a shock-absorbing sling here will mean that any loading to the system created by a fall on the first few moves of the next pitch will be decreased by the sling ripping and protecting the screw placement, which in turn will keep the loading away from the anchor system.

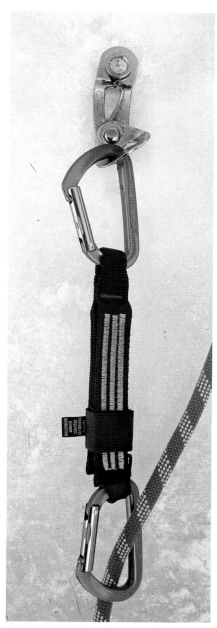

A shock-absorbing sling on an ice screw placement

An anchor system with the first protection of the next pitch clipped with a shock-absorbing sling

CLIMBING STYLE

Swinging a technical ice tool can be likened to the effect of cracking a whip. The tool is brought forward using power from the shoulder and elbow, and a flick of the wrist just at the end of the swing serves to drive the pick home efficiently. It may take a few moves to get used to the ice quality on any particular climb, as it is important that the pick is not over-driven into the ice as this will make it time-consuming and tiring to remove, using up valuable energy. Make the most of ripples on the surface or old axe placements, and resort to hooking on these if possible, maybe just with the slightest of taps. Keep a downwards loading at all times when moving up, otherwise the pick could pop out as you get level with it.

When climbing on steep ground, try to avoid forming a narrow X shape. The main problem here is that there is a chance that tools placed too close together can cause the ice to fracture. As this predominantly happens across the horizontal plane, there is a chance that as you place one, if the ice shatters the other could pop out. It also makes balance difficult as each axe is moved out and up.

Use a staggered tool style, where one is always placed above the other and at the centre line of your body. This is known as the tripod system, where feet are placed apart and at the same level, and a tool swung into the ice to create the top point. Straighten your supporting arm, move your body away from the ice and take a number of small steps to move your feet higher, avoiding the temptation to move up in one big leap. Now straighten your body and swing the other axe in and above the first, so that the hand holding this axe is around the level of the head of the other. By moving in this manner you will keep well in balance, save energy and reduce the possibility of the axes unseating each other through ice fracture.

Place your feet as efficiently as possible, using as little force as you can to get the points to grip, and avoid the temptation to kick in hard. This is both tiring and unnecessary, as the force of your boot going in could shatter the ice or cause the points to bounce straight back out. Make sure that, once they are placed, you do not wriggle them, raise or drop your heels.

Waterfall climbing

Standing straight to swing the axe

Moving the body away from the ice to allow the feet to be moved up

A stable tripod position, with the body in balance and the legs well braced

RESTING

As steep ice is very demanding on both arms and legs, gaining a resting position at intervals is advantageous. The simplest way to rest will be to let go of the axes every now and then, and shake out. This is much simplified with the use of a leashless tool system, although those with fast clipper leashes will be almost as good. Obviously, the axe needs to be well secured into the ice, as to drop one at this stage would not be a good idea. Make sure that the pick is well secured. If this cannot be guaranteed, for instance where the ice is very thin, you may need to hang the axe over a shoulder. Alternatively, although not as efficient, you could clip the axe to your body using a large karabiner or spring clip designed for the job.

Efficient use of your feet will go a long way to help achieve a rest. Bridging will help, and can often lead to a position where both hands can be dropped down by your side for a breather, your weight and balance being taken by your feet. On ice pillars, it is possible to wrap a leg around the back of the pillar and heel-hook it. This will be far simpler if a heel spur is being used, as the foot can be placed at a more natural angle. Free-hanging icicles sometimes offer the chance of a body-wedge behind, perhaps with one crampon on rock and the other on ice.

Resting on gear whilst climbing on steep ice will often be deemed as cheating. However, it may be necessary in order to relieve aching arms and legs, and if the only alternative is to tire to the extent that you are going to fall off, many will not hesitate to do so.

The simplest rest will be to place a good ice screw and have your belayer take the rope in tight. This will allow you to drop your arms down to your side and shake out, relaxing the tension on your calf muscles. If you are going to be there for any time, you may elect to clip a short extender or cowstail to the screw so that your belayer can also relax for a moment. It is essential, though, that they do not let go of the rope at all, as they will be your back-up if the screw you are resting on should fail.

Another alternative is to have the rope hooked over the top of a well placed axe. This can be used as a very quick method of resting, but the axe must obviously be very secure. The rope is simply looped over the top right next to the ice, and the belayer takes in tight.

Careful footwork will go a long way to letting you climb further before tiring

MIXED CLIMBING

This is where snow, ice and rock are present on a climb, often in equal measures. It may be that some sections of the route are totally on rock, requiring the use of the dry tooling techniques outlined below, before transferring to an icicle or snow-filled gully. Alternatively, it may be the ascent of a snow-covered summer rock route, where a variety of climbing techniques, such as using frozen turf for axe placements, are required to succeed. Mixed climbing often presents a climber with the ultimate series of technical problems, often steep or overhanging and with any chances of a rest few and far between. However, for many it is the epitome of movement on technical terrain, and they seek it out to the exclusion of all else.

EQUIPMENT

There is no particularly specialized kit needed for mixed climbing. A hybrid rack from summer and ice climbing will often be adequate, and some sections of rock may even be bolted and simply require the use of extenders. Axes and crampons can also be decided upon according to personal preference and to the conditions expected, and they will usually be those previously used for winter climbing. The exception would be when extended areas of rock are to be crossed, where mono-point crampons, as used for dry tooling, would be better suited.

WARTHOGS

A drive-in ice screw, these are a very useful addition to your rack, particularly when climbing routes that have frozen turf exposed. This is like reinforced ice and can make for excellent protection placements. The presence of rock particles in the turf would destroy any normal ice screw, but the solid-section warthog is strong enough to be pounded in with a hammer without deforming.

Removal is the same as for a conventional screw, with it being wound in an anti-clockwise direction.

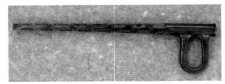

A warthog

PITONS

This type of hammer-in rock protection, also known as pegs, is useful where no other options exist. They are being introduced here, but obviously have uses in other areas such as some summer rock climbing situations or in gullies. Take care when placing them as local ethics may ban their use, particularly on established routes or summer rock climbs being attempted under winter conditions. This is because their placement and removal can permanently scar the rock, changing the route forever.

They are available in a variety of shapes and sizes, so can fit a variety of crack widths. They are best placed in horizontal cracks, although vertical placements are quite secure with some designs. Select the one that you think will fit and place it by hand. It should fit in for just over half its length before being gripped by the rock. Now hammer it home so that the eye is flush with the surface. A ringing tone that steadily increases in pitch as you hammer the piton in is a sign that it is the right size.

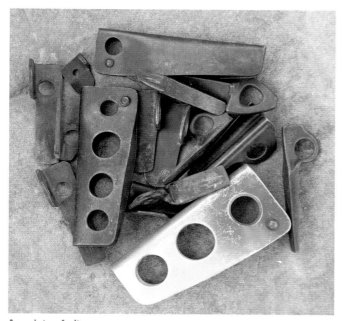

A variety of pitons

A piton tied off with a sling to reduce leverage

If you have no option but to leave a length of the piton sticking out from the crack, perhaps because it has bottomed out, which is when the piton is longer than the depth of the crack, it needs to be tied off to reduce leverage in much the same way that an ice screw would. Use a short thin sling and clove hitch it around the piton up tight against the rock. Inverting the clove hitch (see 'Knots' section) may help to keep it snug, and placing the piton upside down in some cases will allow the eye to help prevent the sling from working its way off.

Pitons stacked to fit a wide crack

It is possible to stack two or more pitons together if you don't have one of the correct width. This works well with angle pitons, but can be a little trickier to achieve with other shapes. Try to arrange it so that the karabiner attaching your rope to the placement is clipped in to the eye of the piton as close to the rock as possible, or tie it off as above if this is not possible.

Removing pitons is where damage occurs to the rock, as they have to be tapped from one side to the other in order to wear away a small groove, allowing them to slide out. Do this as carefully as you can, and watch out as it loosens because it could ping out and be dropped down the route. Having a piece of old cord or tape threaded through the eye will prevent this happening, but don't be tempted to hit a piton that still has a karabiner attached, as the karabiner itself could be damaged by the blows from the hammer.

TECHNIQUES

As mixed climbing is a hybrid between ice and gully climbing, rock climbing and dry tooling, the techniques for climbing these types of route are all relevant here, obviously depending upon the terrain being crossed at any given time. The skill is in knowing which technique is appropriate where, and adapting accordingly.

DRY TOOLING

This is the climbing of areas of rock where either no or very little snow or ice is present for the entire route. Strictly speaking it could be placed under the 'Summer' section, but as the use of axes and crampons is involved, and due to its close ties with mixed climbing, it has found its way into this section.

Dry tooling is a useful skill to practise, as large expanses of rock may have to be crossed on routes even when areas of snow and ice are expected. As a discipline in its own right, it could be said to have parallels with sport climbing, where progress is made up a route using bolted protection as a safeguard against a fall. However, some dry tooling routes also require the placing of protection on the lead, and it is here that traditional rock climbing placements are used.

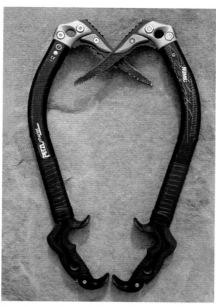

A pair of technical dry tooling axes

A metal-visored helmet

EQUIPMENT

Bearing in mind that a high percentage of routes will be bolted, a rack of extenders, similar to those carried on sport climbs, will be useful. Clothing should be lightweight and snug fitting, as there may be some athletic manoeuvres that need to be completed, and crampons could catch when passing a leg over an arm for a figure of four, for example (see p. 185).

CRAMPONS AND BOOTS

Most dry toolers will opt for mono-point crampons, where a single front-point projects forward rather than the more normal two. This is because the single point can be effectively placed into thin crack lines and small pockets, providing purchase where a twin pointed crampon would be unable to fit.

Those taking the sport seriously will most likely invest in a pair of fruit boots, where boot and crampon are combined. These are lighter in weight than a conventional boot and crampon pairing, and are more sensitive to use when dealing with small holds. They are expensive however, and a happy medium is often sought by fashioning a homemade pair, where the front section of a mono-point crampon is screwed to the underneath of a pair of stiff, semi-retired boots that have had their soles removed.

Heel spurs have become less popular in recent years and they are banned in many dry tooling competitions. Ascents of climbs are now said to be with or without them, sometimes making quite a difference to the grade. You will need to find out the local protocol for the area where you wish to climb before using them either for a serious route or competitively.

AXES

These tend to be quite different to those used for winter climbing, although they do also have their place in mixed and top-end ice climbing disciplines. Firstly, they will just have a pick, with no hammer or adze on the opposite side of the head. This is because these features are not likely to be needed on pure rock routes, and their presence could cause facial injury if an axe slipped off a hold and hit you in the head.

Secondly, there will be no spike at the end of the handle, as they will not be used in a walking mode on snow or ice and also, again, to prevent injury.

Thirdly, the handle section will be radically pronounced, often with an extra protruding thumb grip above the main section. This allows a variety of holds to be made on the shaft while climbing, even with two hands holding the same axe when swapping hands. The pronounced curves also make it easier to hook one axe over the other when performing certain manoeuvres.

As your hand will be holding the shaft at different heights, it is worth wrapping a tape around it from the top of the handle to the head to give you a better grip.

It is very unusual to see dry tooling axes being used with leashes on, as these can cause injury if you fall and the axe is swirling around your head. Also, the very nature of leashless climbing makes a whole variety of techniques become possible, far more than if there is an attachment to each hand. Just don't drop them!

VISOR

This is a very sensible addition to your helmet, and some come with visors attached. The Perspex one recommended previously for ice climbing is a good idea, and it will at least protect your eyes. A better version will be one that uses a metal criss-cross visor which is very strong and protects your whole face.

At the very least, when starting out use a pair of DIY goggles, especially if using your normal climbing tools. Even then, consider detaching the hammer and adze sections, if possible, for your own safety.

GLOVES

These need to be thin and grippy. Your hands will probably get a few knocks when on the route, but it will also be hot work holding on to the tools, so don't go for anything too padded. A snug fit is also important, with a Velcro wrist closure being useful, otherwise they could be pulled off through use after you have been hanging on them for some time.

TYPES OF HOLD

EDGES

These are probably the commonest of holds, and often provide a secure placement. You may find it best to start with the tip of your axe right at the front of the edge and push it back slowly, waiting for it to drop into a hollow or irregularity. If it does so, it is almost always possible to also hook the second axe tip directly alongside it, known as matching. This obviously saves searching for another hold in the same area.

Be very careful when pulling up on tools on incuts, as if you do not keep the pull downwards the tips will fly off without warning. Dropping your shoulder when moving up helps to prevent this, and this is in fact the key to many dry tooling manoeuvres.

Tools matched on an incut

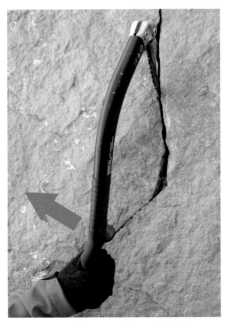

Torquing a tool in a crack, maintaining sideways pressure

CRACKS

The way in which these are used depends upon their depth, width and shape. A thin S-shaped crack, for example, can have the tip of the pick slid into it, and any downward pressure will keep it in place. Take care not to force too much of the pick in here, as it can jam under body weight and be very difficult to extract.

A more uniform straight crack will need a slightly different approach. Place the pick in as far as it needs to go, and then exert a sideways pressure to the shaft. This is known as torquing, and the leverage thus created will be enough to keep the axe in place. Make sure that you keep the same degree of pull on the shaft all the way through the move as you climb up, otherwise grip will be lost.

If there is a small pebble or chockstone in the crack, place the pick above this. It will let you use the hold with far less effort than torquing, and be less prone to popping out unexpectedly.

Thin horizontal cracks can be used in the same manner as edges, with the tip of the pick being placed on them. If this is not possible, the axe can be presented horizontally and the shaft pulled down on, wedging the pick into place. Be careful when doing this though, as a huge amount of pressure is exerted on to the tip of the pick and it could snap.

Wider horizontal cracks can have the entire head and shaft section placed into

The mechanics of a stein pull

them, leaving just a small section of handle to pull down on. Alternatively, the handle can be pushed right in, just leaving part of the head protruding as a hand hold.

STEIN PULLS

This is a very effective way of using the tool, and can be handy in a variety of situations. It uses the pick and the top of the head section of the axe in opposition, a little like the action when using a pickaxe. The tip is placed on a suitable ledge or incut, with the top of the tool pushing against the rock just above. Outward pressure on the handle will keep the tool in place and provide a very secure placement.

Stein pulls can be used on holds overhead, undercuts, or even as side pulls if the direction of loading will be appropriate.

HAMMER AND ADZE PLACEMENTS

It is quite possible to use both the hammer and adze sections of tools to jam into cracks or hook over edges. Although technical dry tooling axes will not have them fitted, you may be starting out with an old pair of ice tools, or perhaps you have come across a section of blank ground whilst on a mixed route.

Their main advantage is the increase in width over the pick, with an adze in particular giving a vast increase in the size range of cracks that can be used. Be extremely careful, even when wearing face protection, as the pick of the axe will be pointing towards you and could cause injury if the axe popped off the hold.

Short tooling to reach a higher hold

TECHNIQUES

There are so many ways in which the thin picks of your tools can be used in cracks and on holds that they are almost countless, and tools can even be hooked on to each other when performing certain moves. What is more important is the way in which you use the placement once it is made, and in particular how you use the rest of your body in order to save energy and avoid tiring your arms excessively.

SHORT TOOLING

This is where you gain extra height by pulling up on the shaft of one well placed tool, using the extra finger grip and the tape around the shaft. With the axe on a hold, store the other one (covered below) and move your hands one at a time as far as is needed up the shaft. Now recover your second axe and make the move to the hold that you want.

SWAPPING TOOLS

This is useful, both when moving up and when traversing to one side. If you have a good hold with one tool, you might as well keep it on there as you go past. Thus, store the other axe, match your hands on the good tool, retrieve the stored axe and place it where required. This demonstrates one of the great benefits of leashless climbing, for climbing ice as well as rock, in that you have the flexibility to perform manoeuvres such as this, which would be impossible to do if you were attached to each tool.

FOOTWORK

Take time and care when placing your crampon points, as it is all too common to hear an awful scrabbling and scraping noise as someone attempts to get their points to stick. They are not magic, and require some thought and precision to get into the right place. Make each movement of your feet count, because while they are not on the rock the majority of your weight will be on your arms, and it will become tiring.

The starting position for swapping tools on a traverse

Stow the left tool over your shoulder and hold the other tool above the finger grip

Edging is quite possible, using the side points of the crampon, and this is often desirable, as it will give your calf muscles the chance to have a rest.

Once you have placed your foot, particularly on small holds and incuts, try not to move it as you deal with the other foot or tools, as any slight change in angle or torsion could be enough to make it slide off the hold.

Heel spurs can be used to good effect (one reason why their use is frowned upon in some areas!) for heel-hooking and resting manoeuvres. In particular, the negotiating of the lip of a roof could be eased considerably if a spurred boot is used in the same manner as a rock boot would be in summer. However, as mentioned before, their use is not tolerated in some areas and, from a purely practical point of view, having the sharp spike sticking out from the back of your foot creates all sorts of possibilities for injury.

STORING TOOLS ON A ROUTE

There may be times when you need to store a tool, such as when short tooling or swapping over. There are a variety of ways to do this, with the main criterion being not to drop it!

Hooking the pick over your shoulder is one way. Some serious toolers add Velcro to both the tool and climbing jacket to avoid dropping it from this position when performing awkward moves. Another option is to hook it over the thumb of the hand holding the securing tool, useful when clipping a piece of gear.

For those with a large mouth, holding the axe between your teeth is an option, although it must be said that many climbers do not like having a shaft in their mouths. Alternatively, simply hooking the axe over the one that is placed, with the pick going over the recessed head or through the eye, will be secure in many situations.

Retrieve the stowed axe with your right hand and place it on the rock

A resting position!

A figure of four

ADVANCED MANOEUVRES

There are so many possibilities for being acrobatic, especially with leashless tools and heel spurs, that anyone who is flexible will have a great time finding out what is possible. There are a couple of techniques that are worth mentioning, both of which serve to gain extra reach where holds have stopped for some distance, particularly on roof sections where keeping your footing is desperately hard, and these are the figure of four and the figure of nine. Although putting a lot of strain on the supporting tool and arm, they are the key to climbing sections of many long roof climbs across the world. Time spent practising them, in a controlled situation on a top rope, will be well spent.

FIGURE OF FOUR

From a hanging position, arrange your leg so that it is across the top of the opposite arm, so right leg over left arm or vice versa. The aim is to get your knee at the same point as your elbow. With the other leg pushing against the rock to keep you steady, you can now reach forwards a lot farther with your free arm and in more control than you would otherwise be.

FIGURE OF NINE

This is similar to the figure of four, except that the same side leg is hooked over the arm. Thus, left leg over left arm or right leg over right arm. This is a useful method for negotiating stretches of roof, where a figure of four is used to start with, and once you have made the next tool placement a figure of nine, using the same leg, is arranged. After the next tool placement, a figure of four is again appropriate, and so on until the end of the section.

RESTING

Apart from obvious hands-off rests where your feet take all the weight, it is possible to use your tools to give your arms a bit of respite. Any secure axe placement can be used, and because of the curved nature of the tool handle, various parts can be hooked around it to give your forearms a rest. Shoulders, knees and upper arms can all be secured, giving you a little time at least to shake out and ponder the route ahead.

Alpine territory

6: ALPINE CLIMBING

Alpine climbing is generally defined as the ascent of peaks in the continental Alpine regions, often in snowy conditions and after a glacier approach, but where extremes of altitude are not usually a major factor. This last feature highlights the difference between Alpine and expedition climbing, the latter being where a considerable amount of time may have to be taken in order to acclimatize to altitude, before the technical climbing begins.

OBJECTIVES

It is important that you have a sensible progression of objectives on an Alpine climbing trip. To expect to be able to climb to the summit of the highest peak in the area a day after arriving is not likely to be a practical target. Don't try to cram too much in. Rest days must be included, and most climbers will find that one rest day after a big two-day trip is needed. Factor in a couple of days lost to bad weather, add a couple of one-day routes accessed by cable car at the start of the trip, and in a two-week holiday you could therefore expect to climb four to six summits of reasonable height, with anything more than this being a bonus.

VALLEY BASE

Most climbers will opt for tented accommodation as a valley base. The advantage here is that you have your own space, and it is easy to uproot and travel to another area if trying to dodge poor weather. Financially, a campsite will usually work out a lot cheaper than other forms of accommodation, and negotiation with the owners will often result in a reduction of the charge for the nights that you are on the hill and not using the camp facilities.

Although rough camping away from commercial sites is a tempting option I always like to stay at a site that offers good facilities, if at a cost, as I know that my property will be looked after whilst I'm away on the hill.

Cable cars and other means of uplift give easy access to the mountains in some areas

A large Alpine hut

USING HUTS

Many of the Alpine regions are well provided with high-level huts and refuges. These provide a very good and often crucial base for the night prior to the ascent of a nearby peak or objective. They range from very basic, offering little more than four walls and sleeping platforms, to those that are more akin to hotels, with restaurant and bar service amongst their attractions.

Bear in mind that stocking a hut is often a costly business, frequently requiring the use of a helicopter to ferry in goods, so the price that you pay will reflect this. The comfort that you gain will often be worth the expense though, as you will be warm and dry, well fed and need only carry up to the hut the gear for the subsequent climb, as blankets and mattresses are often supplied.

Some huts will prepare your own food for you at a small fee. You supply them with the complete raw ingredients, say pasta and sauce, they cook it and charge you for the fuel and time. This will work out cheaper than buying meals on site, but even some huts that offer this service may not be able to provide it at peak times, as the kitchen will be busy cooking meals for restaurant patrons.

Another option that many take is to book bed space in the hut but do the catering themselves. If you choose this option, it obviously means that you will be carrying a little more equipment. However, apart from bivouacking nearby, it often works out as being the cheapest option. Some huts provide an area where cooking can be done, others will not permit it to be done on the premises, so you will have to move away a little and cook outside.

You would normally arrange to arrive at the hut at around midday to mid-afternoon. This will give you time to get settled in, sort out kit, eat and rest. It is also worth taking time to find the best way from the hut to the start of your intended route to save valuable time early next morning.

Many climbers take to their beds at around 20.00hrs or earlier. This is because many will be up at 03.00 or so the next day, particularly if a snow or glacier approach to the climb is involved, so that a lot of the initial approach to the route can be covered before the sun hits the mountains, making the snow soft and the going arduous. Being organized is extremely important, getting as much kit as possible ready the night before, simply leaving getting dressed, breakfast and ablutions to be done in the morning.

Have a head-torch to hand for the morning departure and something that I never stay in a hut without is a set of foam earplugs. As rooms commonly accommodate 20 or more slumbering people, getting a good night's sleep would, for me at least, be very difficult without dulling out the noise of a lot of snoring mountaineers!

Many huts give a discounted rate on their tariff for members of home-nation Alpine clubs or mountaineering councils where a reciprocal agreement has been taken up. Check this with the area before you go, as it can save you a lot of money in the long run.

gives you the chance to meet and talk to other climbers during the day. However, if you prefer not to do this, or are remote from any hut, then you will need to cook for yourself on a good quality stove. If you are intent on saving as much weight as possible, and are sleeping below the snowline so don't need to melt snow for water, you may elect to do without a stove at all. There is nothing wrong with cold pasta, meat, cheese and bread as a meal, along with water, and you may decide that this is the way ahead, especially if you are only spending one night at the bivi site. However, the psychological benefit of having the ability to eat a hot meal, along with hot drinks, will often far outdo the weight concern, and most climbers opting for a bivi will have a stove with them. Indeed, many find the idea of waking up during the hours of darkness and readying themselves for a day on the hill without a hot drink or two inside them to be a nightmare scenario, and would never consider continuing without one.

You will probably not be taking your bivi kit on the hill with you, unless you are doing a traverse or otherwise intending to spend the night out or take a different descent route, so most of it can be left behind at the bivi site. It is worth packing it away into a plastic bag and placing it discreetly away from any paths, making sure that the place is easily identifiable on your return!

Camping is also an alternative way of spending time high in the hills, but of course this will have a weight penalty. It is also very difficult finding somewhere that is flat enough to pitch a tent, especially in areas near heavily glaciated terrain and boulder fields. A tent is a good choice if you are intending to spend two or three days at the same site, perhaps doing a number of routes from a single base. Using a nearby cable car or funicular rail system to take a lot of the walking out of getting there in the first place is a useful idea.

BIVOUACKING

This may be done for a number of reasons, either financial or for convenience near to the start of a route. For the former motive, a bivouac, more commonly known as a bivi, can be done near the site of an existing hut or refuge. You are then able to make the most of waymarking and signposting in the area, making the start of your climbing day easier during the hours of darkness. Some regions also offer very basic bivouac huts, consisting of four walls and a roof, perhaps with sleeping platforms and not much else. Although many of these rely on an honesty system for payment, you may find that they are preferable to carrying your own bivi shelter or tent, and will often be a lot more spacious. However, you may also have to share them with other occupants, and during busy times there may be little

or no room for you at all, leaving you little alternative in poor weather but to descend.

A bivi bag of some description will be the minimum needed for a comfortable and dry night out on the hill if a refuge is not being used. A breathable fabric is essential, otherwise the condensation that builds up during the night will soak you. It should also be large enough so that you can use a good quality sleeping bag inside it, as the nights at altitude will be very cold. A good sleeping mat is also important, both to insulate you from the ground and to help smooth out any bumps.

There is no reason why you can't sleep away from the hut but buy your meals there. This would save having to carry a lot of cooking gear with you, and at least

GETTING TO THE START OF A ROUTE

Route-finding, particularly in complicated lower areas that may include glaciated terrain and large areas of boulders and moraine, is a difficult task at the best of times, and more so in the dark, which is when you will very likely be heading out for your route.

Many of the popular mountain areas have a good network of paths that lead to the huts and refuges, and these often continue on a little beyond towards some of the more popular objectives. Signposting is common, as are paint splashes on boulders, and in busy areas you will see paths made by hundreds of pairs of feet heading in the same direction. However, it is important to check your intended route the day before you leave, taking perhaps an hour or so to make sure that you have the right direction located and that you can easily negotiate it in the dark.

If your approach crosses a glacier, make sure that you have all of the necessary equipment to hand so that there is minimum organization needed in the morning. Have all the kit ready and clipped to your harness, such as ice screws and spare karabiners, and have other items such as your food prepared as much as is possible.

LADDERS

A number of routes from huts or popular end-of-path points rely on the use of ladders to negotiate steep sections of cliff. These will commonly be in place where you need to descend to glacier level, but may also be used to descend/ascend blank sections of rock that bar passage onwards. They are becoming more widespread and of greater length each year as glaciers recede. They are generally of a very sound construction, but take care when using them and make sure that there is no debris around that you could kick on to your partner when starting off, or that they could kick on to you. If you are carrying a large rucksack, thus having a high centre of gravity, you may decide to use a rope as a back-up. An Italian hitch on a short sling around one of the higher ladder supports may well do the job, and you could clip in with a screwgate to the abseil loop on your harness. Once you are down, you can safeguard your companion by simply having the rope running over the top rung of the ladder, and controlling it with a belay device on your harness. This means that the rope will be easy to pull through once they are down.

If you are going up a ladder and feel the need to use the rope, place a sling or two on your way as runners. Alternatively, you may find that extenders fit over the rungs, and these will be an excellent choice.

As the ladders are made of metal, they get very cold so your hands will become numb after only a short distance, particularly early in the morning. Wear gloves with a non-slip palm to save any problems.

Using an extender on a ladder rung as a runner for security

Ascending a steep ladder, using a rope for security

Take great care during descent as you will be tired and mistakes can happen

DESCENT

No climb can be claimed as being totally successful until you are safely back down at base again. Alpine days are long and arduous, and it is worth having a cut-off time for your ascent, in order to allow enough daylight to negotiate at least most of the descent under good conditions. Bear in mind that the heat of the day will have had an effect on the snow and ice, and snow bridges, for example, may have been significantly weakened and be prone to collapse. Regular afternoon thunderstorms are often another reason for getting back to safety in good time.

Exhaustion is another factor, as climbing at moderate altitudes is very tiring, leading to a lot of energy being burnt up and a huge amount of liquid being needed just to stay hydrated. Make sure that you have some high calorific value foods for the descent and don't be tempted just to plod on without taking a break for a bite to eat, as it is here that accidents can happen.

On your way up the hill, and particularly when making your initial way up through the complicated lower sections of ground, keep looking behind you to identify features that will subsequently help you on your descent. A GPS unit will obviously help you here, but if you do not have one take note of any unusual or interesting land forms. Cairns, glacial rock piles, unusual sérac formations and protruding ridge lines will

all help, as long as you can remember them for the descent. On very complicated ground, you could even resort to taking a few digital photographs of features as you pass them and use the review button on the descent to match the features to the ground you are crossing.

Remember that once you are back at the hut or bivi site you will have still farther to descend, most likely carrying the extra gear retrieved from the site of your overnight stop. Once again, take a bit of time to eat and drink, as this will not only help you on the way down but will also provide essential fuel for your body to process, regaining energy for the next mountain day.

EQUIPMENT

Climbing in the Alpine regions requires a little more thought and preparation than routes at a lower level may demand. You need to think carefully about weight as your day on the hill will probably be very long, and carrying a lot of unnecessary and heavy kit will slow you down considerably. Much of the equipment used for winter climbing will be very appropriate and can easily be transferred to the higher mountains, but the amount that is carried and the specifications may have to be altered slightly. There are also a few items of kit that may be carried that you will find are unique to glaciated terrain, such as pulleys and lightweight rope ascenders.

AXES AND HAMMERS

The type, style and length of ice tool that you carry will very much depend upon your chosen objective for the trip. If you are heading for a reasonably simple ascent of a snow peak, you may choose to use one axe, as lightweight as possible, and err on the side of the shaft being a little longer than you would use on steep ground. This will most likely have a classic curve to the head, making it suitable for self-arrest, and a good-sized adze and a grip that is easy to hold. However, if you are going to be making an ascent of a technical route and need two tools, a matched pair of 50cm (20in) reverse-curve and bent-shafted axes may be your choice, and these can be exactly the same as you use for lower-altitude ice climbing (see 'Winter Climbing' section).

CRAMPONS

The same goes for crampons as for axes. For the ascent of uncomplicated snow peaks or when traversing snow and ice terrain, a pair of lightweight but good quality crampons, with a pair of horizontal front-points that project a reasonable distance beyond the front boot sole, will be fine. For more technical routes, higher-specification crampons, perhaps with vertical front-points or even single front-points, along with an aggressive set of supporting points, will be required.

The author in the European Alps

TREKKING POLES

Because you will very likely be carrying a heavy load in your rucksack, you may find that trekking poles are of great benefit, taking a good deal (around 30 per cent) of compression loading from your knees and ankles, as well as helping with your balance. A pair of telescopic poles will be the best, as they can be stowed into or alongside your rucksack when not required. Be careful, however, that you are not using them where an ice axe may be more appropriate, such as on snow slopes where a slip could turn into a slide.

SUNGLASSES

Absolutely essential in order to stop snow blindness, a good quality pair of sunglasses is a must when walking or climbing in the sun on snow or ice. Some will incorporate a nose-flap to help prevent burning and lens side-pieces to reduce the amount of indirect light reaching the eyes. They should be manufactured to international standards and be capable of filtering out 100 per cent UVA, UVB and UVC light bands. Manufacturers commonly use a 1–5 scale of filter grading, where 5 is the standard suitable for very high altitude use, and 4 appropriate for most Alpine areas.

SUNSCREEN

There is a huge amount of ultraviolet radiation present in the mountains, particularly on snow-covered terrain or glaciers. A high-value sunblock is essential to prevent severe burning, in particular to the nose and forehead. On snow or ice there will be a lot of reflected light, so remember to cover the underside of your nose and chin as well.

A total protection lipsalve is also important, and remember to renew it every so often, particularly after drink or snack breaks.

SUN HAT

This is useful in addition to sunscreen, and protects your head from being in direct sunlight, a common cause of severe headaches. Although you will most likely be wearing a helmet when climbing on technical ground, for walking to and from a hut a sun hat with a wide all-round brim is a very good investment.

DRINKING TUBE

This is a very handy thing to have with you when crossing high Alpine terrain. It is simply a metre (yard) or so of plastic tubing, around 6mm (quarter of an inch) in diameter, carried somewhere handy, such as looped through an appropriate part of your rucksack. In the sun, glaciers will have many small pools of water on them, but they are often too shallow for a water bottle or mug to be scooped into. Simply use the tube like a long drinking straw, holding one end in the pool whilst sucking on the other. This will allow frequent water breaks to be taken, but without having to carry a lot of water with you.

An extra safeguard against possible bacterial infection from the melt-water will be the use of a water-filtering straw. These are easy to use, and you just suck up the water and the internal filtering mechanism removes most of the harmful constituents.

Small meltwater pools like this, measuring only a few centimetres across, provide clean drinking water

A swing cheek pulley and one with a locking cam system

PULLEYS

Although not an essential item, a pulley will be found to be indispensable if you are setting up a hauling system, either for equipment or in a crevasse rescue situation. They work by reducing the friction inherent in any hauling or hoisting rig, and come in a variety of styles, weights and sizes.

The most basic is a simple swing-cheek pulley, and this style is ideal for carrying when crossing glaciated terrain. It is very lightweight and easy to clip on to any part of a rope system, as the sides supporting the pulley wheel swing apart and can be connected around the rope with a karabiner. It greatly reduces the friction that would otherwise be caused by the rope running around a karabiner, making the operation of a rescue system much easier.

A variation is a pulley that incorporates a rope clamp. These are heavier than a standard swing-cheek pulley, although they can be connected to any point on the rope in a similar manner. The difference is that a toothed cam allows you to pull the rope in one direction, but locks off when the load is released. This saves the need for so many French prusik or klemheist knots in the system, and makes the whole ropework process a lot cleaner. Ideal for hauling equipment, this type of pulley has its place in glaciated terrain, particularly when the ground to be negotiated is covered with a layer of snow, making progress around and across crevasses more hazardous. Although there is a weight penalty over a standard swing-cheek pulley, you may be carrying one of them anyway for use when on the climb. In that case, it would be worth having it ready to hand.

ASCENDERS

These come in a variety of forms, from the small basic type through to large handled ascenders, suitable for ascending fixed ropes. The former are far more suited to Alpine use, as they are lightweight and take up very little space, with the latter more suited to ascending fixed ropes on big walls.

Small ascenders can be used for a variety of tasks because they grip better than a prusik on icy ropes. They can be used in self-rescue for ascending the rope, should you be unlucky enough to fall into a crevasse, as well as a back-up on a hoisting system if your partner is arranging the rescue. They are useful when setting up hauling systems to move equipment up a route, and can be used for general prusiking. Additionally, they can be used as an intermediate free-running belay device, a technique sometimes deployed when moving together.

Small ascenders

DEALING WITH GLACIATED TERRAIN

At some stage you will come face to face with a glacier. These huge ribbons of ice are part and parcel of mountaineering in the Alpine regions, and dealing with them effectively is one of the most important skills to learn and practise.

Glaciers are complex structures and fascinating places to visit. There are two main types, dry and wet. Dry glaciers are generally of pure ice with no snow covering them, wet glaciers are best described as snow-covered ice sheets where the snow not only makes progress slow but also covers crevasses. Interestingly, dry glaciers tend to be running with water during the day, while wet glaciers do not!

Dry glaciers will often not present much in the way of danger from crevasses, as they will very often be visible and as such avoidable for the most part. However, either early or late in the season there still may be some residual snow covering any holes, so you must take great care. Some technical route finding ability may well be called for, and you will most likely find that you have to cross back and forth over the glacier in order to find the best path to your objective.

Traversing this type of terrain should not present a major problem, as long as sensible precautions are taken and care is exercised at all times. Very narrow crevasses could even be jumped across, although the safeguard of providing a rope for each member of the party would be a sensible move to provide security against slips or in case the far rim crumbles. Also, if you elect to jump across one, take care with your crampons. These not only provide another opportunity for tripping over at the crucial take-off point, but landing with your crampon points dug firmly into the ice and then twisting your body is guaranteed to do damage to your knees or ankles. Only ever jump a short distance and never be afraid to use a rope.

A dry glacier. Note the amount of loose rock debris, often making for awkward walking

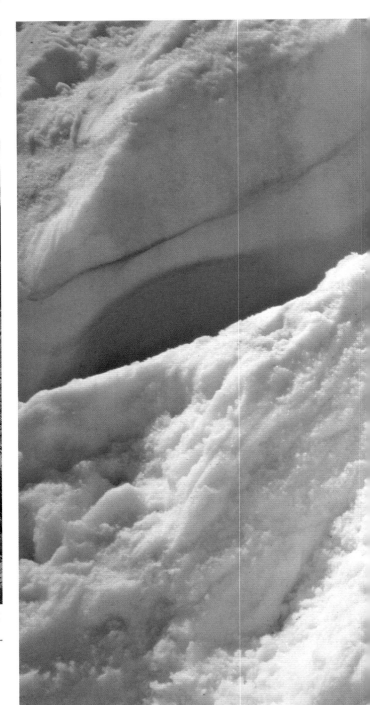

Crevasses may, in some circumstances, be crossed by the use of a snow bridge, but these should always be treated with the utmost caution and are usually best utilized early in the morning when the snow is still frozen and their strength greater. Later in the day, when the heat of the sun has softened the snow somewhat, the same snow bridge that was safe in the morning may now be a dripping death trap, just waiting for you to tread on it. Whenever using a snow bridge to negotiate a crevasse, the use of a rope is essential.

A wet glacier presents potentially the most dangerous terrain, as snow will be hiding crevasses, route-finding will be complicated, and simply walking across the glacier will be hard work if the snow is soft, particularly late in the day once the sun has done its work.

Look for signs on the surface of the snow that may indicate danger. A slight hollow may indicate the presence of holes, and

A snow bridge. Would you trust it?

Obvious depressions in the surface of a wet glacier are a sign of crevasses underneath

areas that look suspect should be avoided completely. Even the smallest depression may be simply the tip of a large cavern that bells out into a huge crevasse. If you do need to cross a suspect area of ground, and going round it is not an option, always approach it at right-angles, as this means that you will most likely be stepping over the crevasse at 90 degrees, thus crossing the shortest distance. Probing with a walking pole or ice axe may well help to uncover any hidden traps, and even having the lead person lie on the snow and crawl forwards, probing at intervals, will help to spread their bodyweight out and lessen the chance of the snow collapsing if a hole does exist. The rest of the party should be ready to hold their weight, in a braced position and with their axes ready to brake.

Falling into a crevasse, with or without a rope, is an extremely terrifying proposition. For this reason, you should never venture on to snow on a glacier without being properly roped up. Falling in for any distance will normally only happen as the result of poor judgment, as incorrect footwear, trusting snow bridges late in the day or deciding to not use a rope may all be contributing factors. If one of your party steps on to an unstable patch of snow, they may well fall only partially through, to be left supported by their rucksack, their feet waving in the cold void below. If this happens, the rest of your party should resist the temptation to gather round to help pull them out, as the consequences of a sudden increase in weight on the snowpack are inevitable. Instead, the rope should be used as an aid to pull them out. If the person has trekking poles, these can be used to help spread their weight, pressing down on the centre of the shafts with the poles held horizontally on the surface of the snow.

Take heed!

PREPARATION FOR GLACIER CROSSING

This should be meticulously prepared and rehearsed, so that no time is wasted either setting up the basic moving-together system or any of the techniques that may subseqently follow. The distances between group members must be carefully calculated to ensure that just the right amount of rope is left to initiate a rescue, and so that a loop of it can be lowered to the person in the crevasse. For two of you travelling together, the distance between you needs to be in the region of eight metres, with the same between each if there are three or even four of you. For two people, taking 12 coils (covered below) of around 1.7 metres per coil will give enough rope to effect a rescue. For three people, the lead and last person can take nine coils, again with the same result. With four on a rope, six coils will work. Remember that, even though less rope is being carried in coils, should one of the group members from any position need rescuing, there will be enough rope to use once everyone has untied.

Put careful thought into your preparation before crossing crevassed terrain, and some practice, done in a controlled situation well before the skills are needed in anger, is essential. Everyone in your party needs to prepare themselves and the rope in such a way that a variety of extraction techniques can be carried out, depending upon what any given situation demands.

Shortening the rope by tying coils off around your body is the standard way to set things up, and the following method is a simple and effective way of doing this. An advantage here is that, if there is any chance of you being suspended by the rope, this method of tying off the coils acts as a simple chest harness, helping to keep your body upright if you are wearing a rucksack.

First, tie in to your harness. To take the coils, which must all be the same size, place either your left or your right hand, pointing out with your palm down, at a point around about hip to waist level. This will act as a measure to get the size of the coils equal. The exact point that you use will be the result of practice, with the amount of clothes that you are going to wear being one factor that may make a difference day to day.

If you are using your left hand as the measure, bring the rope from your harness up around your neck in an anticlockwise direction, round and underneath your hand, keeping the rope and thus all of the coils snug. Continue doing this, making sure that all of the coils are the same size, until around a metre or so more than the desired distance between you and your partner is achieved. In other words, if you want to have 8 metres (26ft) between you and your partner, the total amount of rope between you prior to locking it off, assuming that your partner is also taking coils, will be 10 metres (33ft).

Once you have done this, put your arm, the one that has been used for measuring, through all of the coils so that they sit on

your shoulder neatly and comfortably. After some practice, you should be able to get these so that they neither slide off your shoulder nor restrict your breathing due to them being too tight.

Using a bight of the main rope from close in front of you, pass it around the back of the coils and up next to your chest, and tie a small overhand knot on the bight around all of the coils, making sure that the resulting tail loop is as short as possible, and that there are no loose coils or flappy bits of rope left around.

Now clip a small screwgate karabiner into either your abseil loop or tie-in loop, and clip the overhand knot loop into this. If you have tied it correctly, you will find that you have to stoop forwards slightly in order to clip it in and, as you stand up straight again, the coils around your shoulders will be pulled snug as the knot comes tight.

Bear in mind that carrying hand coils should never be done. All that these do is to simply increase the distance that a victim will fall and makes the resultant shock-loading on the person remaining on the surface far greater than if they had been simply roped together conventionally. If you see coils being carried, chances are that they are being used for the technique known as short roping, something that should only be carried out by professionals or those with a high degree of training, but is still not appropriate for glacier travel.

If you are travelling as a party of three or more on the same rope, those between the ends can tie on, using a rethreaded overhand knot on the bight, keeping the resulting loop end short and clipping

Taking coils

Locking off coils for glacier travel

The finished coil system, locked off

this back in to the rope tie-in loop with a screwgate karabiner to stop any chance of it unthreading. To make things a little more comfortable, they can first create an isolation loop by tying an overhand knot or an Alpine butterfly in the main rope, and tie the overhand on a bight at the end of this. When completed, the distance between the two knots should be about waist- to knee-length. Doing this allows the middle person to walk slightly to the side of the rope, and they will not be pulled around by the motion of their companions.

Other items to prepare will include three or four screwgate karabiners, one or two ice screws and slings, a pair of prusik loops or small mechanical ascenders and maybe a lightweight pulley per person. Whatever you carry should be tailored to the terrain and the number in your party.

Once you have taken the coils, it would be a good idea for at least the first and last person to have a prusik loop clipped with a short sling to the front point of your harness, and this goes for all of your group members. This can be arranged as either a klemheist or a French prusik, as if need be these knots can be quickly altered from one type to the other. The klemheist attached to the front person's harness would be of use should they fall into a crevasse and need to ascend the rope to get out, and therefore they have one prusik attached and ready. The French prusik on the harness of the person or persons left on the top of the glacier would be directly to hand so that a method of transferring the weight of the victim from them to an anchor system could be quickly and efficiently carried out. You may decide to use a small mechanical ascender in place of the prusik loop, but bear in mind that these are often non-reversible.

Another option, for two or more climbers, is to use the knotted rope method. This can provide security via a number of small overhand knots on the bight tied at intervals along the length of the rope. The idea is that, should the lead person fall into a crevasse, the knots will cut into the snow and ice at the lip as they

Tied on to the middle of the rope using an isolation loop

drop, and stop them from falling in for any distance. The length of rope between the front two climbers should be in the region of 20 metres (60ft) once a series of overhand knots on the bight have been tied. This method works well in a number of situations, particularly if the person in the crevasse is able to clip into each of the overhand knots in turn as a means of self-rescue, using a sling as a foot loop and a shorter sling to their harness. However, there are a couple of drawbacks with this system. Firstly, having knots in the rope may prevent the fallen climber from being able to efficiently prusik out, as the knots will stop the klemheist and French prusik from being slid up the rope. Secondly, the knots will negate the use of a hoisting system, as they would not allow the rope to run through a pulley, a French prusik or mechanical device.

It is obviously up to you to decide whether this system is appropriate enough to be used in any given situation. However, if you are with a party of three or four inexperienced members and have to cross crevassed terrain, the security provided by this system is quite high. The main rescue criterion is therefore the ability of the group members remaining on the surface to collectively pull on the rope and drag

their companion up and out of harm's way. However, the drawbacks will, for many, preclude its use.

20m
(60ft)

Two people prepared for glacier crossing with the knotted rope method

CREVASSE RESCUE

If any member of your party is unlucky enough to fall down a hole and is not able to climb back out by their own efforts, by far the simplest and quickest method of extraction is for as many people as possible to gather around (not too close to the edge!) and pull on the rope. This will frequently result in the person at the end of the rope eventually being hauled out.

If you were walking as a pair and your partner disappeared down a hole, it would be worth calling for help from other parties in the vicinity. Shouting may get the required help, but if not the international distress signal of six long blasts on a whistle, a minute's pause, then another six may get a response.

If the above methods are not working or are inappropriate, then you need to do something a little more proactive. There are a variety of ways in which the rope may be organized for use as a rescue system on crevassed terrain, and some of these are covered below.

Carefully negotiating a dry glacier

SELF-RESCUE

If the person at the front of your group ends up hanging inside a crevasse, by far the quickest method by which they can get back on to firm ground, assuming that a group pull will not work, will be for them to ascend the rope under their own steam. As they will most likely be wearing a rucksack, this should be taken off and clipped to the rope that is in front of them running to their harness with a karabiner so that it can slide freely. Alternatively, they can take off their coils and clip the rucksack to these. This means that the rucksack will weight the rope, making moving the prusiks a lot easier. It will also help their balance, as having a heavy rucksack on your back makes prusiking up a rope quite awkward, as your centre of gravity is a lot higher than normal.

HOISTING SYSTEMS

These are complicated, at least when compared to self-rescue by prusiking or simply pulling the victim out. However, maybe the victim has been incapacitated in some way, or has lost the equipment that they need to prusik up the rope. If all else has failed, then a hoisting system will have to be set up.

We will assume that two of you are travelling together and that your companion, who was in the lead, has fallen into a crevasse a short distance and is unable to extract himself.

The first thing that will happen is that you realize that your companion is no longer there! This may be accompanied by a short tug from in front, but it is unlikely that you will be pulled far forwards as the rope will cut into the lip of the crevasse under their body weight.

Your initial task, once you have decided that a hoisting system is the only way ahead, is to escape the system. This will be far easier to accomplish if there are two of you on the surface, one to hold the victim's weight and the other to construct the anchor. However, this is not the case here and you need to persevere alone.

As soon as you realize that your partner has disappeared you should fall on to the ground, thus making it easier for you to hold their weight. There will most likely not be a great deal of loading on you at this point. You now need to construct an anchor system. As long as the glacier surface is made from good quality ice, place two ice screws at your side and equalize them with a sling if appropriate. It is absolutely essential that these ice screws are totally solid, as the security of the entire hoisting system relies on them. If there is any question regarding the quality of the ice, such as on a wet glacier, a system such as a buried axe anchor should be constructed. This will be far more difficult to achieve from your sitting position, but you may decide that the screws will provide enough security to hold the victim while you construct a more

substantial axe anchor nearby.

Once you have got a good anchor set up, unclip the French prusik from the front of your harness, along with its sling, clip it into the anchor, and push it as far as possible down the loaded rope. You can now ease your way forwards a little so that your partner's weight comes on to the prusik, giving you some relief from the strain. Now undo the locking-off knot on your coils and pull through a short length of rope, perhaps also one wrap will need to be taken off. It is extremely important at this stage that only a small amount of rope is undone in case the French prusik fails and the system starts to slip.

Clip an HMS karabiner into the anchor, and into this place an Italian hitch that is then locked off. This Italian hitch acts as a back-up in case the prusik slips, and is a better option than a clove hitch as it can be released when under load. You can now take off the rest of the coils, best done one by one to avoid tangles, and you are then out of the system.

Although you are now free to move around, you must be extremely cautious when doing so. If your partner fell into the crevasse because it was hidden by snow, there may well be other crevasses before it that they stepped over.

It is therefore important that you protect yourself, and the best way to do this will be to clip on to the dead rope coming out of the back end of the anchor, with a clove hitch to an HMS karabiner on your abseil loop being the simplest option. You should then be fairly safe as you go to the lip of the crevasse to assess what to do next. Another possibility will be for you to attach a prusik or mechanical device on to the live rope, extended with a sling, and make your way to the edge of the crevasse protected like that.

Hopefully, communication will not be too difficult and you will be able to call to each other to sort out options. The best scenario here, for both of you, is that the crevasse is in fact very shallow and simply lowering your partner to the bottom means that they can walk out of one end. This is where having the locked off Italian hitch comes in really useful, as it can be released under load and your partner lowered to the floor. However, if the crevasse is not so accommodating, another technique will have to be put into place.

Even if they have only fallen in a short distance, the rope will have cut into the lip of the crevasse quite deeply and this will have to be sorted out before any hoisting system can be put into action. If you decide to cut away some of the surrounding snow and ice to help the rope to run, take great care when doing so as not only would there be a risk of your partner being hit with debris, but there is also the concern that a rope that is under tension can be cut through extremely easily.

Whether or not the rope has initially bitten into the lip of the crevasse, a method whereby the rope will not be able to cut itself in deeper when you have set up the hoisting system needs to be constructed. The simplest way to do this will be by placing an ice axe under the rope as close to the edge of the crevasse as possible. If your axe is not to hand, as maybe it has been used as part of the anchor system, a rucksack, tent pole or any similar item can be used. Whatever it is, make sure that it cannot be dropped into the crevasse and be lost, perhaps by attaching it to a spare ice screw with a sling or spare prusik.

The simplest hoisting system will be the assisted hoist, where your partner pulls on a section of the rope and shares the job of extracting themselves. Lower a loop of rope down to them, taken from the dead rope coming from the back of the locked-off Italian hitch. They then clip this to their abseil loop with a screwgate karabiner, which you may also supply on the rope that you lower to them. At the anchor end, run the rope through a system whereby you can hoist with the minimum friction, such as a pulley. If one is not available, two karabiners of the same size and shape placed together will help to reduce drag.

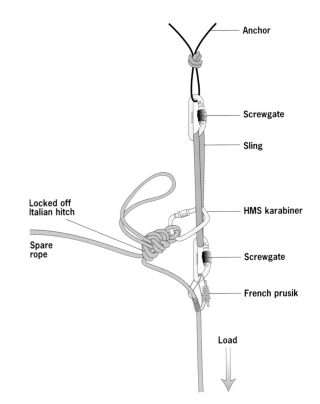

The anchor used for escaping from the system on a glacier

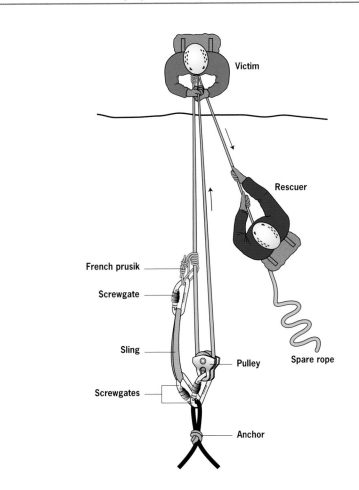

An overview of the assisted hoisting system in practice

You can now undo and remove the Italian hitch, remembering to keep a firm hold on the dead end of the rope, the section coming back out of the crevasse. Pull through the slack rope from the hitch as you untie it, which will in turn take up the slack through the karabiner at your partner's harness. It is now easy, with a combined effort, to start hoisting your partner up and out.

Keep an eye on the French prusik during the hoist, as if it is lying flat on the surface of the ice its operation may be hampered and it won't lock off properly when required. Also, make sure that it will not ride up and either pull through a karabiner, if one is being used, or otherwise jam in the pulley. Make very sure that the original rope to the victim is moving through the French prusik, because if it is not and you stop for a rest, the victim will drop right back down to the start point. When it is all running smoothly, if either of you need a rest, the prusik can be pushed down the rope and the weight of the victim lowered on to it gently.

In some situations, you may not be able to rely on the assistance of your partner, and this could be due to insufficient rope being available for you to lower down to them or them being incapacitated in some way. In this situation, an unassisted hoisting system will need to be rigged. This can be rigged in exactly the same way as for the rock climbing system (see 'Emergency procedures), whereby an extra attachment is made to the live rope with a klemheist or mechanical ascender and you hoist with the pulling rope clipped through there. Once again, this can be made much easier by the use of a lightweight pulley, and a self-locking pulley will also be found to be of value.

If you have a spare sling to hand, or a short length of rope, you can use a slight variation that gives an increased advantage to the rescuer. Including the extra sling increases the mechanical advantage of the hoist, and makes things a little easier. Using a pulley on the dead rope will also help.

If the rope that is holding your partner has become completely jammed in the lip of the crevasse, you will need to set up a different system that will allow them to be pulled up. This uses a section of the remaining rope, and is set up as follows.

You escape the system as normal and the rope is then securely fixed to the anchor. This could be with a clove hitch or a figure of eight, as the rope that your partner is hanging on will be, to all intents and purposes, redundant for the rest of the procedure.

Drop a loop of rope down to them. This will be connected to their abseil loop via a screwgate karabiner and a pulley, items that they may well have with them already. If not, lower these down on the loop as well. The section of rope coming back up to you from the loop is connected to the anchor in a manner that means that it will lock off when it is loaded. A self-locking pulley would be ideal, as would a simple French prusik, but for the benefit of the diagram we will use an Alpine clutch.

Clip another screwgate, preferably with a pulley as well, into the dead rope coming down from the clutch. This is connected to the rope running down to your partner with a klemheist or small ascender. Pulling on the free end of the rope results in your partner being raised, but every now and then you will need to relax your grip, let the Alpine clutch take the weight, and push the klemheist further down the rope.

You may find it easier, for any of the hoisting methods described, to clove-hitch the rope onto a screwgate on your abseil loop, face away from the crevasse and, leaning forward, use this attachment to help you pull. This means that the strong muscles in your legs are doing much of the work as you walk away from the crevasse.

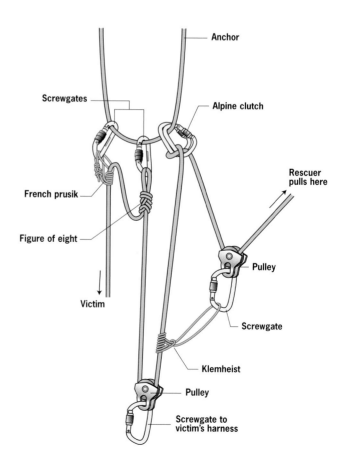

Using an unassisted hoisting system that increases the mechanical advantage of those pulling

Klemheist or lightweight ascender

Self-locking pulley

Pull

An improved hoisting method, useful if the main rope is jammed in the lip of the crevasse

Anchor

Screwgates

Alpine clutch

French prusik

Figure of eight

Rescuer pulls here

Pulley

Screwgate

Victim

Klemheist

Pulley

Screwgate to victim's harness

MOVING TOGETHER ON STEEP GROUND

The ability to move efficiently together on moderate and technical ground is a fundamental skill for an Alpinist, and one that is key to the success of completing a team's objective.

Walking across a glacier is one example of where moving together is a crucial skill, as all team members have to be able to pace themselves to the rate of others within the group. They must also have a degree of technical knowledge about appropriate rope systems, and have practised them so that they can be put swiftly into action should the need arise. Another example will be where the team moves from a gearing-up area at the base of a route to the point where the technical climbing begins. Finally, moving together encompasses the technique whereby all party members climb at the same time on moderate or technical ground, stopping only for the occasional rest, to swap leads and to move any gear from the rear person to whoever is at the front.

It is this final example, continuous movement on Alpine terrain, which will very likely be the key to the completion of a route in reasonable time. It is also the most serious, with prior practice and a high degree of understanding between the climbers essential for it to be safely carried out.

DISTANCES

There are a series of recommended distances apart that a team could be once they have tied themselves on and taken coils. These go up in three metre (9ft) increments, but are purely there as a guide and many will have their own idea about what suits them in any given situation. If there are more than two on the rope, the distances between members will stay the same. The extra people can attach themselves to the rope in the same way as for glacier travel mentioned above, with an isolation loop leading to an overhand knot rethreaded and clipped back to itself.

Moving together on a snow slope

SNOW SLOPES

The suggested distance between you and your partner on a snow slope is three metres (9ft). This allows you to maintain a safe distance between each other, but not be so far away as to create a problem if one of you should slip.

When moving up or down the slope, it is up to whoever is in the lead to set a pace that is comfortable for both of you, and keeping the pace slow and constant will be far better than random bursts of speed. The second person needs to match the leader's pace, ensuring that they never get too close to the extent that the rope droops and touches the surface of the snow. This means that there is too much slack in the system, and controlling a slip would be a lot harder as the rope would jerk tight on the leader as the load came on to them. Equally, the pace of the person at the back must be such that the leader is never in danger of being constantly tugged, as this would make progress very difficult indeed.

Should one of you slip, the first line of defence will be a swift self-belay, and if this fails, a self-arrest (both covered in the 'Winter' section). The short length of rope is there to ensure that the person who has fallen cannot accelerate down the slope before their slide is checked.

If you are climbing up a wide snow slope and both of you are of equal technical ability, it would be fine for you to ascend or descend side by side, obviously ensuring that the rope stays clear of the snow between you.

Knowing the limitations of yourself and the system is important, and one of the advantages of this method, and indeed all of those that follow, is that it is easy to set up a belay whilst tied on. Simply rig an anchor, clip into it with a cowstail, take off the coils and you are ready to climb the next pitch conventionally, climbing one at a time.

A snow ridge, ideal territory for moving together

SNOW-COVERED RIDGES

The distance apart on this type of ground is suggested to be in the region of six metres (19ft). On a sharp-edged snow ridge the plan is simple. If your partner falls off to the right of the ridge, your immediate reaction should be to throw yourself off to the left. This all sounds wonderful on paper of course, but having the wherewithal to do this thousands of feet up focuses your mind somewhat. However, it is a very effective method of stopping your partner slipping down the hill, and probably the only method of stopping a slip on a sharp snowed-up ridge, particularly as the provision of belay points will be far less than on a rocky ridge.

This is the only instance of moving together where you should carry a couple of hand coils each. This not only gives warning of your companion's slip, but gives you a chance to stop them with a sharp tug and, if that fails, an extra couple of metres of rope to jump off the side with.

Once you have completed the technique, you will end up in a counterbalance situation with you supporting each other's weight. The rope will be cutting into the snow at

the crest, and this will create some friction. Get yourselves back to the ridge as soon as possible, but coordinate the final couple of metres so that the weight of one of you does not pull the other, who has just successfully stood up again, over the opposite side.

ROCKY RIDGES AND SLOPES

This type of ground will usually allow some sort of running belay systems to be used. In its simplest form, as you pass a suitable rock spike or block you can flick the rope over it to provide security. Alternatively, you could step left and right of any spikes and blocks as you make your way up or down. If a slip occurs, the rope will be held by the rock and the distance fallen will only be double the distance from the climber to the spike, plus a bit of rope stretch.

On this type of ground, the rope length between you should be around nine metres, (30ft), although you may decide to increase this to 10 or even 15 metres on steeper ground. This distance allows the rope to be used around spikes and blocks en route, but is not so long that a lot of friction occurs, which could result

in the rope jamming. You could place conventional runners, such as slings, nuts and cams, on the way, and stop every now and then to collect the gear from the person at the back, or simply swap leads. Having a number of long slings is very useful here, not just to use on spikes and threads but also to extend other placements into line, reducing the friction that would otherwise be caused.

If you are using the moving together system on steep ground, there will most likely come a point where it ceases to be a sensible option and conventional pitching becomes the thing to do. This can be done until the area of technical ground is passed, then you can go back to moving together for the easier sections.

You may want to use a different method of tying off coils when moving on this type of ground. So-called scrambler's coils can be locked off without using any knots, and this then gives quick access to the coils around your body should you need to take any off. It also means that any loading is at the harness waist belt area, which may be more comfortable in some situations than tying off as for glacier travel.

Once you have taken coils, clip an HMS karabiner through the central part of your leg loops and waist belt, so that it opens at the front and at the top. Take a bight of rope from in front of the last coil and pass it up through your tie-in loop and around the back of all the coils. Bring it out to the front and down to the karabiner, clipping it in and doing the screwgate up. Pull on the main length of rope to get the rope to lock off. If you need to take off any coils, simply undo the screwgate and take out the loop, pull it through the coils and you can now unwrap as many as are needed.

It is a good idea with this method to practise getting the coils exactly the right length, as too long will mean that the loop will not lock off and too short means that you will be pulled downwards in the event of a fall. A compromise between the two is what's needed. An alternative is to take and lock off coils as if for glacier travel, and then clip the rope from the lock-off knot into a screwgate karabiner on your abseil loop. This means that the coils are not compressed around your shoulders in the event of a

fall – which is sometimes a problem with short coils when using the scramblers' coils method.

The use of direct belays is key to completing a fast ascent, and these should be used as and when appropriate. The simplest method, where the rope is run around a suitable rock and taken in hand over hand is all that is needed in most cases, and the time that this saves over setting up a conventional belay system will be considerable. However, always err on the side of safety, and if you need to construct a proper anchor system then don't hesitate to do so.

The completed lock-off

Starting to lock off scrambler's coils

A small ascender being used to protect the leader when the team is moving together

PROTECTING THE LEADER WHEN MOVING TOGETHER

If you are in the lead climbing up relatively steep ground and the person behind you falls, there is a good chance that you will be pulled backwards off your footing and will also tumble a distance. If you pass any short sections that give you cause for concern you should stop and provide a belay for your partner until they have climbed past the problem.

However, another option is for you to place runners that incorporate small mechanical ascenders, orientated so that the rope runs smoothly upwards but not down. This means that, should your partner slip and fall backwards, their weight will be taken by the ascender and not be transferred to you. They should be attached to runners that are designed to take both an upwards *and* downwards pull, as they need to be held in both directions.

Rigging this type of system will make a large difference to your safety, but will also take a bit of time and judgment. There is also a limit as to how many ascenders you will carry, with two per person often being the maximum, giving the leader a chance of four placements. If things are getting to the point that you are worried about being pulled backwards by your partner, you may well be on ground that demands to be pitched rather than climbed by both of you at the same time. However, this technique works very well in a variety of situations, and bears investigation if you are going to seek out this type of terrain.

Classic big wall territory

7: BIG WALL CLIMBING

This is categorized as being the ascent of a climb, very often rock for its entire length but not exclusively so, that will take a minimum of one day and often much longer to complete. Some hard big wall routes may take a week or more, with the team either sleeping at each day's high-point on a suitable ledge or on a platform carried for the purpose, or descending to base and then re-ascending on fixed ropes to their high-point the next day.

These techniques, used for years on some of the hardest and longest rock routes across the world, have also been transferred to the huge walls of the Greater Ranges, allowing some extremely hard ascents to take place. This requires a mixture of big wall and expedition techniques to be used and reflects, for many, the ultimate in climbing achievement.

EQUIPMENT

This will depend upon the length and style of climb that is going to be undertaken. A fast party on a full day climb that is bolted throughout will need little more than normal sport climbing equipment, food and water. However, a team attempting a multi-day route with sections of aid climbing and all protection needing to be placed by hand will end up having to carry or haul a huge amount of equipment, not least to keep themselves fed, watered, warm and dry overnight.

ÉTRIER

This is a ladder made from rope or tape, consisting of a number of rungs on to which you can step to gain height when on blank ground. The top of the étrier is clipped into a suitable point, such as a piton, bolt or leader-placed gear such as a wire or cam, and the extra height that you can gain may be enough to reach holds some distance above. If not, a second étrier is placed above the first and you climb up on to this, clipping the climbing rope into the gear placements as you go, subsequently moving the first one up above you to climb a third section. This continues until you have reached easier ground.

A Fifi hook

Étriers are also used where large roofs have to be negotiated, as it gives you a place on which to stand whilst making your way along the section.

FIFI HOOK

This is a curved device that can be used to connect the top of an étrier to its attachment point. A length of cord is connected from the top of the Fifi hook to your harness, and this serves two purposes. Firstly, it ensures that you cannot drop the étrier. Secondly, when using a series of étrier moves, it allows you to climb past the first one and then retrieve it by simply pulling up on the cord. Being curved, the Fifi hook will lift from the attachment point without any unclipping having to take place.

BASHIES AND COPPERHEADS

These are used in cracks where no other type of wire or conventional protection will work. Coming in various sizes and consisting of a swaged wire with an aluminium, copper or similar soft metal head, they are placed against the crack and pounded into place with a hammer. This pounding causes the metal head to deform and grip the interior contours of the crack, giving purchase. There is quite a judgment call from the climber's point of view as to how solid the placement is, and it may only be able to hold body weight, just adequate for aid climbing purposes.

They can, unsurprisingly, be very difficult to retrieve, and are often left in place, causing an unsightly mark on the rock. The act of hammering can also damage the rock, causing scarring that will never heal. For this reason, their use is frowned upon in some areas.

SKY HOOKS

These are small hooks, often with a short length of tape attached, that are used to find purchase on small incuts and other inconsistencies in the rock surface, where other forms of protection would be useless. They are useful in aid climbing, where your body weight will keep them in place when moving up on a sling or étrier.

As only a very small amount of the tip of the hook is in contact with the rock, huge forces are applied to it if shock-loaded, easily enough to cause the rock to shatter. For this reason, great care should be taken if electing to use them in a situation where they could be subjected to any type of impact load.

They are sometimes used as a running belay, where no other option exists. This type of protection will usually offer extremely marginal security, as a fall from any height would most likely cause the hook to fail on its placement. To keep it from falling off its edge when climbing above it, sticky tape or a rubber compound, such as used for mounting posters on a bedroom wall, can be used.

An étrier

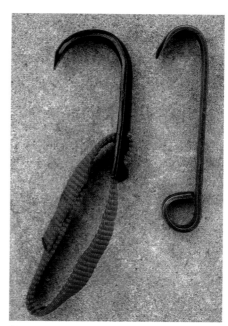

Sky hooks

ASCENDERS

These are usually essential on big walls, both for following pitches and for rigging hauling systems. They come in a variety of styles and sizes, but for prolonged use a matched pair of left- and right-handled ascenders will be ideal.

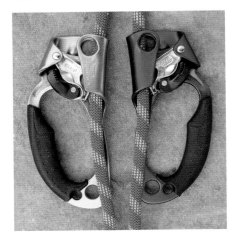

A pair of matched ascenders

PULLEYS

These are invaluable for use in hauling systems, as they help to reduce friction, thus making your task easier. In particular, the type with a built-in locking mechanism is handy, as it will hold the weight of the hauled load without needing to add an ascender to the rig.

A variety of pulleys. The one bottom left has a self-locking capability

HAUL BAGS

It is very rarely possible or desirable on long steep routes to carry a rucksack conventionally. This is where a haul bag will be needed. This will contain all of your requirements for climbing, sleeping and eating, and on long trips, or where there is a large group, more than one bag may have to be used.

A good quality bag will be cylindrical in shape, so that there are no corners to catch when it is being pulled up a route, and it will have a detachable conventional carrying harness for getting to the bottom of the climb. It will be made from a very strong, waterproof and durable fabric, and the top closure should render it totally waterproof, essential in wet weather so that all of your kit stays dry. Importantly, it will have a very strong three- or four-point attachment strap system at the top that allows it to be pulled up the route.

PORTABLE LEDGES

Some routes offer no ledges at all on which to sleep, so an option is to take your own. These will have to be hauled up behind you as you go and be erected when needed for the night.

A haul bag also makes a handy rest point on steep ground

Natural ledges can be narrow, demanding good kit management and a high degree of safety awareness

Consisting of a strong but light metal framework covered in a tough lightweight material and coming in one- or two-person models, they provide an exciting way to spend the night, suspended from a single point above. Although they may feel insubstantial, ledges of this type are very strong and with the inclusion of a waterproof cover, give a comfortable and weatherproof night.

Although they are normally suspended from a single point, which allows them to hang in the correct manner without tilting, there will be a number of other attachment points provided for both yourself and your equipment. Having an extra safety rope trailing from the ledge to a suitable anchor point on the cliff will also be most people's choice.

WASTE DISPOSAL

The consideration of what to do with human waste on a multi-day route becomes important, as any other team climbing below you will not be impressed if you relieve yourself over the edge of your bivi ledge every morning! There is also the environmental and health issue to be considered, as waste is an undesirable addition to the mountain environment.

In its simplest form, waste can be managed by using a strong plastic bag in the first instance, which is then placed into a second strong bag, finally into a large screw-top container, ready for

appropriate disposal when you get back to the ground. Another option is to use a purpose-made human waste carrying system. This includes a bag with decay catalyst and odour neutralizing properties already in it, which is then placed into a larger container for appropriate disposal. Some kits also include medicated hand wipes, and it would be worth taking some along anyway to improve personal cleanliness.

HAULING

Hauling is the hard work part of big wall climbing, but it will be the only way to get your kit up to you. After each pitch a haul system will have to be set up and the bag or bags hoisted up to you and made safe, ready for the next section.

There are a host of ways of arranging a haul, from simply pulling up hand over hand, not very efficient or effective, through to complicated systems that take a little time to set up but make the actual work of hauling a lot easier. Some of these options are covered below.

SIMPLE HAUL

Sometimes known as the Yosemite hoist, this is the quickest to set up, and will be fine for dealing with light loads, although anything very heavy will need a different system. The anchor is equipped with a screwgate karabiner and a pulley, preferably one with a self-locking capability. On the dead rope coming out of the pulley, add an ascender with sling attached. This will create a foot loop on to which you will push to lift the bag upwards. You may want to put another ascender on to the live rope so that you can pull up with your hands as you push down with your foot. Once you have moved the bag up slightly, the self-locking pulley will take its weight whilst you reposition the ascenders on the rope, and repeat the process.

IMPROVED HAUL

For heavier loads, the system can be improved by rigging it in a slightly different manner. The top section remains the same, with the rope running through a self-locking pulley. An ascender is now clipped on to the live rope so that it will grip when pulled upwards, and a section of the dead rope is clipped on to this using a smaller pulley. Pulling up on the dead rope now lifts the load, with the top locking pulley allowing you to move the ascender back into position when needed.

The advantage with this system is that you only need a force of around half the load to lift it, meaning that for a load of 80kg you will be able to move it with a pressure equivalent to less than 40kg. This is a distinct improvement over the simple haul system above, where you need nearly half as much force again to make the load move. The disadvantages are that the load will move a shorter distance for each pull, due to the way that the rope runs, and that you are now using arm muscles instead of the stronger leg muscles.

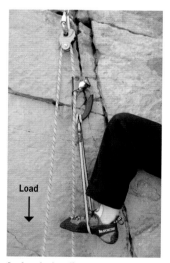

A simple hauling system

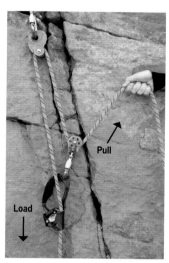

The improved hauling system

The technical haul, with the rope being pulled upwards to lift the load

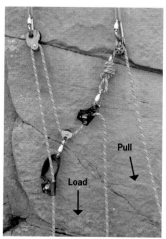

The technical haul with the rope being pulled downwards to lift the load

TECHNICAL HAUL

This method will deal with very heavy bags and make pulling them up relatively effortless. Its downside is again that the bag will move only a short distance for each pull of the rope, but you may decide that the advantages make rigging it worthwhile.

The system is set up as for the improved haul above. The end of the dead rope, or another suitable piece of rope, can now be used to increase your mechanical advantage. It is clipped in to a suitable anchor, most likely with a figure of eight knot. Another ascender or rope clamp (or self-locking pulley) is attached to this rope with a pulley, the clamp now being attached to the dead rope coming from the first system so that it will lock with an upwards pull. Pulling up on the dead end of the rope now lifts the bag.

It is possible to rig the system for a downward pull if that would suit the anchor system better. Instead of tying the end of the spare rope to the anchor, it is attached to an ascender or rope clamp on the dead rope from the original system. It is now taken through the anchor, and it is the dead rope from here that you will pull to move the load.

AID CLIMBING

Many routes will necessitate the use of one or more points of aid. This is the term used where you pull on, or stand up on, anything that is not part of the rock itself. This may be as simple as pulling on a wire placement to enable you to reach a hold a little higher up, through to prolonged days of fully equipping the route with gear that is used, along with slings and étriers, to make upward progress.

Any route that involves aid moves as part of its makeup will have the fact detailed with the route description, so that it is not a shock when you reach that point. It would be worthwhile having experienced using aid points before needing them on a big wall, and indeed many single-pitch climbs will have one or more aid moves on them. If you have not tried them before however, finding a short section of suitable ground and spending time practising with slings and étriers would be worthwhile.

Make sure that you have enough gear to hand, either on you or retrievable from your belayer via a haul rope. Have a couple of étriers clipped to you, and keep some slings in a suitable place. A very short cowstail, the length of a short extender, attached to your abseil loop would also be useful.

When you reach the aid moves, place a piece of gear as high as you can and clip in an étrier, best done using a Fifi hook so that it is easily retrievable as you move up. Place your weight on it to make sure that it holds and, once you are happy, you can also clip your climbing rope to it as a running belay. Make your way up the étrier until you get to a point where your balance is being thrown out by your height. You can now make yourself stable in a couple of ways. Firstly, get your second to take in tight. This will pull you on to the top runner and stop you from falling backwards. Alternatively, and a better option on overhanging ground, clip yourself in to the runner with the short cowstail from your harness, and then sit back on it. You can now reach up high, place the next piece of gear and repeat the process with the second étrier. As you move up, the first one, if you used a Fifi hook, will lift from its placement, pulled by the cord to your harness.

Take a lot of care when standing on an étrier, as your body weight may be enough to rip the placement out. Only once you are happy with it should you also clip in your climbing rope, as to do so before this and have the whole lot come away from the rock could result in a very long fall.

Some climbers like to use a long daisy-chain, a sewn sling with a series of loops incorporated in it, instead of the short cowstail. This gives a variety of options as to where you clip in as regards the distance from your body to the placement and it works well, but be sure that you cannot fall any distance and shock-load the sling.

There are many ways in which to vary the above method of aid climbing, but the one detailed will provide a good starting point, from which you can find what works for you. Remember that a

Using an étrier for an aid move

large roof will demand different tactics to steep face climbing, with almost total commitment to your placements from the outset.

Once you have completed the pitch, unless the section of aid was very short it will be unrealistic to expect your second to follow in the same manner. They will normally climb up the rope using one of the techniques detailed below, and then lead on through to the next pitch. For that reason, a second rope, most likely low-stretch, may be trailed that allows them to climb up without using the main lead rope and causing wear. This second rope can then be used for hauling the bag up if the second is not carrying the gear themselves. Alternatively, the leader may trail a thinner rope for hauling and their second ascends the main lead rope. This is useful when clearing an overhanging pitch, as the second will be kept close to the rock by the gear placements, because otherwise they would be swinging out quite some distance from it.

PLACING BOLTS

It may be that the area of rock that you are on is so blank as to preclude you from placing any conventional protection, and the use of a bolt is the only way to make progress. Alternatively, you may need to rig a very sound anchor system for one reason or another, and natural placements are non-existent.

I should say from the outset that the placing of bolts should only be done if you are completely aware of the local ethics that dictate how they should be used, and that generally they should never be placed on an existing route (known as 'retro-bolting') without either very good cause or permission from the first ascensionist. Only on new routes are bolts tolerated by most, but even here only when no other option exists and there is a local history of bolts being accepted.

Sport climbs are almost exclusively bolted with the use of a powerful battery-powered drill, often from abseil and usually with no immediate concern about the weight being carried. Although cordless drills are sometimes used on the first ascent of a long route, in a remote situation the only option will be to hand drill the placement, a very tiring and time-consuming process. You will need a specially designed hand drill, drill bits, a hammer, spanner, expansion bolts and hangers.

Select a suitable area of rock, one that is solid and reasonably flat. Place the drill bit in the drill, align it perpendicular to the rock, and start to drive it in by hitting the end of the drill with the hammer. Some purpose-made drill holders have an internal twist to their working, which means that every time you hit it, the drill bit is rotated slightly in the correct direction. Even so, it is still worth rotating the drill by hand a little at each strike, in order to let the bit bite in.

Keep driving it in until it is deeper than the length of the expansion sleeve on the bolt. Remove the drill and put it somewhere safe. Give the hole a blow to remove any dust, taking care of your eyes as you do so. The bolt and expansion sleeve can now be placed into the hole and tapped into place with the hammer. Once it is fully seated, the hanger and nut are placed on it and it is all tightened up with the spanner.

Kit for placing a bolt by hand

Make sure that the hanger ends up in the correct direction for loading, and that you do not over-tighten it all, otherwise there is a chance that the expansion sleeve or bolt could be damaged. If there is any question about its solidity, or any movement of the hanger, the placement might need to be redrilled nearby.

Typical big wall terrain

FOLLOWING ROUTES BY ASCENDING THE ROPE

Some climbs will take a very long time to lead, and the second may wish to ascend the rope instead of following each pitch. Generally known as jumaring, it allows time to rest before leading through, as well as letting them clean the gear from the pitch without too much effort. There are various ways to do this, with the two most common being detailed below.

USING TWO ASCENDERS

Using two ascenders is a matter of coordination. One will be attached to the harness, the other will have a sling into which a foot is placed. This second ascender will also have a sling from it to the harness, to act as a back-up should the first slide or somehow become detached. To ascend the rope, slide the top ascender up and then sit back in your harness. This takes the weight off the lower ascender that can now slide up the rope. Using its handle for support, stand up in the sling. The top ascender is now unweighted and can slide up again, and so on.

When there is sufficient slack rope, another back-up could be made by tying a clove hitch from the main rope below the second ascender on to an HMS karabiner on the harness. This will prevent the climber from falling any distance should the ascenders fail to grip, such as on icy ropes, and any slack can be taken in at intervals as they ascend.

If there is any chance of the rope not entering the ascender in a straight line, clip it to the rope with a second karabiner, either through the top holes above the cam or through the lower karabiner hole at the end of the handle, so that the rope is unable ride up over the cam section.

A karabiner clipped through the top of an ascender to keep the run of the rope straight

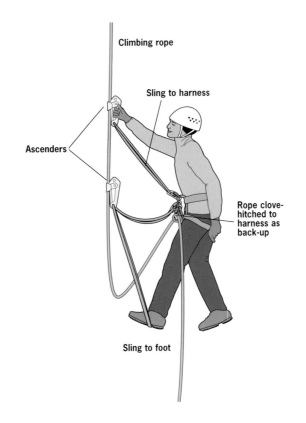

Climbing rope

Sling to harness

Ascenders

Rope clove-hitched to harness as back-up

Sling to foot

The basic set-up for using ascenders

USING AN ASCENDER AND A DEVICE AT THE HARNESS

In some cases, a higher mechanical advantage will be useful. This may be because the ground is very steep and a large load is being carried rather than hauled, or because altitude and exhaustion have played their part and the climber finds the normal method of ascent tiring. It is possible in this case to set up a system that gives a mechanical advantage to the climber, with the proviso that the distance that can be ascended at each pull of the rope is reduced slightly, thus requiring more pulls to ascend a section of ground. This system will need the use of a self-locking pulley or, better still, a self-locking belay device. It should be noted that this technique is unsuitable for use on icy or frozen ropes, as the devices used will not grip properly.

An ascender is clipped on to the rope, which has been passed through the locking pulley or belay device, which in turn is clipped to the harness. The dead rope coming from the harness device is taken up and through a screwgate on the handle of the ascender and allowed to hang free. An extra length of line connects the ascender to the harness as a back-up.

To ascend, sit back and weight the rope, so that the device at the harness takes your weight, and push the ascender up the rope. Now pull up on to the ascender, using the handle to help, feet on the rock, at the same time as pulling down on the rope through the ascender's screwgate. Once this has been done, sit back in your harness and repeat the process.

One of the advantages of this method is that a sling can also be attached to the ascender, long enough for the climber to put their foot in to aid moving up. This will be necessary on very steep or overhanging ground, where foot contact with the rock will not be possible. Back-up clove hitches can also be tied on the rope under the devices as an extra safeguard.

It is worth having a cowtail attached to your harness as well, as this can be used as a safeguard when reaching the stance or ledge where the rope is attached. It should be clipped in to keep you safe while you take off the ascenders.

The rig for ascending the rope using a mechanical advantage

8: EXPEDITION CLIMBING

Expedition climbing covers activities in the mountains where you are remote from home or help for long periods of time, often working in pairs or small groups from a tented base camp, making your way up a peak of substantial size at altitude. Reliance on your companions is paramount, as is your own preparation for the trip, as assistance from outside bodies may be many days away, or even non-existent.

An expedition may not have steep technical climbing as its goal. With many expeditions just overcoming the logistics of getting to base camp, in an unfamiliar country with poor infrastructure and a host of administrative problems to be overcome, will be the hardest part of the trip. I remember a companion on my first ever trip to the Himalaya saying, 'Anything beyond base camp is a bonus.' And I've always remembered that. Get yourself established at base, and from there on in you can enjoy the total change of pace and scenery, concentrating on the job in hand. Many expedition climbers, myself included, enjoy the logistical side of big trips, with the planning, preparation and approach march all being key elements that go to make the entire trip an overall success. But how is success marked? The ascent of a new peak? A hard new line on a long remote buttress reaching thousands of feet into the sky? Or perhaps the relatively simple ascent of a lower level peak with a group of friends and without the concerns created by technical climbing at altitude? Once again, my companion on my first trip said, 'As long as we all come back talking to each other, that's fine.' And that is probably a very wise way to look at it. No mountain is worth a life or a limb, and good friendships will last far longer than any climbing trip possibly can.

EQUIPMENT

There are a number of specialized items that you will need when making a foray into expedition territory. If you are just going away for a short period of time, you may elect to hire the equipment rather than purchase it, and a number of outlets, both at home and at the main town near your destination, will allow you to do this. However, watch out as the quality of some equipment can be variable, and never be tempted to hire items such as ropes or other software as these could be quite old and unsafe to use.

There is a huge amount of equipment needed for even a small expedition of any length

CLOTHING

Clothing for high altitudes needs to be of the best quality available. At lower levels, you can get away with the same equipment as for winter or some Alpine climbs. However, the extreme weather encountered on expeditions to large peaks means that any poorly designed or badly insulated clothing could have its properties compromised by high winds or low temperatures. It is important also to consider the effect of physical exertion, inadequate food intake and lack of sleep on the body, as these factors cause a lowering of resistance to cold.

Many towns and starting-off points for expeditions offer a variety of places where clothing can be purchased or hired. This latter option is a good avenue to take if you are heading to an area that you are unlikely to be revisiting in the near future, in particular for highly specialized pieces of kit such as down trousers. However, the quality of both hired and purchased goods obtainable locally at expedition departure centres can vary dramatically in quality, sizing and availability, so taking gear that you know is fit for purpose with you from your home country will often be the safest choice.

There is such a variety in the type and style of clothing, which needs to be tailored to each individual trip, that it would be very difficult to come up with a full list here. However, a number of pointers may be worth mentioning as far as purchases are concerned, with particular regard to insulation and footwear.

A good quality insulated jacket will be high on any purchase list. Down is a superb insulator, and this garment will most likely be used in base camp as well as on the mountain. Sitting around camp in the luxurious folds of a well-designed garment is one of the great pleasures of expedition life, and even for those not intending to actually climb on the mountain

a down jacket is a must-have. Ensure that it fits a number of criteria before committing to a purchase. It needs to fit over the other clothes that you are intending to wear on the hill in a manner that does not restrict movement but also is not so loose as to allow the wind to enter at any point and cause cooling. The hood should fit over a helmet but still have sufficient adjustment to keep it on the head when one is not worn. Sleeve length needs to allow you to reach up high without any noticeable ride-up, and it should be of a length that covers as far down your body as possible, in particular covering the lower back and kidney area efficiently.

The material from which the outer is constructed will not normally be waterproof, as it would be unusual to come across much rain at altitude However, it should be a water-resistant fabric, as snow will most likely be encountered and it would not be

good to get the insulation damp. Finally, a high-visibility colour is a good idea, and the addition of reflective strips so that team members can easily see each other at night could be considered.

BOOTS

The choice of which mountain boots to wear will depend very much on your objective and area of intended use. They tend to be designed with steep snow, ice and expedition climbing in mind, so you need to think about what the main use will be. Insulation is generally incorporated into the boot, and this will make quite a difference to your comfort when wearing them. Boots for extreme cold used to be almost exclusively a plastic double boot style, but many climbers now opt for a composite material boot, with an inner and outer section, which keeps your feet both warm and dry.

Good expedition quality double boots

A high camp below the north face of Everest

TENTAGE

Tentage used on the mountain should be of the highest quality. It is possible to get away with cheaper accommodation at base camp, but even here wind and snowfall can be considerable and the destruction of sleeping and messing tents is not uncommon. However, the morale-boosting properties of a large communal tent at base camp are not to be overlooked, although a similar shelter may be constructed from a large tarpaulin and the remains of a semi-permanent stone shelter, often improved upon over time by subsequent visitors.

There are a number of features that are desirable in a high-altitude mountain tent, worth considering before making a purchase or hiring one. Lightness of weight is obvious, although this may be compromised slightly by having a flysheet that incorporates a snow valance, useful for securing it down in high winds. A number of high-altitude tents are made from a breathable material, which allows them to be of a single wall construction, compared to the more normal inner/fly

combination. Although lighter overall, single-skin tents will tend to be colder as there is no air trapped between the two outer layers. They are, however, very breathable and may prove to be a good choice in cold altitudes, where efficient vapour transmission is important.

A small footprint, the area that the tent takes up when pitched, should be considered especially if you will need to dig a platform to pitch it on. The less digging at altitude the better, as it is a very tiring and time-consuming process.

Plenty of guy ropes will be found useful, although these can always be manufactured in situ, using spare rope or accessory cord. Having suitable attachment points is obviously important, and the option for adding more should be investigated prior to leaving home. The lightweight skewer-type pegs often supplied with tents are next to useless when used in snow, so make sure that you have a suitable supply of specialist pegs with a large surface area. Small angle-section aluminium stakes are very useful for more permanent securing,

with any larger snow stakes, possibly even salvaged from previous occupiers of the camp site, being excellent.

Almost anything that can be buried can be used to secure the tent. Even a handful of thin pegs, buried under the snow which is then stamped into a solid mass on top of them, will do. Lumps of very hard snow or ice can have the guy rope tied around them and then be buried under more snow. A very good anchor can be made by filling a bag with snow, tying a guy line on to it and burying it.

A lot of cooking will most likely be done whilst in the tent, so a porch area that allows the storage of spare equipment and provides a ventilated cooking area is very useful. Ventilation is very important, especially if a snow valance is being used, as air circulation may not be sufficient to disperse moisture and fumes created by preparing food and drink. The amount of air in the porch will normally be regulated by opening upper zips, which let steam out of the tent. However, ensure that the porch design has taken this into account, and that the opening of the upper zips will not result in any snow on the tent being dumped into the porch area – a possibility that, surprisingly, has been overlooked by some manufacturers.

Hanging points are a useful addition to the inner, and you can add these yourself to suit, prior to setting off on your trip. Best manufactured from a small loop of narrow tape, they can be used to hang equipment on to dry, as an attachment point for lighting, or simply to provide extra off-floor storage space.

Take a couple of pole repair sleeves with you, as these can prove to be indispensable if a pole is badly bent or snapped by the wind or excessive snow loading. They consist of a metal tube that is slid along the pole to cover the offending section, allowing the tent to be used for longer. Without them, a damaged pole could cause the camp to be abandoned.

Abandoned oxygen cylinders on Mount Everest

OXYGEN

This is a specialist item, reserved for trips to the higher peaks, most often above 8,000 metres (26,000ft). It is sometimes carried in small quantities for medical reasons, and can be administered as a temporary remedy for potentially fatal conditions such as HAPE or HACE (see below) during casualty evacuation.

Oxygen is delivered via a regulator to a face mask, which can be used both when climbing and when sleeping at altitude. The oxygen cylinders are small enough to be carried in or on top of a rucksack, and the extra physiological benefit that they give more than makes up for the increase in carried weight.

Using a fixed rope over a section of rock step

FIXED ROPES

The use of these may vary from the semi-permanent protection of a short section of technical ground, perhaps through an icefall or a hazardous section of an approach route, through to hundreds of metres of rope being fixed for the safe ascent, and more importantly descent, of steep snow or technical terrain.

The rope can be of either dynamic or low-stretch construction, although those used during a long-duration expedition will often tend to be low-stretch, as they are more resilient to the rigours of frequent use. They are also available on handy reels of a couple of hundred metres or more. On technical ground, they have the advantage that when weighted they will not bounce as much as dynamic ropes, not only making the ascent easier, but also preventing the rope from rubbing too much at crucial wear points, a problem with stretchy ropes.

The thickness of the rope will depend on a number of factors. The thinner the rope the lighter it will be, obviously important at altitude, but it will be less strong, harder to handle, especially with ascenders and when using thick gloves, and it will be less resistant to abrasion and general wear and tear. This final factor is extremely important, and anyone choosing to use ropes of around 8mm (3/8in) or less in diameter should take great care.

Many low-stretch ropes are white, so have a think about the ground over which the rope is to be rigged. If it is to be set up on a snow slope, a coloured rope would be far easier to locate in times of drifting snow or darkness. If you are rigging the rope over sections of rock, a white colour will be fine as it will be easy to locate.

The final choice comes down to the terrain that you are going to cross and the amount that it will be used. For instance, the rope that you rig for just a couple of days on a short section of snow slope as a safety line will differ from that which you rig on a long section of steep ground, which will be used by climbers and support staff over a period of a month or more.

AXE AND CRAMPONS

These will often be very lightweight, particularly those that are to be used at altitude. Technical routes at lower levels may demand some that are more robust, most likely the same that are used for ice climbing, but as every tiny increase in weight

really does make a difference at higher elevations, light alloys and uncomplicated systems will be preferred. Check the usage guidelines of any extra-lightweight kit that you purchase, as some gear that is designed to be used on snow will very quickly become damaged if any rock is crossed, as it will not be manufactured from strong enough materials.

ASCENDERS

These are a staple of many expeditions, and allow a number of tasks to be carried out with relative ease and security. The negotiating of fixed ropes is the prime use, although they also have their place when setting up hauling systems.

Handled ascenders are best suited to use on fixed ropes, and these should be chosen so that they can be used when wearing thick gloves. Moderately angled ropes, such as those placed on long snow slopes, will just need one ascender, whereas steep ropes, perhaps placed in order to regain high-points on technical routes, may require the use of two. They come in left- and right-handed versions, in order that the thumb can be used to operate the release switch, so make sure that you purchase the correct type.

Attachment to the climber will commonly be with the use of a cowstail to their harness. This can either be clipped to the ascender with a screwgate through a hole at the end of the handle, or by using a larksfoot around the base of the handle.

DESCENDERS

The most practical here is a figure of eight descender. This is easy to operate with gloves on, and will work well when the rope is covered in snow. More technical descents may warrant the use of conventional abseiling techniques, such as with a belay device and prusik back-up.

A small figure of eight will do the job well, and will weigh a lot less than its larger companion. It should be furnished with a

A figure of eight descender

Connecting an ascender to a cowstail

screwgate karabiner and its use is covered under the 'Descending fixed ropes on snow' section (see p. 227).

LADDERS

These are most often used where the negotiation of severely crevassed terrain will have to be made on a frequent basis, such as on a siege expedition. The classic terrain for this can be found in the Khumbu Icefall below Mount Everest. Here expeditions routinely place ladders across hazardous areas to allow teams of climbers and porters to carry loads of food and equipment up to higher camps. However, as icefalls are constantly on the move, a safe ladder one day may be a twisted mass of metal the next, or a reasonably safe crossing may be turned, just a few hours later, into one that is severely threatened by sérac fall. Thus, although ladders may be seen as a 'permanent' answer to crossing crevasses, the reality may be very different.

Purpose-built ladders tend to come in short sections, designed to be bolted together to attain the required length. Because they are most commonly made from aluminium, the longer the span the more flexible and springy the ladder becomes, not something that is desirable when carrying a heavy load across a seemingly bottomless abyss! To combat this, vertical struts can be placed at various sections, which are in turn linked to each end of the ladder with non-stretch rope or cable, in order to allow the ladder to retain some rigidity, in a similar fashion to a suspension bridge. This vertical support hangs down into the crevasse, with other, shorter vertical supports being placed facing upwards, on to which a handrail can be attached to allow increased security for the person crossing.

Spans of any length will also have a second safety system in place, in the form of an independently secured rope on to which the crosser can clip a free-running karabiner cowstailed to their harness. This means that, should they slip from the ladder, or it turns or otherwise becomes dislodged, they will be kept from falling into the crevasse.

Ladders are sometimes used to make passage over vertical sections easy, taking away the need for technical climbing. In this instance, intermediate supports may still be used. The top of the ladder will be secured to the top of the ice, and a safety handrail may again be put in place. In this instance, an ascender will be used, so that a slip does not result in the climber falling all the way back to the ground.

Any ladders found in situ that have no obvious provenance should be treated with caution. Also, any ladders that are bought locally which show any signs of buckling or other damage should not be used, as they could potentially collapse under use.

WANDS

Marker wands are very useful. They can be used to identify the ends of fixed ropes, gear dumps, campsites, the path through crevassed terrain, in fact all manner of things. They are best purchased locally, as they are quite unwieldy to carry any distance. Ideally, they will be made from bamboo or similar material, and measure about two to three metres in length and have a diameter of a centimetre or two. The top needs to be furnished with a noticeable marker of some type. This can be cloth or plastic, and be well secured so that it cannot blow off in the high winds that are inevitable at altitude.

When choosing the length, bear in mind that it may be secured by being pushed a metre or so into the snow. Thus, although a two-metre wand may appear to be very long when viewed at the market, when used on the hill there may be less than a metre left protruding, making location tricky.

PULKS

A type of sledge that is pulled behind you, these are useful items where heavy loads have to be carried over long sections of horizontal ground, such as glaciers and long snow fields, in order to establish a base camp. Commonly used along with skis, they are very efficient, particularly if soft snow is going to be encountered on the way.

They are most often made from a polycarbonate or similar plastic material, and shaped like a shallow bath.

Having used a ladder to cross a crevasse, the climber is now using the rope for support

They will be attached to you at hip height by two rigid traces, which allow the pulk to be pulled but will not let it run over your skis on downhill sections of ground.

Using pulks on flat terrain can save a lot of time and effort when ferrying loads

EXPEDITION LIFE

One of the biggest differences between Alpine trips and expeditions is the time scale, not just from a planning and travelling point of view but also from the amount of time that you will spend just doing nothing! This may be for reasons of acclimatization, waiting for transport links, sitting out poor weather, or just relaxing and having a day off from a heavy schedule. Other factors, such as the amount of time that you will spend trekking to your base camp and dealing with any staff that you employ, all go to make life on an expedition, large or small, quite different to any other type of trip that you may have been involved in.

OBTAINING PERMITS

Many countries that have the highest mountains within their borders use a permit system, where a fee is paid to the government, often through their mountaineering association. This can range from many thousands of dollars for a peak such as Mount Everest, through to a few dollars for a trekking permit for lower level objectives. Full details of current fees can be found on the country's tourism websites, or by contacting a trekking company who operate on site.

USING A TREKKING COMPANY

The vast majority of expeditions will use the services of a trekking company to help sort out the logistics for their trip. This could be a complete service, which will include items such as gaining a climbing permit, making hotel bookings, picking you up at the airport, employing local staff and hiring you all the equipment. Alternatively, you may just wish to use the services of a company to help you fight through the mound of bureaucracy that accompanies trips to many parts of the world, and do the rest of the organizing yourself. Queuing at the mountaineering headquarters of the host country and waiting for endless forms to be stamped by people who really don't care is one of the least appealing aspects of a trip, and many climbers will happily pay for a company to go through this process for them.

Most areas of the world have a licensing system for local companies, so find out about the area to which you are travelling in advance, and see what the local regulations are for the registration and running of trekking firms.

STAFF

You will most likely wish to have a few local members of staff to help with your trip, so that you can concentrate on the job of preparing for the climb and getting fit in readiness. Your key person will be a sirdar, elder or headman, depending upon where you are travelling, and they will be in charge of the rest of the staff. Generally very experienced in dealing with expeditions, they will most likely have worked their way up through the ranks of portering and cooking to gain the top job. Thus, they will have a wealth of knowledge about man-management and dealing with climbing teams, and you should respect their advice and judgment when dealing with the myriad issues that crop up on a trip.

You may also want to use a cook, who will then usually require the services of a cook-boy or assistant. Cooks are skilled at preparing vast quantities of food with a variety of ingredients, many of which they will purchase locally, all cooked on an ancient stove that appears to produce more smoke than heat! However, they understand that food is key to a successful trip, and you will be amazed at the quality of the meals they produce in little time. The purring of a kerosene stove making the evening meal is one of the most comforting sounds that you will ever hear on a trip!

USING PORTERS AND ANIMALS

Most expeditions will employ the services of local porters or animal-owners to help transport their equipment to base camp. This is because the amount of food and equipment needed could not possibly be carried by the team members, as it will have to be enough to last them for the duration of the trip, possibly a month or more.

Most of the more popular climbing and trekking areas are well regulated, with official procedures in place for hiring licensed porters that stipulate the maximum load that can be carried, daily wages, living conditions and the like. Although it may seem that people working as porters are being paid very little money and are having to carry heavy loads for long periods of time to earn their keep, this is not necessarily the case. Portering for expeditions is generally a very lucrative profession and one that is highly respected, not only in their own country but also by mountaineers the world over. The small amount of money that expeditions appear to pay per day will very likely be considerably more than the average wage for that country, and even the weights that they carry will be little more than if they were at home carrying supplies to their village or when employed in other areas of work. All expeditions should have the greatest of respect for anyone working in this way, as they are invariably friendly, helpful and have a wicked sense of humour!

When employing porters it is important to make sure that they are indeed registered and licensed, if that is the local convention. Many trips abroad will be using the services of a trekking company, and they will use staff that they know. This helps to smooth out any employment problems that you may have, as well as ensuring the wellbeing of the porters whilst on the trek. Be wary of using staff that present themselves to you looking for work without having any official paperwork, at least in the more popular areas, as there have been problems in the past with unregulated staff absconding with expedition supplies, as well as staged pay disputes, often calculated to happen at the point of no return along an approach march. Always agree the fees up front, and be prepared for a little leeway in your negotiations.

Using herders or pony men tends to be less regulated, and this can pose a risk if the person you happen upon is unscrupulous. However, beasts can often carry a lot more than a man, and so the overall cost when all is considered may be a lot less than using porters. Horses, donkeys, camels and yaks are the commonest

A yak, essential when transporting heavy loads at altitude to base camp

types of animal that are used, depending upon the area that you are visiting.

Always check the welfare of the animals before agreeing to use them, and if they appear to be malnourished or mistreated then use another supplier. Don't let the owner overload them, and make sure that they get regular food and water breaks, particularly during the heat of the day or when at altitude.

LIAISON OFFICER AND GOVERNMENT OFFICIALS

Expeditions in some areas, and particularly those visiting the higher peaks, may need to be accompanied by a government official. These will most often be members of the tourism ministry of the host country, and their job is to ensure that visitors to their country adhere to the climbing regulations. They also make sure that no militarily sensitive sites are visited and that behaviour does not offend religious practice. They can also be helpful by liaising with local village headmen and government officials, often smoothing the way when all else seems to have failed.

In most countries, you will be expected to equip your 'LO' at the outset with the same quality clothing and tentage as the rest of the team, and this will be made clear in your initial approach to the host mountaineering association or ministry.

Apart from their given task, they usually do not take part in any other aspect of the expedition, and may even mysteriously disappear for a week or more while you are climbing. They do have the power to stop an expedition if they think that a team is overstepping the mark in some way, for instance climbing a peak without permission, and they will always send a report in to their ministry at the end of the trip. Generally, I have found them to be very good company and not inhibiting in any way. As their role is purely observational and they don't have a great deal to do, they are very keen to chat about you and your country, and can offer a fascinating insight into their own world.

TREKKING IN

This is the term usually given to the journey from the roadhead or airstrip to your base camp. Depending on where you are starting and finishing, the trek in, or approach march as it's also commonly known, may take from a few hours to a couple of weeks or even more.

Life on the approach march tends to be at a moderate pace, particularly if you are employing local staff to cook and provide tentage for you, as they will be doing most of the hard work. This will be the commonest style of walking in to a climb, as it allows the group members to get fit and acclimatize whilst walking, at the same time as saving energy and being able to relax into the expedition environment.

A typical day will start early, maybe just before sunrise, and often with 'bed tea', brought to you by the cook's assistant. After this, you can wash and have breakfast before setting out on the first section of the walk for the day. Your staff will pack everything away and soon overtake you (remember that they are used to this style of life!), and be ready to meet you farther along the trail with lunch. After a short rest it's back to walking until you reach the camp for the night. There will normally be plenty of opportunity to explore surrounding areas as you trek, and as the night's camp will be reached early, there is time to relax and acclimatize to your surroundings and the altitude.

I always make the most of the approach march to hone my fitness levels, but at the same time being careful to not get too tired or pick up an injury. I carry a few items in my rucksack, such as camera gear and water, along with essentials such as sunscreen and spare jacket. Given time, I normally make the most of any side trails that go uphill off the main path, as these not only provide an interesting diversion from the main route and a good photo point, but also let you do a bit of uphill walking with a rucksack on, thus improving your fitness. After a bit of uphill I come back down again to join the main route. Be careful if you choose to branch off the main trail like this however, as the maze of paths can become quite confusing and you could easily become lost.

Some bridges in remote areas can be less than solid

AIR SUPPORT AND TRANSFERS

Some areas of the world are suitable for support and base camp approach by air. This may be by fixed wing aircraft, where a glacier or ice-cap landing can be carried out, or by helicopter, which gives access to remote and more rugged terrain. Although air support may seem to be very expensive at the outset, it should be compared against many days trekking with porters, or the hardship of pulling sledges over great distances. However, if the climb is to be at any altitude the positive effect of a slow walk in and correct acclimatization should not be underestimated, with a quick ascent to base camp by mechanical means possibly contributing to the rapid onset of altitude sickness.

Travelling from your home country, you may choose to airfreight out extra equipment well before your team are due to arrive. This not only avoids expensive excess baggage charges on the day, but also ensures that your gear has already arrived when you reach your destination.

Two main fare structures are relevant to aircraft usage. The first will be per person and per kilogram of equipment carried, sometimes given as per cubic metre. This may mean that you end up sharing the craft with another climbing team heading out to a similar area, and it can prove to be quite cost-effective. The second is to hire the craft outright. You will be told the maximum passengers it can carry along with the payload, and this often means that there is plenty of leeway in planning what gear (and indeed which people!) to take along. Although this may be the most expensive way of paying for uplift (though not necessarily so, as some 'per-passenger' and 'per-kilogram' fares are imaginatively constructed), it will often be the most flexible, and the only option if you are flying out as a single team to a remote location.

Packing gear for carrying as freight on internal flights need be no different to the method used for international carriers. The advantage is that any products purchased locally, such as foodstuffs or tentage, can usually be carried in whatever containers it was supplied in and needs no special repacking or sealing. The company with whom you are travelling will give you the best advice as to how to pack large or bulky items, and will often supply packing cases or sacks for the task.

There are many suppliers of local air transport across the world, but make sure that the one that you choose has the relevant safety certificates, air warranty paperwork and is licensed with the appropriate authorities. Although non-registered carriers may prove to be cheap at the outset, should anything go wrong, such as cancellation or

A supply plane fitted with skids

loss of equipment, you could lose out both financially and maybe with the ultimate abandonment of your trip. Also, make sure that any insurance that you have taken out for the expedition includes cover when travelling by air on internal flights.

ON THE MOUNTAIN

BASE CAMP

This is where you will be living for quite a long time, and recuperating during rest visits after spells of climbing on the mountain. So it is nice if base camp is situated somewhere pleasant and flat, allowing you to relax on your days off. However, this is not always possible, as you will need to be quite near to the start of the climbing, so you may be based on a large area of moraine, for instance, or on the flat area of a glacier.

I always carry a few luxuries to be used at base, as this just makes the whole experience a little more relaxing. Although it may sound strange, some good quality chocolate or sweets will always be welcome, as these are often not available. A good book, music and a comfortable sleeping mattress are also an essential part of relaxing and recharging your batteries. If possible, having a tent to yourself allows you to stretch out and make the place your own.

Take the opportunity to eat and drink well, and catch up on the sleep that you will most likely have missed out on when on the hill. If you have just arrived at base camp at the start of a trip, make the most of the opportunity to go high during the day and return for the night, as this will help acclimatization.

CAMPING AT ALTITUDE

When on the climb you may be camping, snow-holing or simply bivouacking on a ledge. Whichever you end up doing, it is important to have a system that allows you to make your night as comfortable and restful as possible, as this will allow you the maximum chance to recuperate, ready for the next day.

If you are going to snow-hole, the techniques that you have used at lower level in winter will see you through most eventualities. Bear in mind, though, that digging a snow hole is hard work at the best of times, so to dig one of any size at altitude is a very hard task indeed. However, a snow hole will give you a windproof and, compared to a tent, warm night.

Bivouacs are cold affairs, and are often only carried out when there is no other alternative and light is fading. To sit out a bivi when the weather is poor and at altitude, possibly without means of cooking or preparing drinks, is to leave oneself open to hypothermia and the onset of altitude sickness. However, a bivi that is planned may well be a comfortable

experience, with the added advantage that the rucksacks will be lighter as a complete tent will not be carried, perhaps just a rudimentary covering for the climbing party. Organization is very important here, and having spent time practising the skills of cooking and managing a bivi site at lower levels will certainly pay dividends. A bivi such as this will often be done just for a few hours, while a team rests before making a summit attempt or a push up a particularly technical section of ground.

Camping will be the most common way of spending the night out, although this does of course mean carrying tentage up the route, adding considerably to the weight of your rucksack. However, the flexibility of pitching that a tent allows, along with a very quick set-up time, means that it is normally first choice.

Finding somewhere flat to pitch will be the main problem, and you might have to dig a platform out of a snow slope in order to get somewhere reasonable enough to spend the night. Ridge lines, although often windy, will be an alternative. The chance of pitching your tent in beautiful geometric lines, just like in the catalogue, is extremely unlikely!

Keep as much snow as possible out of the tent, otherwise this will melt and make everything sodden. A small toothbrush is a good way to remove snow from boots, as these will be best stored inside the tent to stop them from freezing.

Take care when cooking, as fire is a real possibility, as is asphyxiation from unburnt fumes where the hot flame reaches a cold pot and not all of the vapours ignite. Make the effort to get as much liquid in you as possible, as well as any food that you can prepare. Do this from the comfort of your sleeping bag, as you will keep warm during the long time it takes to get a meal ready.

Once inside the tent, try to not have to go outside unless it is absolutely necessary, or the weather is decent enough to let you do so. You may have to rig an anchor rope so that you can move around outside in safety.

A pee bottle is one of any expedition's essentials, and it is worth having one for each person. These can be used by both sexes, and it saves having to trek out of the tent in the middle of the night. Make sure that the bottle is easily identifiable by putting tape round it and writing your name in large letters, so that no one else uses it by mistake, as confusing a pee bottle with a drinks bottle can easily happen at night!

Those with a tight screw top are the best, with plastic being the material of choice.

Make sure that you have everything ready for departure the next morning, to save as much time as possible and so that you can get ready with the minimum of effort. Cooking is notoriously slow at altitude, seemingly more so in the mornings, but do make the effort to drink and eat appropriately before you set off.

CLIMBING STYLES

There are three main types of ascent, as far as expeditions are concerned, and these are siege, capsule and Alpine. The siege style of ascent is usually reserved for large expeditions on big mountains, and relies on a constant stream of men and materials being moved up the mountain to various camps, with each one being well stocked and able to support a number of people. Having a large amount of logistical support means that the lead climbers have a good chance of being well rested and fed before making their summit attempt from the highest camp. The logistical chart of a siege expedition looks like a pyramid, with a large number of people involved at lower levels, all working to maintain the efficiency at the top of the pyramid, the climbers out front.

Capsule style is where a small group of climbers, perhaps even just two, work to stock a camp with everything for the climb, move on up to the next camp and spend time ferrying the gear up to there, and so on. This is almost like a miniature version of a siege expedition, but with the participants working a lot harder and without any logistical back-up should anything go wrong.

Alpine style is seen by many to be the purest form, where everything needed by the team is carried on their backs, and no extensive load carrying and stocking of camps is carried out.

Solitude? A busy camp one on Cho Oyu

CLIMBING ON FIXED ROPES

This is a feature of many expeditions, and may be only for a short way over an awkward section of ground, or for quite some distance up the flank of a huge snow face. You should never underestimate the seriousness of using a fixed rope for an ascent or descent, and always make sure that the rope is safe and secure, checking any knots and rub points for signs of wear and tear.

The commonest type of rope will be the low-stretch variety, where the weight of a climber will not cause much elongation. Dynamic ropes could be used, but they will stretch when loaded, and there will also be the problem of the sawing action, caused by frequent loading and unloading of bodyweight, across a section of rock, which could damage or even cut right through the rope over time.

A fixed rope that crosses a section of snowy ground may be relatively easy to negotiate. It will be anchored at each end, and probably by a variety of points along its length. This can be done by using snow stakes, deadmen or even buried oxygen cylinders in the highest areas. A snow bollard as the top anchor would also be suitable, but would only last a short time due to the cutting effect of people pulling on it constantly as they made their way up and down the rope.

Ropes that cross steep rocky ground tend to be put under a lot more pressure, as the weight of the climber is usually committed to the rope as footing can be hard to gain. The techniques for negotiating them will often rely on using just the rope for ascent, with two jamming devices being used, one each for a hand and a foot.

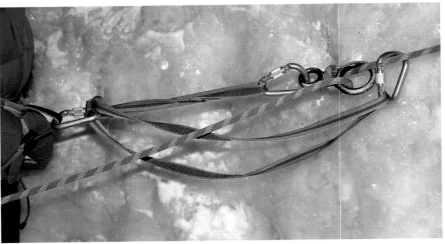

A figure of eight device and a cowstail set up for an abseil

Hand-over-handing when descending easy ground. Note the cowstail clipped to the rope

ASCENDING FIXED ROPES ON SNOW

This will be the way in which fixed ropes are most commonly used, and is often deployed by commercial companies to facilitate their clients making it to the top of their chosen mountain. It is also used where loads are being ferried up from camp to camp, or just as a general back-up. The line is there as a safeguard, with the climber making progress by walking up. They will be attached to the fixed rope with a mechanical rope clamp, with the version incorporating a handle being the best and easiest to operate, especially when wearing gloves. This clamp will be attached to the climber with a short length of rope or sling, which allows for freedom of movement. To ascend, the clamp is simply slid up the rope as the climber moves forwards, and it locks when pulled backwards, such as in the event of a slip. In their other hand, the climber may well be carrying an ice axe which is used as a walking aid, and is obviously there as an extra safeguard in an emergency.

Also attached to the climber's harness is a cowstail with a karabiner. When they reach an intermediate anchor point, the cowstail is clipped above it on to the new section of rope, before the clamp is taken off the rope just ascended, then placed on the next section. This ensures that the climber is at no time unprotected, as if they just took the clamp off the rope without the cowstail back-up, and slipped, they would have the possibility of falling quite some distance.

Resting is important, especially at altitude, and in hard snow conditions having a few ledges cut out of the snow along the length of the fixed line will allow the climbers to get their feet flat and have a breather.

The top of the fixed rope needs to have been set up at a place that is safe enough for the climbers to unclip and move away from their security, so care should be taken when doing so that there is no chance of a slip causing a long slide back down the hill.

DESCENDING FIXED ROPES ON SNOW

The top of any fixed rope section needs to be clearly marked and locatable, even in bad weather. Tall marker wands, purchased locally for the purpose, serve to do this very well, with the rope being tied to a secure anchor immediately adjacent to them. A large pyramid of snow may also help, or the use of oxygen bottles. If the rope is anchored low to the snow surface, such as with a deadman, it can easily become drifted over and impossible to find, even in relatively good visibility.

A figure of eight abseil device will commonly be used for descent, as this will be easy to handle with large gloves on, and will not jam up on snowy ropes. It is important that this, too, is backed up with a cowstail and screwgate, to provide security at changeover points. Once the first section of rope has been descended, the figure of eight device is taken off the top rope and placed on to the next section, with the cowstail remaining on the upper rope. Once the device is secure, the cowstail is transferred to the rope just above it, and the descent can continue.

A snow stake being used as a fixed-rope anchor. Note the sling attached low down to reduce leverage

ASCENDING FIXED ROPES ON ROCK

This style of ascent usually means that the rope will be loaded with the climber's weight for at least part, if not all, of the ascent. For that reason, not only must the rigging of the rope be done in a very safe manner, but care should be taken to avoid any chance of the rope fraying on sharp sections of rock when in use. If there is the possibility of a problem occurring, the rope should be routed in such a way as to miss out the suspect area altogether. Remember that the action of the wind, rubbing the rope on to any sharp areas of rock, can also cause a great deal of damage even when the system is not being used.

The prudent use of intermediate anchors can go a long way to preventing this problem. For instance, even if the main anchor point is close to the area that is to be avoided, placing a wire or chock a short way to one side will have the effect of redirecting the rope away from the problem.

In some cases, and to give absolute security, it may be necessary to double up areas of concern by using a sling or spare length of rope. For instance, if the main rope is going to unavoidably be running past a sharp area of rock, that section can be bypassed quite simply. A sling or length of spare rope is attached to the anchor, along with the end of the fixed rope. At a point beyond the obstruction, an Alpine butterfly or similar knot can be tied in the main rope, and the sling attached here. This means that any wear will be on the sling section, and should it wear through, the whole rig will still be supported by the main rope. Obviously, this is not a remedy that should be used for a long period of time, but it will certainly allow the use of a fixed line to be considered in problem areas.

The actual ascent of the rope very much depends upon the nature of the terrain. On the simplest ground it may be very similar to ascending a rope on snow, where a single ascender or rope clamp is used as a back-up, and the climber is easily able to make their own way ahead. On any other type of ground though, the use of two ascenders or a hybrid system will be found to be most appropriate. These techniques are the same as those covered in the 'Big wall climbing' section. A cowstail should once again be used, for extra security when swapping from one rope length to another.

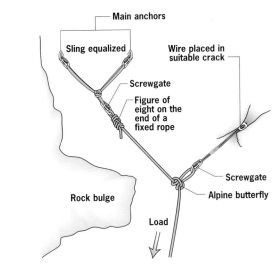

A wire keeping a fixed rope away from a rock bulge

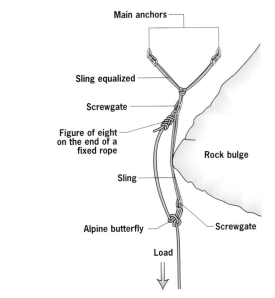

A sling backing up the top of a fixed rope

The author on a previously unclimbed summit in the Himalaya

ALTITUDE ISSUES

As expedition climbing often explores terrain at altitude, an understanding of the problems associated with it should be gained. This is a very complicated subject and high-altitude medical specialists, with research ongoing, still do not completely understand many areas. The same people can react differently at different times, and it seems to have no relation to age, sex, fitness or diet. There are some prescribed medicines that will, for some, go towards aiding acclimatization. Knowledge of what to avoid is also important. The three main areas of concern are as follows.

AMS

Acute mountain sickness. This is the body's inability to deal with the decreasing oxygen pressure as altitude increases. Symptoms include headache, loss of appetite, vomiting, loss of sleep, fatigue and dizziness. Although many climbers maintain that a headache is part and parcel of climbing at altitude, it is not, and it should certainly be treated as a warning sign that your body is starting to react to the change in height. Descent to an altitude where you previously felt well is the best remedy.

HAPE

High-altitude pulmonary oedema (the acronym comes from the American spelling, edema) is a major killer in the greater ranges, and a condition that can make its presence felt at relatively low levels. It is caused by the constriction of vessels in the lungs, which in turn cause those that are not restricted to be subject to high pressure and subsequently to leak fluid into the lungs. Signs and symptoms include extreme fatigue, breathlessness, fast but shallow breathing that is possibly noisy, a productive cough, tightness of chest, drowsiness and blue lips or fingernails.

Immediate descent, or the administering of oxygen, is the answer, and any delay can be fatal. As exertion leads to a worsening of the condition, sufferers may need to be carried to lower altitudes. Research has shown that this condition affects mainly fit and young climbers, and its onset is rapid. Although sometimes confused with AMS, there may be no connection and AMS signs may not be present.

HACE

High-altitude cerebral oedema is another serious condition, and is the swelling of the brain to the extent that normal cerebral function is impaired. Sufferers will often seem to be confused, unable to think for themselves, and their manner of walking becomes like someone who is severely intoxicated.

Immediate descent is essential, even during the middle of the night, when both HACE and HAPE tend to manifest themselves. Oxygen and drug treatment, along with a hyperbaric bag may help, but failure to act quickly can result in death in as little as a few hours.

ACCLIMATIZING ON A TRIP

As different people acclimatize at different rates, it is very difficult to accurately chart an acclimatization programme that will suit everyone. The maxim of 'climb high, sleep low' should be remembered, as it is during this sleep phase that the body can rest and adapt to the altitude. Going high during the day, perhaps during a rest day on a trek in, and then returning to sleep at a lower level, will do a lot to help you get used to the rarefied atmosphere.

The following are general guidelines, based on the average rate of acclimatization for trekkers and climbers, but remember that everyone will be different. Having had a night at an elevation below 3,000 metres (10,000ft), when continuing above this height you should not sleep in increments of more than 300–500 metres (1,000–1,500ft) per night. Additionally, it is suggested that for every 1,000 metres (3,000ft), a second night should be spent at the same location. It is here that, should you feel well enough, you can go high during the day, returning to the camp at night.

It is important to remember that, if you feel at all unwell at altitude and there is no obvious reason for being like that, such as diarrhoea or other illness, then the altitude is affecting you and descent is the only sensible option. Descending to the last point where you felt well, usually the last sleeping place, will often be enough to reduce the symptoms. After a period of rest, maybe a day or so, re-ascent may be possible, and this can often be done without any more altitude-related problems for the rest of the trip.

Take it easy when trekking at altitude and have regular rest stops

APPENDIX I
GRADES

The tables that follow indicate various climbing grades, both summer and winter, for a number of countries worldwide. These are for guidance only, as there will always be an ongoing healthy discussion about which grade is equivalent to another.

VIA FERRATA

	FRENCH	ITALIAN	H/W	F/S
The easiest grade with simple climbing.	F	1	A	1A
A little trickier, suitable for beginners and children.	PD	2	B	2A
A grade for beginners with experienced companions, where technique is becoming important	AD		C	
		3	D	3B
Suitable for those used to Via Ferratas. Many sections will be inescapable.	D	4	E	4B
Physically demanding, can be long and in remote locations.	TD	5	F	5C
The highest degree of stamina and physical fitness is required.	ED		G	
NOTES	Can be sub divided into + and − grades. Difficult to tell the difference between very short hard routes and remote long easy ones.	Common system, but like the French it is hard to quantify technical difficulty against seriousness or commitment.	The Höfler/Werner system, with similarities to the French and Italian methods of description.	The Fletcher/Smith system, where 1-5 indicates the technical difficulty and A, B and C the commitment. Grades can be interchangeable, with 2C and 4A as examples.

You can see from the table that the final column gives more information than the others about the route, although it is not currently in common usage. The flexibility of the system allows a route with hard moves but a short and safe overall trip, for instance, to be given a 5A rating. Conversely, a Via Ferrata that is easy but long and remote could gain a 2C rating.

Other grading systems do exist, but the first two columns indicate the most popular forms currently. The F/S system may come into more mainstream use, and this is up to guide writers and pressure from Via Ferrata users.

ROCK CLIMBING GRADES

UK SERIOUSNESS	UK TECHNICAL	FRENCH/ SPORT	RUSSIA	NORWAY	USA	UIAA	SOUTH AFRICA	POLAND	AUSTRALIAN
Moderate	-	-	III	1	5.1, 5.2	I, II			4, 5
Difficult	**3a**	2	III+	1, 2	5.3, 5.4	II		I	5, 6
Very Difficult	3a, **3b**	2	IV-	1, 2	5.4	II+		I	6, 7, 8
Hard Very Difficult	3b, **3c**	2+	IV	2, 3	5.4, 5.5	III-		II	8, 9
Mild Severe	3c, **4a**	3	IV, IV+	3	5.5, 5.6	III		II, III	9, 10, 11
Severe	**4a**, 4b	3+	IV+	3, 4-	5.6	III+, IV-	13	IV	11, 12
Hard Severe	4a, **4b**, 4c	3+, 4	IV+	4	5.7	IV-	14	V-	12, 13
Mild Very Severe	**4b**, 4c	4	V-	4	5.7	IV, IV+	14, 15	V-, V	13, 14
Very Severe	4b, **4c**, 5a	4, 4+	V-	4+	5.7, 5.8	IV+	15, 16	V	14, 15
Hard Very Severe	**5a**, 5b	5, 5+	V	5-	5.9	V-, V, V+	17, 18	V+	15, 16, 17
E1	5a, **5b**, 5c	5+, 6a	V	5, 5+	5.10a, 5.10b	VI-, VI	19	VI	17, 18, 19
E2	5b, **5c**, 6a	6a+, 6b	V+	6-, 6	5.10c. 5.10d	VI+, VII-	20, 21	VI+	19, 20, 21
E3	5c, **6a**, 6b	6b, 6b+	V+	6+, 7-	5.10d, 5.11a	VII-, VII	22, 23	VI.1+	21, 22
E4	**6b**, 6c	6c, 6c+, 7a	VI-	7	5.11b, 5.11c, 5.11d	VII+, VIII-	24, 25	VI.2	22, 23
E5	6b, **6c**	7a, 7a+, 7b	VI	7+	5.11d, 5.12a, 5.12b	VIII, VIII+	26, 27	VI.3	23, 24, 25
E6	6c, 7a	7b+, 7c, 7c+	VI+	8-, 8	5.12c, 5.12d, 5.13a	IX-, IX	27, 28	VI.3+, VI.4	25, 26, 27
E7	6c, 7a, 7b	8a, 8a+	VI+	8+, 9-	5.13b, 5.13c	IX-, X	29, 30, 31	VI.5, VI.5+	27, 28, 29, 30
E8	6c, 7a, 7b, 7c	8b, 8b+	VII	9	5.13d, 5.14a	X, X+	32, 33	VI.6, VI.6+	29, 30, 31
E9	7a, 7b, 7c, 8a	8c, 8c+	VIII	9+	5.14a, 5.14b	XI-, XI	33, 34	VI.7 VI.7+	31, 32
E10 and up	7b, 7c, 8a and up	9a and up	IX and up	10 and up	5.14c, 5.14d	XI+, XII	34, 35 and up	VI.8 VI.8+	32, 33 and up

The UK system is two-tiered, with a letter prefix and number suffix. This system allows you to find out details about the severity and seriousness of a climb, and this takes into account factors such as protection and how sustained the route is, as well as informing you of the grade of the hardest technical move or sequence. For the purposes of the table, UK technical move benchmark grades are in bold. Thus, on a VS climb you would expect the technical standard to be at 4c. However, it could vary up or down by a couple of places or more, with VS5a giving a well-protected but hard route and VS4b denoting an easier route but with fewer runners than usually expected at that level of technicality. Longer climbs will often have an overall seriousness grade but several technical grades, showing the difficulty of moves on individual pitches, for instance a five pitch climb may be graded at VS 4b, 4c, 4c, 5a, 4b, with the hardest moves on the fourth pitch being the crux of the route.

BOULDERING GRADES

There are two generally accepted systems of grading boulder problems, but specific bouldering areas may also have their own systems in place. There is a lot of variation in how problems are graded, as people of differing heights will approach the rock from different perspectives. Sitting starts are common, and these will shift the difficulty of a move up a few places.

V GRADE	FONT GRADE
V0-	3
V0	4
V0+	4+
V1	5
V2	5+
V3	6a, 6a+
V4	6b, 6b+
V5	6c, 6c+
V6	7a
V7	7a+
V8	7b
V8+	7b+
V9	7c
V10	7c+
V11	8a
V12	8a+
V13	8b
V14	8b+
V15	8c

AID CLIMBING GRADES

A0	Equipment is already in place and used with ease.
A1	Relevant equipment is easy to place, and will provide some security in the event of a fall. Progress is often made simply by pulling on the placement.
A2	Awkward placing of some aid equipment. Some placements may be of questionable strength.
A3	Difficult aid climbing, taking time to place equipment. Poor placements likely, resulting in some gear being stripped out in the event of a fall.
A4	Very difficult placement of gear, which will usually only hold bodyweight. As such, the consequences of a fall are severe.
A5	Extreme aiding, with placements only just holding body-weight and little chance of realistic protection along the pitch. A fall may result in the gear on the entire pitch stripping out.

The table above displays the generally accepted categories, but a number of variations exist. The addition of a + sign may be used to denote sub-levels between grades, a popular format in the USA. The letter C may occasionally be used in place of A to represent a clean ascent, where no intrusive marking or damaging of the rock will occur, such as when using camming devices instead of pitons.

EUROPEAN ALPINE GRADES

F (Facile – easy)	A straightforward climb, maybe with a simple glacier approach. The route, if snow and ice, will be consistently of an easy angle. Any rock climbing will be low-grade scrambling.
PD (Peu difficile – not very hard)	Possibly comprising an awkward glacier approach or retreat, routes with tricky scrambling or snow and ice slopes of 35–45 degrees. The length of the route and the altitude may be more than that encountered at F.
AD (Assez difficile – fairly hard)	Snow and ice slopes of up to 55 degrees, with short sections of UIAA grade III rock possible.
D (Difficile – hard)	Snow and ice slopes of up to 70 degrees and rock climbing in the region of IV and V.
TD (Tres difficile – very hard)	Serious routes, with snow and ice of up to 80 degrees, rock in the region of V to VI, possibly including aid moves. The objective danger may be high.
ED (Extremement difficile – extremely hard)	Very hard and serious routes, displaying 90 degree snow and ice, rock of grade VI to VII, aid pitches and high objective danger.

The ED grade is open-ended, and categorized as ED1, ED2 etc, to cope with the continual rise in climbing standards and equipment. Some guide books may use the ABO grade at the very top end, standing for 'Abominablement difficile', and this is reserved for routes of the most extreme difficulty and seriousness.

ALASKA GRADES

AK1	No technical difficulties, with simple glacier crossings.
AK2	No major technical difficulties, but may include narrow ridges, altitude and accompanying weather-related problems.
AK3	Big routes with steep ground requiring technical climbing and possibly the passage of corniced ridges.
AK4	Difficult, sustained climbing.
AK5	Difficult, involving sustained technical climbing and bivouacking.
AK6	Very hard, with long distances over technical ground and little option for retreat.

The Alaska system is cumulative, where a grade, for instance AK3, will include all the elements of those coming before it, in this case AK1 and AK2. It takes into account overall seriousness, including factors such as avalanche hazards, cornicing, the poor weather often found in the region, altitude and extreme cold. Thus, a route with few technical sections may in fact get a high grade if the team have to move fast whilst making constant snow-structure evaluations and needing to cope with cornice hazards.

NORTH AMERICAN AND EUROPEAN ICE CLIMBING GRADES

This two-part system consists of Roman numerals giving the seriousness of the route (encompassing the length of approach, objective danger and duration of the climb), and numbers to denote the technical difficulty (graded for the hardest pitch). These two scales are denoted in separate tables below. The first table gives the prefix to a grade, denoting the type of climbing that is being described.

WI	Water ice.
AI	Alpine ice, often formed from a metamorphosed snow base.
M	Mixed ground, indicating that both rock and ice are encountered.

SERIOUSNESS

I	A route only taking a couple of hours, with non-technical climbing and an easy descent.
II	A route with an easy approach and climbing of moderate technical standard. Time for completion in the region of three to four hours. Easy descent, often by abseil.
III	A route taking half a day, involving a longer approach, more intricate descent and low-altitude multi-pitch climbing. There may be a rockfall or avalanche hazard.
IV	A climb at altitude or in a remote area, taking most of the day to complete. Multi-pitch in nature, objective hazards may be high and descents complicated.
V	A route that takes at least a day to complete, often only attainable by a fast and competent party. Objective dangers are likely to be high and the climb long and technical, often at altitude. Descents may involve multiple abseils.
VI	Taking over a day to complete, this grade contains climbs of a high technical severity in Alpine-like settings with sustained technical difficulties and serious rock fall, avalanche, crevasse and extreme weather possibilities. Only the most technically competent and physically fit parties are likely to succeed.
VII	The hardest and most serious of climbs, involving great personal risk and the need for high technical, physical and mental competence. Only attainable by the few.

TECHNICAL DIFFICULTY

1	Water ice of up to 50 degrees or a long snow slope requiring basic skills.
2	Water ice, including sections of up to 70 degrees, including good protection and belay opportunities.
3	Sustained water ice climbing at between 70 and 80 degrees, possibly with short steeper sections, followed by a rest. Protection is still good.
4	Sustained climbing on 75–85 degree ice, or vertical sections of around 25 metres (80ft) with periodic rests. Protection is reasonable.
5	Sustained multi-pitch ice climbing on vertical terrain, giving little or no chance of rest. Generally good or reasonable quality ice.
6	Serious multi-pitch routes with sustained difficulties over long distances on vertical ground. Protection can be hard to place due to the ice being poor in places. Mixed ground may be encountered.
7	Poor quality thin vertical or overhanging ice smears, with poor or purely psychological protection. Very technical climbing needed to produce upward movement, including sections of extreme mixed ground. High possibility of ice failure on icicles or chandeliers.
8	The most extreme ice routes possible, involving all the above factors and more.

The scale is commonly left open-ended for mixed routes.

The above system is designed to be consistent across the different media. For instance, WI6 should be the same difficulty as M6, which in turn will be the same as AI6. On routes with a large variation of terrain, various prefixes and suffixes may be used, for instance M5, AI3. As an addition, routes that may display a tendency to fall down, such as fragile chandelier ice, can be given an X rating, and those that have a particularly committing run-out can be labelled with an R. This then allows a lot of information to be given about any route, although the result may look like a scientific calculation: VI/AI3, WI5, RX.

In some areas, where the climbing is in a non-remote setting such as a roadside icefall, just the technical grading may be applied, as there would be no seriousness commitment such as a long approach or avalanche hazard.

SCOTTISH WINTER GRADES

This is a two-tier system, where the Roman numerals denote the seriousness and difficulty of the climb and the number denotes the technical grade of the hardest section of the route. The two tables below list the features of each element.

SERIOUSNESS

I	Easy ridges and snow gullies of around 45 degrees. Cornices may be present.
II	Routes with short sections of difficult ground, either ice pitches or rock steps, followed by good resting areas. Ridge climbs would equate to easy summer scrambles.
III	Routes that give a more sustained outing than at grade II, with mixed routes equating to around Moderate summer standard.
IV	Completion of a route involves the climbing of long sections of steep ice of up to 70 degrees, or shorter sections of vertical ground. Mixed routes, of Difficult or Severe summer standard, will need good axe technique, including technical torquing, to overcome them.
V	Sustained routes with ice of 70 degrees or more for long distances, as well as vertical ground. Mixed routes will be very hard, up to around summer Very Severe standard.
VI	Ice pitches will be vertical for quite some distance, and the ice often of dubious quality. Mixed routes will be technical summer Very Severe in standard.
VII	Extremely hard routes, offering technical moves on overhanging sections or very thin ground and mixed routes of a very high technical nature.
VIII and up	Harder than grade VII, very few climbers will attempt this grade and fewer will succeed.

Grade VIII is open-ended, allowing for the addition of IX and X as the need arises. There may be a wide variation in winter conditions over adjacent years, so the grade shown for a route may often be split, such as II/III, for example.

DIFFICULTY

1	Easy-angled snow and ice or mixed ground with no technical difficulty.
2	Steeper ground than that found at grade I but generally with excellent quality ice and good protection.
3	Ice of up to 60 degrees, but still giving good opportunity for sound runners and belays.
4	Ice of up to 70 degrees, still of good quality.
5	80 degree ice, with less chance of resting than before. Ice quality may not be particularly good and protection tricky to place. Steep, mixed ground.
6	90 degree ice, giving tiring technical climbing and with protection being difficult to place securely.
7	Very steep, sustained and poor quality or thin ice, with protection opportunities few and far between.
8 and up	Extreme climbing, at the very highest standard.

This system allows the description of a route to be reasonably precise, given the obvious constraints of the winter environment. Grades such as VI 5 or VI 6 work in a similar fashion to summer UK grades, where some flexibility is attainable within the system to describe routes that may have the same seriousness but offer separate degrees of difficulty.

MIXED GRADES

These are often used to categorize dry tooling climbs, where ice may or may not be encountered. If the route is completely dry, the grade will be prefixed with a D instead of an M. The C prefix is used for climbs on chalk.

GRADE	DESCRIPTION	
M1–M3	Low-angled, easy routes with little technical skill required.	
M4	Ground up to vertical, requiring technique to progress.	
M5	Sustained vertical dry tooling.	
M6	Ground that may be overhanging for some of its length, necessitating good technique.	
M7	Difficult, overhanging ground, involving hard climbing of up to 10 metres in length.	
M8	Ground presenting overhangs verging on the horizontal, requiring powerful and technical tool technique. May include cruxes longer than those encountered on M7 ground.	
M9	Sustained vertical or overhanging ground with difficult tool placements, also ground with roofs of 4–6 metres.	
M10	Horizontal ground of 10 metres or more, or 30 metres of overhanging ground, providing no opportunity for rests during a series of extremely powerful moves.	
M11	Extreme climbing of 40–50 metres on overhanging ground or across 15 metres of roof.	
M12 and up	Extreme climbing, encompassing all within the M11 grade and more, as well as questionable placements.	

RUSSIAN GRADES

They have a system different to that laid out in the rock climbing grade comparison table, and it has parallels with the UIAA system which is noted here using Roman numerals.

1B	Roped climbing of a low technical nature.
2A	Several pitches of moderate roped climbing.
2B	Multi-pitch routes at around UIAA II+ and III standard.
3A	Up to two pitches of grade III climbs, making up a section of a multi-pitch route.
3B	A long route, typically taking a day to complete, which includes up to two pitches of III+ or IV climbing.
4A	IV+ climbing on a multi-pitch route that will take a day to complete.
4B	A route with a number of pitches at IV+ and up to V+.
5A	Grade V climbing on routes that may take one, two or three days to climb.
5B	Routes of 48 hours length encompassing ground at grade VI+ level.
6A	Long routes taking two or more days to complete, with sustained sections at grade VI or VII.
6B	Extremely long sustained and difficult routes, with climbing at VII and VIII or harder.

DEEP WATER SOLOING GRADES

DWS grades are extremely subjective, as they rely on external factors such as the state of the tide, section of the route the climber fails on, etc. It should be remembered that a fall from any height into water is potentially extremely dangerous.

S0	The shortest of falls, generally over deep water with no obstructions.
S1	There may be a boulder or ledge hazard, and the height of the tide will affect the landing area.
S2	Great care must be taken to get the sea state right and not to fall from above any hazards, of which there may be many. Correct landing area and posture are critical, as the fall could be of some distance.
S3	The highest category, extremely dangerous falls from height into shallow water or above many exposed ledges and similar hazards.

APPENDIX II
FACTORS AND FORCES
FALL FACTOR

The fall factor is the name given to the sum of the equation used to calculate the hardness, or severity of loading, of a fall. The higher the value, the more severe the fall. For most rock and ice climbing situations, the highest fall factor obtainable is 2, the lowest is 0. The exceptions are mentioned in a moment.

The fall factor is calculated by dividing the length of the fall by the length of the rope deployed. It can only be fully calculated when climbing in a multi-pitch situation, as on a single-pitch route the ground is in the way for some of the examples!

The calculation comes in two versions. The Theoretical Fall Factor gives a number based on the simple mathematical equation mentioned above. The Actual Fall Factor is a much more complicated equation, which takes into account such variables as the line that the rope takes between runners, the friction caused between placements and the effect of it rubbing over rock or ice. It is the Theoretical Fall Factor that is used as the simple calculation of the value in each given situation.

Let's say, for instance, that 2.5 metres of rope have been run out from the belay, and that you have not placed any protection. If you fall off, the distance you will go will be 5 metres (16ft). The fall factor, therefore, is 5 metres divided by 2.5, which gives a total of 2. This is not, as you will appreciate, a pleasant experience.

Having learnt by your mistake, you are now 5 metres from the belay, but this time have placed a runner at 2.5 metres up the pitch. If you now fall, you will drop 5 metres which, divided by 5 for the length of rope run out, will give a factor of 1. This gives a much lower shock-load on the system, in particular the belay rig.

It is very important to reduce the fall factor as much as possible when climbing from a stance on a multi-pitch route. The placing of a running belay as soon as you leave the stance, or even before setting off if there is a suitable placement, will do a lot to lessen the loading on the anchor system, belayer and yourself.

Be aware that factors far higher than 2 can occur in some climbing-related activities. Via Ferrata cables, for instance, clipped with karabiners that are then towed up alongside you for security can give rise to huge fall factors if you slip. As an example, if you are 5 metres above a cable attachment point, as well as towing up a 1 metre lanyard, if you slip the fall factor would be 6. It is for this reason that Via Ferrata safety equipment (as well as a lot of industrial access kit) is designed with a built in shock-absorbing device. This will most commonly be achieved either by a progressive and controlled ripping of stitching, or by the attachment rope being pulled through a metal plate to achieve a smooth braking effect. Never be tempted to make up your own Via Ferrata protection lanyards, unless you know what you are doing, as a system with no give in it is asking for disaster when subjected to a high fall factor.

KILONEWTONS

This is the value used by equipment manufacturers for stating the strength rating of their equipment. For instance, a karabiner may be rated to have a strength of 25kN. The karabiner will in fact have its actual physical breaking point a lot higher, but 25kN will be its tested rating and seen as encompassing its safe working loading range. For us as climbers to put a load of 25kN on to a karabiner under normal usage will be almost impossible. Many ropes are tested to a rating of 12kN, as this is seen as the maximum force that the human body can take. A climber experiencing anything over 4kN when taking a fall is likely to experience extreme discomfort.

The Newton is a unit of force used by the International System of Units (SI), and this has as its basic components mass, length and time. The Newton is equivalent to the force required to produce an acceleration of one metre per second squared on a mass of one kilogram.

1,000 Newtons equal one kiloNewton. Thus a piece of climbing equipment with a 25kn stamp on it would have a strength rating equivalent to 25,000 Newtons.

Gravity exerts a force on the human body, which is why we accelerate when we fall off a climb. This force is approximately 9.8m per second squared. Thus someone that weighs 70kg exerts a force of approximately 686 Newtons. However, these values are rounded up or down for most uses, so it would be acceptable to talk of a 25kN rated piece of gear having a strength of 2,500 kilograms.

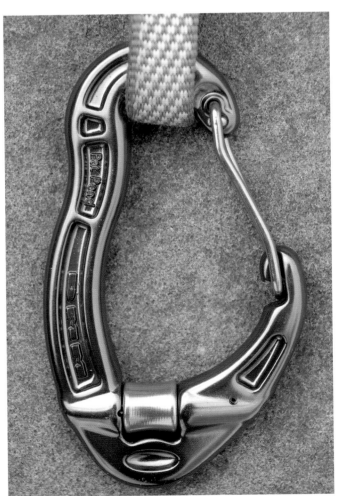

IMPACT FORCE

This is the name given to the loading experienced by certain sections of the protection system, such as the top running belay, in the event of a climber falling off. The lower the impact force the better, as high impact forces can cause runner failure or injury to the climber.

It is therefore essential to do everything possible to reduce the impact force on runners, particularly on marginal placements or in winter. Climbing with a rope rated with a low impact force will help, as will using a semi-direct or indirect dynamic belaying method and allowing a little rope slippage through the device or around your body when a load is taken. Keeping the run of the rope straight with appropriate length extenders helps, as this allows the rope to use the maximum amount of stretch when loaded and thus absorb energy. Tests have shown that a ground anchor where the belayer can have up to a metre (39in) of lift helps to reduce the impact force, as the belayer's body weight lessens the shock of the braking effect as they rise from the ground slightly. The use of shock-absorbing slings should be considered where you know that marginal placements exist, such as some ice screws, as these will tear at a known load, once again reducing the impact force. Karabiners with built-in pulleys can be used to help reduce friction in the system, thus allowing the rope to perform correctly. Even small changes, such as the use of figure of eight knots instead of clove hitches when tying on at anchors, will make a difference, as the figure of eight will tighten slightly when loaded, absorbing energy as it does so.

COMPARISON OF IMPACT FORCES CREATED BY A FALL OF 8 METRES WITH A FALL FACTOR OF 1.4

RATED IMPACT FORCE FOR ROPE USED	FORCE ON RUNNER IN KN
Using dynamic belay device	
7.2kN	5.6kN
12kN	8.25kN
Using auto-locking belay device	
7.2kN	8.85kN
12kN	14.35kN

You will note from the above table that there is a marked difference in results between various rope ratings and belay methods. Using a dynamic belay device and a 7.2kN rated rope will give a massive 250 per cent reduction in impact force loading when compared to a 12kN rope and an auto-locking belay device. This will obviously have consequences for the equipment that you choose for certain routes, as the former would be the best for those with marginal placements such as ice screws, the latter would be fine for bottom rope and very well protected climbs with solid gear.

A karabiner with a built-in pulley will help in reducing friction, thus lowering impact force, when used on an extender

VECTORS

This is best described as being the angle that a belay rope, sling or section of a rigging system makes where all load-bearing points meet, such as at a knot or where they are connected together with a karabiner. The narrower this angle the better it is, as each element of the system will be stronger, a very important consideration when using marginal anchors or in winter. Generally, the wider the angle the greater the load on each individual anchor point.

You can see from the diagram that it is easy to quickly reach a critical loading on each anchor, such as when a sling is forced over a spike, for example, with the karabiner attachment point creating a wide angle. An example of the loading is given below.

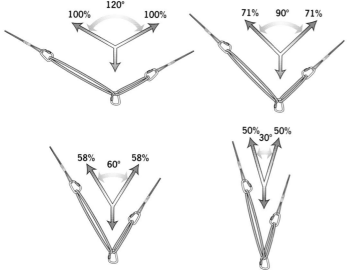

The relationship between angle and loading percentage

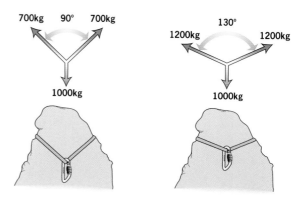

The relationship between sling angle over a spike anchor and the loading in kilograms

At the end of the day, there's nothing quite like skiing a companion back down to the valley

INDEX

Learning Resource Centre Stockton Riverside College

Pete Hill MIC, FRGS

Pete has climbed in many continents and countries across the world, including first ascents in the Himalaya. He is holder of the MIC award, the highest UK instructional qualification, and has been delivering rock and mountain sports courses at the highest level for a number of years. He is a member of the Alpine Club, Honorary Life Member of the Association of Mountaineering Instructors and a Fellow of the Royal Geographical Society. A lack of common sense has found him on the north faces of the Eiger and Matterhorn in winter, as well as a number of other extreme routes climbed in extreme conditions in the European Alps, Africa, Nepal and India.

Pete lives in Scotland and has two daughters, Rebecca and Samantha. A frequent contributor to various magazines and websites, he is author of *The International Handbook of Technical Mountaineering*, *Sport Climbing*, *Rock Climbing* and co-author of the globally successful *The Mountain Skills Training Handbook*. He runs both summer and winter skills courses from beginner through to advanced levels and can be contacted via his website at www.petehillmic.com.